Flint Mines in Neolithic Britain

To Jane and Russ,
Glynis, Bronwen and Megan.
Thank you all.

Flint Mines in Neolithic Britain

MILES RUSSELL

TEMPUS

First published 2000

PUBLISHED IN THE UNITED KINGDOM BY:

Tempus Publishing Ltd
The Mill, Brimscombe Port
Stroud, Gloucestershire GL5 2QG

PUBLISHED IN THE UNITED STATES OF AMERICA BY:

Arcadia Publishing Inc.
A division of Tempus Publishing Inc.
2 Cumberland Street
Charleston, SC 29401
1-888-313-2665

Tempus books are available in France, Germany and Belgium
from the following addresses:

Tempus Publishing Group
21 Avenue de la République
37300 Joué-lès-Tours
FRANCE

Tempus Publishing Group
Gustav-Adolf-Straße 3
99084 Erfurt
GERMANY

Tempus Publishing Group
Place de L'Alma 4/5
1200 Brussels
BELGIUM

British Library Cataloguing in Publication Data.
A catalogue record for this book is available from the British Library.

ISBN 0 7524 1481 X

Typesetting and origination by Tempus Publishing.
PRINTED AND BOUND IN GREAT BRITAIN

Contents

The illustrations

Text figures

Colour Plates

Preface and acknowledgements

Today we are used to being surrounded by huge buildings, structures and monuments. The modern world is characterised to most by large urban centres and dense concentrations of people. It has not always been like this. For much of humankind's existence, there were no substantial built forms to speak of. Human groups foraged, hunted animals (and each other), made stone tools, and cut down trees, but did not appear to significantly alter their immediate environment architecturally. Around 6,000 years ago, things began to change. Humans started to modify the natural world around them through the construction of new and large-scale architectural forms. Specific areas of the landscape were now enclosed with ditches and banks of spoil. Deep vertical cuts were made into the ground to extract flint. Large earthen mounds with parallel ditches were constructed. This was the beginning of the Neolithic or 'New Stone Age'.

Monuments represent the major defining element in our understanding of the Neolithic period. Monumental architecture structures and permanently alters the landscape. It changes the way in which particular locales are visualised, perceived and understood. It enhances the importance of place. It controls the way in which people move through the landscape. It generates a framework of shared experience. It imposes order.

Although much has been said in recent years with regards to two forms of Neolithic monument, namely the enclosure and the long mound, there has, in comparison, been little discussion surrounding the third form of early monumental construction: the flint mine. Flint mines represent one of the earliest prehistoric type-sites to be archaeologically investigated in Britain. Many areas of mining have now been identified and most have been at least partially examined. Excavation and recording has, in more recent years, concentrated upon one site in particular: the well-preserved sequence of deposits at Grimes Graves in Norfolk. Despite the extensive work conducted here by the British Museum and others, however, the process and nature of flint extraction and the significance of mining within the Neolithic still receives comparatively little consideration within general texts on British prehistory. Recent work, especially that conducted by the Royal Commission on the Historical Monuments of England, has gone some way to altering this scenario, though it is clear that mining is still generally treated as a footnote in most overviews of Neolithic society. Worse, when flint extraction processes are discussed, the Sussex and Wessex mines often receive scant attention, weightier consideration being given to apparently later Norfolk series.

This book hopes to go some way towards redressing the balance, for there are a number of important questions that deserve consideration with regard to these early forms of monumental structure. Where were the mine sites and how were they used?

What did they mean to the people that created them? How do they relate to other monuments being built at the same time? What form did they take? What would it have been like to work in them? How were they first discovered and interpreted? It is time, therefore, to bring the Neolithic flint mines of Britain to centre stage.

This particular text has developed from a number of current research interests and fieldwork programmes developing at Bournemouth University. As a consequence there are a large number of people who have provided me with advice, inspiration and guidance and (without wishing to sound like an Academy Award speech in which everyone, including the cat's dentist, is thanked) I would like to acknowledge at least some of that help here.

For access to archive material relating to John Pull's excavations at Blackpatch, Church Hill, Cissbury and Tolmere, and for permission to discuss and publish information derived from that archive, I would like to thank Dr Sally White, Principal Curator of Worthing Museum and Art Gallery, and Mrs Beryl Heryet. I would also like to acknowledge the help of Dave Field, Martyn Barber, Peter Topping, Al Oswald and Dave McOmish of the Royal Commission on the Historical Monuments of England (now merged with English Heritage) for their help and advice and for allowing me constant access to information derived from their 1994-7 survey of flint mines in England. Thank you also to Gillian Varndell of the British Museum for access to the Grimes Graves archive, Emma Young and Barbara Alcock of the Sussex Archaeological Society for access to the Blackpatch and Harrow Hill photographic archive, and to the Royal Commission and English Heritage staff of the National Monuments Record in Swindon and Fortress House in London, for dealing with some of my more unorthodox telephone and email enquiries. Special thanks to all those at Tempus, especially Peter Kemmis Betty, who first invited me to prepare this current work and who patiently awaited its arrival throughout the trauma of a PhD thesis, three terms of teaching and structural repairs to a bathroom.

All line drawings presented here were produced by the author and I have acknowledged source material and copyright where appropriate. All photographic sources, and ownership of image copyright, have been acknowledged within figure captions. Thank you to everyone who gave their permission to reproduce those images here. Thank you also to the editors of the *Oxford Journal of Archaeology* for permission to reuse and rework some ideas first aired in an article appearing in Volume 19, no. 1 of the journal, entitled 'Of Flint Mines and Fossil Men: the Lavant Caves deception', for chapter 2 of this present work. The Research Committee of the Archaeology Group at Bournemouth University made a number of generous grants throughout in order to facilitate photographic reproduction, data collection and travel.

A number of friends and colleagues read various chapters and sections and were able to correct errors in spelling and help modify some of the more abstract theories (any remaining mistakes, inaccuracies or strange idiosyncrasies that remain hidden in this book are of course entirely my responsibility). In particular I would like to thank the following people for their help, criticism and information: Con Ainsworth, Mike Allen, Kevin Andrews, Martyn Barber, Martin Brown, Chris Butler, Amanda Chadburn, Jeff Chartrand, Philip Claris, Tim Darvill, Roger Doonan, Dave Field, Linda Fransen, Andy Fulton, John Gale, Julie Gardiner, Oliver Gilkes, Francis Healy, Iain Hewitt, Robin

Holgate, Alex Hunt, Peter Kendall, Ian Kinnes, Glynis Laughlin, Mark Maltby, John Manley, Fiona Marsden, Dave McOmish, John Mills, Al Oswald, Louise Pearson, Liz Pye, Colin Richards, John Roles, David Rudling, Derek and Jane Russell, Gale Sieveking, Helen Smith, Jeff Spencer, Gareth Talbot, Mark Taylor, David Thackray, Peter Topping, Gillian Varndell, Jon Wallis, Sally White, Alasdair Whittle, Keith Wilkinson, Andrew Woodcock and Emma Young. Congratulations also to Kate Macdonald for successfully combating the index monster. Acknowledgement must also be made to the many archaeology undergraduates at Bournemouth University who have coped with my enthusiasm for Neolithic mine sites, usually on a snow covered Sussex hill in December or early January. The greatest debt of thanks, however, must be to my wife Bronwen and daughter Megan, who have successfully dealt with the real world whilst I was more concerned with the minutiae of the past.

1 The evidence revealed

Before the introduction of metal technology into Britain the majority of tools used by human groups were fashioned from flint. Flint is a stone which in hardness and durability is second only to diamond. Flint possesses excellent flaking properties and can be chipped or worked into a variety of shapes, sizes and implement types. It is a substance which occurs naturally within the Upper Chalk, a sedimentary rock outcropping across much of the south and eastern lowlands of Britain (**1**), where it may be found on or just under the surface as separate nodules or deep underground as horizontal tabular sheets or seams. Mining for deeply bedded, unweathered seams of flint begins in Britain at the same time that humans were building the first forms of monumental architecture, such as the ditched enclosure and the linear mound. This is a period characterised by a gradual if significant change in human subsistence, from hunting and gathering to the domestication of animals and plants. It is also marked by the arrival of new forms of artefact, such as the polished stone axe, the leaf-shaped arrowhead, sickles, grinding stones and pottery. This is a period defined by modern archaeologists as the 'Neolithic' or New Stone Age.

Flint mines, together with enclosures and long mounds, represent one of the oldest and most distinctive forms of archaeological earthwork recorded from the British Isles. Unfortunately the characteristic crater-like hollows of the backfilled mine sites were not fully understood by the earliest of British antiquarians who, in the eighteenth and nineteenth centuries, were still coming to terms with the fact that the world might be older than anyone had previously dared think. The distinctive surface form of the mine sites in particular gave the earliest antiquarians something of an interpretational headache. What were these features and how on earth could they be fitted into the established framework of human history?

In the beginning

When the Rev Francis Blomefield described the site of Grimes Graves, Norfolk (**2**), in 1739, he suggested that it was in all probability 'a very curious Danish incampment [sic]', the larger pits at the centre probably representing the former position of a tent belonging to the commanding officer. As to why their tents had been sunk so deeply in the ground, Blomefield observed that 'they are capable not only of receiving a very great army, but also of covering and concealing them'. Quite why a marauding Danish army would have required such an elaborate form of concealment is never made clear, and Blomefield does not seem to be concerned that the huge chalk spoil heaps surrounding their hideout may have been considered something of a give-away.

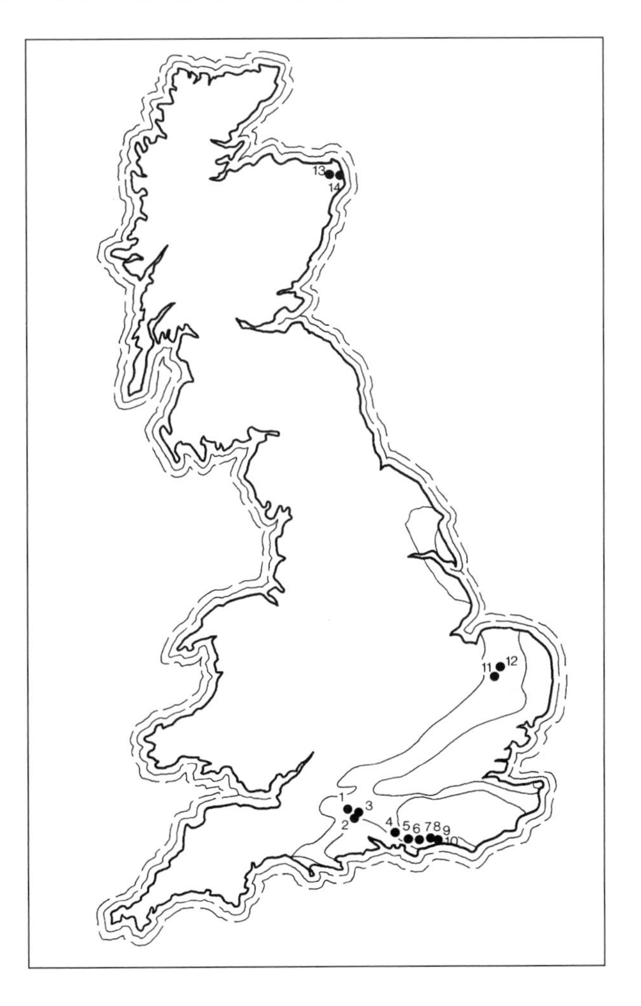

1 Location of confirmed Neolithic flint mines in mainland Britain in relation to the major deposits of chalk:
1 Durrington
2 Easton Down
3 Martin's Clump
4 Nore Down
5 Stoke Down
6 Long Down
7 Harrow Hill
8 Blackpatch
9 Church Hill/Tolmere/High Salvington
10 Cissbury/Mount Carvey
11 Grimes Graves
12 Buckenham Toft
13 Skelmuir Hill
14 Den of Boddam
Redrawn from Barber, Field and Topping 1999

Excavations into some of the pits by the Rev C.R. Manning and the Rev S.T. Pettigrew (Manning in 1852 and Pettigrew in 1852 and 1866), did not significantly expand upon Blomefield's interpretation. Pettigrew reported to the British Archaeological Association that Grimes Graves 'was formerly the seat of war between the Saxons and the Danes' whilst Manning informed the Norfolk and Norwich Archaeological Society that the site was 'a fortified settlement of the Iceni; probably of a date anterior to the arrival of the Romans'. Neither Manning nor Pettigrew appear to have excavated beneath the topmost layers of fill, finding only animal bone and pottery relating to a period of site use significantly later than the original digging of the pits.

Interpretation of the flint mines of Cissbury, in West Sussex, fared little better at this time. The depressions covering the western slopes of the hill, within the area enclosed by the Iron Age hillfort (**3**), were at first viewed as being the remains of 'rude huts' or a form of ancient reservoir. In 1849, whilst addressing the Sussex Archaeological Society, the Rev Edward Turner stated confidently that the hollows were undoubtedly a form of barrow or holy place 'formed for the special purpose of forwarding the celebration of the religious ceremonies of the ancient Britons'. Turner believed that the features possessed strong

2 *The distinctive 'crater-like' appearance of the flint mines at Grimes Graves from the air in July 1997. Greenwell's pit, now capped with concrete, is visible at the bottom of the mine group, just before the trees. NMR 1846/076. English Heritage © Crown Copyright*

Druidical connections, though quite what Druids were thought to have done in them was never explained. No doubt something unpleasant involving goats.

George Irving was the first to excavate at Cissbury and record his findings. Irving failed to bottom any of the four features opened in 1857, being deceived, as Manning and Pettigrew had been at Grimes Graves, by the hard chalk rubble fill in the upper levels of the shaft. Nevertheless, Irving felt that enough had been revealed during the course of his excavations to interpret the Cissbury pits as animal pens, noting that 'the remains found are exactly what one would expect to be thrown down about a pig pound'. There the matter rested for another decade.

In the summer of 1867, Colonel Augustus Lane Fox began a long and detailed survey of all the hillfort enclosures on the Sussex Downs. Turning his attention to Cissbury and Highdown, another enclosure lying to the immediate north of Worthing, Lane Fox decided to investigate the origins of hillfort construction through excavation. He had already noted the density of stone tools lying on the surface of a number of Sussex enclosure sites and was keen to ascertain whether such implements could provide 'evidence of having belonged to the people who constructed these forts'. In other words, were the hillforts of the South Downs Stone Age in date or were they, as many other antiquarians believed at the time, the product of the Roman army.

Lane Fox oversaw two phases of investigation into the Cissbury pits, in September 1867 and January 1868, the later visit being accompanied by his colleague and former mentor, Canon William Greenwell. At least 30 pits and a number of minor earthwork

3 *The backfilled mine shafts and later Iron Age enclosure circuit of Cissbury from the air. NMR CCG 8492/306. English Heritage © Crown Copyright*

enclosures were examined by Lane Fox and Greenwell, the majority of pits lying along the north-western slopes of the hill. The nature of the chalk infill again proved deceptive and the excavators, believing that they had reached the bottom of the features, cleared most to a depth of no more than 2m. Lane Fox recovered a considerable amount of flint work from his excavated pits, 'the majority of a very rough description', suggesting that 'Cissbury was the place in which the implements were worked'. The excavated form of the opened pits also deserved comment, for the absence of clay lining when combined with their deep, basin-like bottoms, made it clear that the features could not be reservoirs, pig-pens or huts. 'For what use then were they formed?', Lane Fox pondered, 'I am inclined to think for the purpose of obtaining flints'.

The realisation that the Cissbury pits had been cut to procure flint was an important one and the 'evidence of habitation' in the form of animal bone, pottery and charcoal from the fills, which had bedevilled so many of his predecessors, could now be dismissed as waste belonging to a period of later reuse. These pits were clearly not Roman in origin. The features belonged to the mysterious world of the 'Ancient Britons'. A single piece of polished axe, from investigations conducted to the east of the mines, provided a link with the period of the Stone Age which had only then recently been termed the Neolithic. Limited excavation within the ditch of the hillfort at Cissbury revealed a small number of worked flints and a flaked axe, something that appeared to imply that 'the intrenchment [sic] belongs to the Stone Age, or at any rate to the age of the flint manufacture'. The possibility that the flints could predate the construction of the hillfort, and may accidentally have been incorporated into ditch backfill, is one that does not appear to have occurred to Lane Fox.

At the same time that Lane Fox and Greenwell were investigating the Cissbury pits in 1868, Ernest Willett was opening a series of similar features on the opposing slopes of Church Hill. As with the Cissbury investigations, Willett appears to have been deceived by the hardness of the chalk rubble fill in the shafts he investigated, and consequently does not appear to have bottomed any of the features. Though disappointed with the results of his work, Willett came to the same conclusions as his colleagues at Cissbury, in that the pits had originally been cut for the purpose of extracting flint.

Grimes Graves and after

In 1868 Greenwell moved his attention from Sussex to Grimes Graves in Norfolk. The Norfolk site presented a range of surface features similar to those recorded from Cissbury (**colour plate 4**), and, presumably, Greenwell felt that here he could safely devise his own programme of excavation and analysis, developing ideas that he may have had whilst working in Sussex, without potentially alienating his former student. Greenwell never explained, at least in print, why he commenced the excavation of Grimes Graves so soon after finishing at Cissbury. It is probable however that the trigger may have been the reports, then just circulating in Britain, of spectacular discoveries made at the Belgian flint-mining site of Spiennes.

The flint mines of Spiennes had first been noted in the 1840s, when a combination of quarrying and landslides had exposed a number of subterranean tunnels. The full nature of these tunnels was not revealed until 1867, when a cutting for the Mons to Bencke railway was dug through the site, exposing some 25 vertical shafts in the process. The shafts measured around 1m in diameter and descended to a depth of between 9 and 12m. Galleries extending outwards from the base of certain shafts contained red deer antlers, flint tools and sandstone hammers. Archaeological examination of the site continued into 1868, with a detailed report being published the same year. The discovery proved to be something of a revelation for those interested in prehistory, for it was abundantly clear that the quest for subterranean flint had led some early communities to burrow deep into the earth. Hearing the reports, Greenwell must have wondered whether the pits that he and Lane Fox had opened at Cissbury were really so shallow and insignificant after all.

Between 1868 and 1870 Greenwell oversaw the excavation of a single shaft at the south-eastern edge of the site of Grimes Graves, then still heavily wooded. He was assisted by Lord Rosehill, who, in the final season of work, undertook the partial examination of a second shaft at the north-western margins of the mining area. The pit that Greenwell chose to examine was emptied to a depth of 12.2m. The final 5.5m of the fill consisted of densely packed chalk rubble, exactly the material that earlier excavators at Grimes Graves

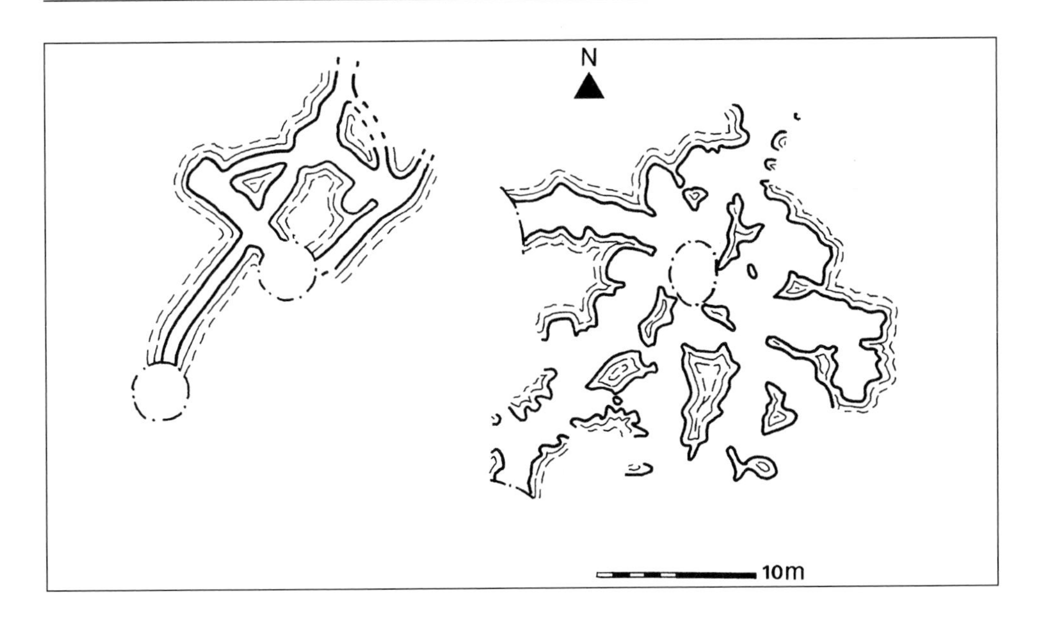

4 Plan of Greenwell's Shaft and radiating galleries at Grimes Graves, as originally recorded between 1868 and 1870 (left) and as redrawn by the Prehistoric Flintmines Working Group of the Dutch Geological Society following more complete excavation between 1974 and 1976 (right). Redrawn from Longworth and Varndell 1996

and Cissbury (including both Greenwell and Lane Fox) had interpreted as comprising undisturbed bedrock. At this point Greenwell must have been elated. Here there was clear evidence that prehistoric flint extraction pits in Britain were far more substantial than anyone had previously envisaged. The early investigations in Sussex and Norfolk had barely scratched the surface.

Three horizontal seams of flint had originally been cut by Greenwell's shaft. Using terms employed by the nineteenth-century flint miners of Norfolk, the Canon described these seams as 'topstone', 'wallstone' and 'floorstone'. The basal floorstone represented the desired layer of unweathered, good quality flint that, in Greenwell's pit, had been removed by the original miners through the cutting of niches and galleries extending out from the base of the shaft. The working conditions for Greenwell and his team during this exploration were severe, the Canon noting on at least one occasion the difficulties surrounding the removal of rubble from cramped subterranean tunnels with little light or air and the ever-present threat of roof collapse. As a consequence Greenwell and Rosehill did not fully excavate the area of the shaft, neither did they fully expose or empty the network of subterranean gallery systems, as reinvestigation of the feature in the early 1970s have shown (**4**). Enough of the mine and its workings was revealed, however, to demonstrate the substantial nature of prehistoric flint extraction in this part of Britain. The range of artefacts from the mines, including flint and antler tools, the bones of domesticated animals, worked chalk and a ground greenstone axe, suggested to Greenwell that the flint working dated to the Neolithic period.

Greenwell and Rosehill presented papers on their discoveries at Grimes Graves in 1870, Greenwell to the Ethnological Society of London, and Rosehill to the Society of Antiquaries of Scotland. Augustus Lane Fox was present at the meeting in London, afterwards publicly congratulating Greenwell on his work. Lane Fox's comments, following the presentation of Greenwell's paper, and recorded in the Journal of the Ethnological Society, however suggest that he continued to view the Cissbury pits as being distinct from those investigated at Grimes Graves. Both sites were clearly flint quarries, but the pits at from Sussex were, in Lane Fox's mind, shallower and likely to be contemporary with the hillfort of Cissbury Ring. Greenwell, it would appear, did not agree. In 1873 he met with Ernest Willett, and advised him to instigate a deeper and more detailed investigation of the Cissbury pits. Willett was already aware of the potential problems surrounding the examination of prehistoric features cut into the Sussex chalk, having already partially investigated the upper levels of pits on Church Hill between 1868 and 1870.

Return to Cissbury

Willett began work at Cissbury in the autumn of 1873. He specifically targeted one of the 30 shallow pits opened by Lane Fox and Greenwell during the 1867-8 season (**5**) and discovered, just as Greenwell had predicted, that the feature had not been bottomed. The hard packed chalk that Lane Fox had taken to represent the base of the pit, actually represented a layer of redeposited rubble within the upper half of a much larger cut. Once through this compacted layer, Willett was able to follow the feature to its real depth of 4.2m. As at Spiennes and Grimes Graves, the base of the cylindrical shaft was punctured by a series of chambers or galleries. Unfortunately, though he made 'careful notes and memoranda' regarding his work, Willett was unable to later detail the exact nature of his discoveries due to the subsequent loss of his site notebook.

January 1874 saw the excavation of a new shaft at Cissbury by Plumpton Tindall. Tindall's motives for opening a shaft are lost to us for he died before being able to report his findings to the Society of Antiquaries. Fortunately both Lane Fox and Willett were able to recount certain details from original information that Tindall had communicated to them at the time. Tindall's shaft was a large one, descending to an overall depth of 12m. No galleries or other subterranean features were observed. Willett noted that the majority of artefacts deriving from Tindall's work passed, after his death, to Lord Rosehill, Greenwell's collaborator at Grimes Graves. In 1924 the Rosehill Collection of flint implements went on sale at Christies and was purchased by Lewes Museum. Though the context of these finds was given only as being 'from Cissbury' it seems likely that it must at least in part represent material derived from Tindall's excavation.

The examination of a third shaft at Cissbury was commenced by Willett in August 1874. Willett presented the results of this and Tindall's earlier work at Cissbury to the Society of Antiquaries of London in 1875. At the end of the paper he concluded that the shafts had been dug to extract deeply bedded flint and that the traces of domestic refuse that some earlier excavators had found in the upper fill probably related to later activities conducted

5 An aerial photograph of the Cissbury mine shafts taken in 1936, looking south. The spoil generated from Willett's and Tindall's examination of three shafts between 1873 and 1874 remain visible as large patches of white chalk rubble from the centre to the top left of the photograph. Unlike today, there was no concern, following an excavation, to backfill trenches or stabilise the spoil in order to return the site to its natural appearance. © The Sussex Archaeological Society

within the abandoned and half backfilled features. Willett also gave reason to doubt Lane Fox's earlier assertion that the shafts at Cissbury were broadly contemporary with the hillfort, the circuit of which had, in his view, 'abruptly severed' the mine group. Unfortunately, the exact nature of the debate that followed the presentation of the paper were not recorded in detail, though Willett later observed that 'in consequence of the discussion that arose', Lane Fox decided to return to Cissbury. No doubt the Colonel hoped to resolve all the issues surrounding the site in one final, definitive season of investigation.

In June 1875 Lane Fox, assisted by J. Park Harrison, oversaw the reopening of two pits which he and Canon Greenwell had examined between 1867 and 1868. Presumably he wished to check for himself the nature of the upper chalk rubble fill that had earlier proved so deceptive. No detailed account of the reopened pits is provided in Lane Fox's subsequent site report. Even the exact whereabouts of the features remain unknown, though they may have lain on the south-western slopes of the hill, just outside the hillfort. The only comment that Lane Fox makes concerning the shafts is that both extended to a 'greater depth' than either he or Greenwell had first supposed. The realisation that he had, after all, only superficially explored 30 shafts during the 1867-8 season must have been extremely sobering.

6 *The earliest photographic record of an archaeological section: No.1 Escarp Shaft at Cissbury, in the process of excavation by Lane Fox and Harrison in 1875. The excavation clearly demonstrates that the enclosure ditch (beneath shovel B) cuts through the upper fill of the shaft (beneath shovel A), making it the later of the two features. Chalk rubble derived from the examination of the Skeleton Shaft may be seen in the background of the picture, whilst in the distance are the tree-capped slopes of Church Hill. © The Sussex Archaeological Society*

Having cleared two of the earlier pits to their full extent, Lane Fox and Harrison, now aided by Professor George Rolleston and Sir Alexander Gordon, turned their attention to a portion of ditch within the south-western portion of the hillfort (**6**). Here both pits and rampart met and Lane Fox was keen to ascertain whether the two features were in any sense contemporary. When cleared it was apparent that the ditch cut through, making it later than the upper fill of buried shaft, identified here as No.1 Escarp. Lane Fox illustrated this relationship by publishing a drawing of the vertical section cut through the fills of both shaft and ditch. Such a use of vertical stratigraphy to demonstrate the relative phasing of particular structures, though a commonplace archaeological technique today, had never been used to such effect before. To the immediate east of No. 1 Escarp, and similarly cut by the hillfort ditch, lay a second shaft, identified as No. 2 Escarp. Only half the soil layers within this feature were removed by Lane Fox in order that a section through the accumulated fill could be retained, an archaeological recording practice which was again years ahead of its time.

Four further shafts were partially examined within the area of the south-western rampart circuit. These were named by Lane Fox as No.1 and No.2 Counterscarp, the Rampart Shaft and the Skeleton Shaft. Both the Rampart and Skeleton shafts were first detected from their lower fills during the preliminary examination of gallery systems extending from other pits. This meant that the excavators were faced with the problem of clearing the lower levels of the two shafts whilst the majority of shaft fill remained in place over their heads. This form of inverted spoil removal, from the bottom up towards the modern ground surface, presented the excavation team not only with extreme concerns over health and safety, but also with some interpretational problems which were frankly bizarre. On one occasion, whilst removing soil from the base of a shaft, Lane Fox observes that 'a well formed and perfect lower human jaw fell down from above, and on looking up we could perceive the remainder of the skull fixed with the base downwards . . . between two pieces of chalk rubble'. The sudden discovery unnerved Lane Fox who 'hollowed out so loudly that Mr Harrison, who happened to be outside at the time . . . thought that it must have tumbled it, and came with a shovel to dig us out. It was some time before I could make him understand that we had added a third person to our party.'

Having largely resolved the chronological issues surrounding the relationship between the shafts and the hillfort enclosure, Lane Fox and his colleagues moved on to a feature known as the Large Pit. Already excavated to a depth of about 3.6m during the course of an earlier period of exploration, the Large Pit measured around 20m in diameter. The lower half of the shaft was now excavated in half section, again in an attempt to retain a representative slice of fill accumulation, to a depth of around 13m. At this point a sudden collapse of the section edge, which had been without shoring or scaffolding, made further examination extremely hazardous.

At the close of the 1875 season, Lane Fox moved on from Cissbury, presumably having made a series of interpretations that he was now happy with. In his absence, the further investigation of shafts was, until 1878, overseen by Harrison and Rolleston. The first shaft to be opened, and referred to as the Cave Pit, proved to be somewhat unusual. Harrison's description of the shaft is frustratingly vague at times, something not helped by his repeated interpretation of the feature as a form of subterranean hut or dwelling. At one point, for example, when describing Gallery E, Harrison ventured that the narrowing of the gallery walls could be explained as a form of defence for those living in the end chamber for it would have 'hindered a pursuer from using his flint weapons'. Rolleston and Harrison went on to open an additional four shafts at Cissbury, the latter becoming increasingly drawn to a series of strange markings found upon the walls of the subterranean workface.

The legacy of Grimes Graves and Cissbury

The discoveries made at Grimes Graves and Cissbury had a massive impact upon antiquarian and early archaeological thought. Now it appeared that any hole in the ground could represent the remains of a prehistoric flint mine. Shafts of all shape, size and age were grouped together with genuine prehistoric mines as the early archaeologists attempted to define and understand this new class of field monument. For the next sixty years, a variety of marl pits, chalk quarries, dene holes, wells and natural solution pipes were all at some time classified as being Neolithic. Some examples, such as Easton and Weybourne in Norfolk, Bow Hill and Lavant in Sussex, Hackpen Hill in Wiltshire, and Crayford and St Peter's in Kent have been shown to be of post-Neolithic date and may now be removed from the list of potential flint mines. Other sites, such as Great Massingham, Buckenham Toft and Whitlingham in Norfolk remain of uncertain origin and derivation.

A possible mine was observed at High Wycombe, in Buckinghamshire, during the digging of a railway cutting in 1902, but, unlike the pits at Spiennes which had been discovered in similar circumstances, no further examination of the feature was conducted. At least two shallow pits were investigated at Peppard Common, in Oxfordshire, by Dr A.E. Peake (1912-13) and Reginald Smith (1913) and interpreted as an area of prehistoric flint extraction. The limited amount of archaeological work conducted here, when combined with the observation that there has been much gravel extraction in the immediate area, means that the pits cannot however be viewed as Neolithic flint mines with any certainty. A series of pits on Skelmuir Hill, Grampian, were partially investigated by G.S. Graham-Smith in 1918. The possibility that these features represented flint quarries was discussed, but their nature and extent was not to be revealed for another 70 years.

A number of shafts examined before the late 1930s did however prove to be Neolithic, most notably Stoke Down in Sussex and Easton Down in Wiltshire. At Stoke Down, Major A.G. Wade oversaw the excavation of three ungalleried shafts and a smaller Bronze Age pit from 1910 to 1913, publishing the results in the *Proceedings of the Prehistoric Society of East Anglia*. Two shafts (B1 and B1a) and at least three flint working floors were examined at Easton Down by J.F.S. Stone, an employee of the Royal Engineers Experimental Station, in 1930. A further four shafts (B19, B45, B49 and 67) and two floors were opened by Stone between 1931 and 1932, the results being published in the Wiltshire Archaeological and Natural History Magazine. None of the shafts investigated appeared to have possessed galleries, though the basal walls of pits B1 and B49 were punctured by 'deep undercuttings'. Stone suggested that four of the six shafts at Easton Down (namely B1a, B19, B45 and B67) had been abandoned before they had been finished.

The dating controversy

Forty-four years after Greenwell and Rosehill had completed work at Grimes Graves, the second major phase of investigation at the Norfolk site began on behalf of the Prehistoric Society of East Anglia, under the directorship of Dr A.E. Peake. The return to Grimes Graves was motivated by a desire to address a series of issues that had begun to cause prehistorians some unease: How were the mines originally worked? Were the pits all dug at the same time? Were the miners specialists, agriculturists or transitory hunter-gatherers? Were the bones of animals recovered from the mine sites those of domesticates? What evidence was there to suggest the former environmental conditions that the mines were worked in? Tied in with all these questions was one overriding concern: just how old were the mines?

7 *The 'southern gallery' of Pit 1 at Grimes Graves showing the intended prize of the Neolithic mine, the basal floorstone deposit, still preserved in the walls of the shaft.* © *The British Museum*

Since the monument class had been first identified, a diverse range of dates had been suggested for the first forms of large-scale flint extraction. Greenwell, Lane Fox and Willett had all proposed a Neolithic origin, based on the observation of stone tools (most notably polished axes), pottery and the bones of what appeared to be domesticated animals. However, doubts concerning the date of certain axe forms recovered from Cissbury and Grimes Graves had, in some circles, been growing. Reginald Smith, Keeper of the British and Medieval Antiquities at the British Museum, set his concerns down in a paper in 1912, published in the journal *Archaeologia*, that the flint artefacts recorded from both sites were more likely to be of Palaeolithic date than Neolithic, thus making the mines thousands of years older than anyone had previously supposed. Other protagonists in the debate favoured a date in the Bronze Age. Either way a Neolithic date was beginning to seem increasingly doubtful.

Excavation at Grimes Graves commenced in March 1914, two shafts, or 'pits' as Peake referred to them, being cleared to basal levels (**7**). The fills within both pits were initially examined in half section, before the subterranean galleries were explored. Peake notes that during the course of gallery excavation 'all objects found were recorded in a notebook at the time with the level and layer in which they were found', providing the first opportunity to examine the original extraction process in some detail. The 1914 excavations were also the first to deal substantially with surface areas of flint knapping debris around the mouths of the mine shafts. Referred to as 'floors', such accumulations of waste flint provided an indication of the sort of tools that may originally have been manufactured at the site. Unfortunately, Peake's examination of Pits 1 and 2 did not fully resolve issues concerning the date of the Grimes Graves flint mines. Lack of resolution may in part be ascribed to Reginald Smith, the main advocate of a Palaeolithic date, whose involvement in the published finds report served only to further confuse the issue.

In his report on the flint work derived from the 1914 excavation, Smith argued that the clear absence of distinct Neolithic forms, such as the polished axe and the leaf-shaped arrowhead 'is strong evidence against a Neolithic date'. If Neolithic man was responsible for the manufacture of tool types at Grimes Graves, Smith asserted, then it was noticeable that 'he eschewed his native patterns and modelled his output on Le Moustier [Palaeolithic] forms of which he can have had no models and no memory'. The presence at Grimes Graves of pottery, thought to be a clear indicator of the Neolithic period, did not deter Smith who noted that 'the occurrence of pottery in late Palaeolithic deposits has long been a subject of discussion', especially in France and Belgium where the debate raged most strongly. British archaeologists would be more likely to discount the existence of pre-Neolithic pottery, observed Smith, 'but negative evidence is of little weight in such matters, and the undoubted discovery of a few sherds in an undisturbed Palaeolithic deposit would suffice to turn the scale'. The determination with which an early date for flint mines continued to be embraced by some, may have strongly influenced certain members of the excavation team at Grimes Graves. It is certainly interesting that the scale of Palaeolithic-style fakes emanating from the site began to escalate at precisely the time that the Old Stone Age hypothesis was coming under fire.

The continued and at times heated debate inspired further work at Grimes Graves, excavation and survey continuing under the umbrella of the Prehistoric Society (which dropped the 'of East Anglia' suffix in 1935) until the beginning of the Second World War. A considerable number of shafts and working floors were examined at this time, under the varied direction of Peake (notably Shafts 3, 4 and 5), E. Lingwood, the Rev H. Kendall, Derek Richardson, Dr R. Favell and A. Leslie Armstrong. Throughout the 1920s and 30s, it was Armstrong who oversaw the majority of work at the site, directing the overall research programme. Armstrong, initially a supporter of Smith's Palaeolithic hypothesis, opened at least twelve shafts, Pits II, III, IV, V, VI, 8, 9, 10, 12, 13, 14 and 15, during his time at Grimes Graves, and partially examined several others. Armstrong compiled a mass of data relating to prehistoric mining techniques and, by the late 1920s, was able to postulate an evolutionary sequence for the extractive process. In this sequence, the earliest shafts were thought to be those without basal workings. These were consequently termed 'Primitive Pits'. The sequence ended with the deeper and, to Armstrong's mind, technologically more advanced deeper shafts, possessing a complex network of subterranean gallery systems. This progression from primitive to complex was, Armstrong argued, a clear indicator of the evolution from the earliest Palaeolithic extraction techniques.

Not everyone agreed with Armstrong's hypothesis however. W.G. Clarke had already argued, in two separate papers published in 1917 and 1921, that the stratigraphy and faunal remains at Grimes Graves did not compare at all favourably with sites of pre-Neolithic date. In 1933, Grahame Clark and Stuart Piggott published an article entitled 'The Age of the British Flint Mines' in which they rebutted all suggestions of a Palaeolithic date for the mines, clearly reaffirming their belief in a Neolithic origin. Armstrong reacted almost immediately, arguing that Clark and Piggott's assertion that all the mines belonged to a single period (ie. the Neolithic) 'can only be reached by ignoring or distorting the evidence, which the cited article very skilfully accomplishes in numerous ways'. In fact, so strong was Armstrong's attack on Clark and Piggott, that the editor of the journal in which his article of 1934 appeared, felt it necessary to append a note hoping to clarify, and to some extents calm, the argument on both sides.

Armstrong continued to excavate at Grimes Graves until 1939, when the outbreak of the Second World War effectively closed operations down. Three shafts, identified as Pits 13, 14 and 15, were cleared in this final phase of examination (**8**), but the results were unfortunately never published by Armstrong himself. The absence of a definitive account for the 1934-9 season is particularly frustrating, not least because of the potentially explosive nature of the finds recovered from Pit 15 in the very final days of excavation. Here, in the base of the shaft, a large artificial platform constructed of mined flint appears to have been found, in close association with a number of carved chalk pieces, the most famous of which, a female figurine, is now in the British Museum. No firm evidence exists, but it is likely that this so-called 'ritual group' was part of an elaborate and somewhat cynical hoax designed to reaffirm a Palaeolithic origin for the mine shaft. Unfortunately, as we shall see, both the perpetrators and intended target of the forgery remain obscure.

Controversy and conflict in Sussex

Controversy and argument, on a scale similar to that at Grimes Graves, also surrounded the pre-war examination of flint mines on the South Downs in Sussex, though here a Neolithic date for the mine sites had never really been in doubt. The main phase of investigation began in the early 1920s, when John Pull, then a plumber and part-time gramophone salesman from Worthing, noticed a series of interesting surface depressions on Blackpatch Hill. The hollows proved to be flint mines, and Pull wasted no time in reporting his discoveries to the local press. Unfortunately his trial excavations seem to have angered certain elements within the local archaeological community, and a series of increasingly vitriolic attacks were launched upon Pull and his colleagues. One particular critic, employing the pseudonym 'Antiquary', wrote to the *Worthing Herald* in November 1923 to suggest that sites such as Blackpatch 'should be opened under the supervision of experienced people, or under the supervision of some society, and not by those who have no experience whatever'. Herbert Toms, curator of the Brighton and Hove Museum, replied to Antiquary's letter almost immediately, chastising him for his tactless comments and noting that 'if there be in the district archaeologists of wider experience and riper judgement, then from them should emanate encouragement and sincere criticism . . . rather than badly veiled snubs and censure'. The written attacks did not end there, however, and continued to focus on Pull's age (then 24) and perceived lack of archaeological experience. W. Dilloway, replying to further anonymous outbursts, commented that such letters presumably left Pull feeling like 'an ambitious young constable who has been asked to fetch a policeman'.

8 The western galleries of Pit 15 at Grimes Graves, originally exposed by Armstrong in 1939 and re-examined by the British Museum between 1972 and 1976. © The British Museum

From the end of 1922, Pull supervised the complete excavation of a mine shaft at Blackpatch (**9**) on behalf of the Worthing Archaeological Society, who at that stage were providing substantial material and financial assistance. Pull presented a report on the excavation of Shaft 1 to the newly formed Earthwork Subcommittee of the Worthing Archaeological Society, which included Dr Eliot Curwen, Dr Millbank Smith, C. Goodman and Marian Frost amongst its members. The committee deemed the report as unsuitable, and, excluding Pull from any further input, published their own account of the excavation in the *Sussex Archaeological Collections*. Both Pull and Herbert Toms resigned from the Worthing Archaeological Society in protest, Pull writing to the local press, noting that the published version was 'not recognised by the authorised excavators'. Distancing himself further from the actions of the earthworks subcommittee, Pull added that their report was a piece of pure fiction that had 'ignored all necessary and no doubt troublesome data'. In response, the Worthing Society withdrew all support from the Blackpatch excavations, leaving Pull to his own devices. The schism between the archaeological 'old guard' and the new breed of archaeological working class enthusiasts was complete.

In 1924 the Earthworks Committee of the Worthing Archaeological Society commenced examination of the flint mines of Harrow Hill (**10**), across the other side of the valley and less than 2km (1 mile) away from where Pull continued to work at

9 *John Pull at the entrance to gallery vi, Shaft 1 at Blackpatch in 1922. © Worthing Museum and Art Gallery*

Blackpatch. One can only imagine the mood in the two camps at this time. Rarely in the history of archaeology has the concept of site intervisibility ever seemed so intimidating. For all their differences, however, Pull and the Curwens both achieved high standards of recording and interpretation. The Curwens report on the 1924-5 examination of Pit 21 at Harrow Hill was published with commendable speed in the 1926 edition of the *Sussex Archaeological Collections*. Pull, presumably after his experience with the archaeological establishment, preferred to disseminate data produced from Blackpatch through the medium of lectures, seminars and local newspapers. As a consequence, much of his work remains largely unknown and ignored today.

Between 1922 and 1932, the investigation of at least nine mine shafts (Shafts 1, 2, 3, 3a, 4, 5, 6, 7 and 'Barrow' 2), four flint working floors, eleven round mounds and a number of other associated features were overseen by Pull and his colleague C.E. Sainsbury at Blackpatch. A series of detailed and well-illustrated articles describing the results of fieldwork, written by Pull and Sainsbury, appeared in the Magazine of the *Worthing Herald*, between 1923 and 1928. A summary of the main results was later published by Pull in his book *The Flint Miners of Blackpatch* in 1932. This book, a popular work for 'experts and general readers', was not intended to be an authoritative description of the excavations. Unfortunately this point was not acknowledged at the time, and Pull found himself once more under attack by the archaeological establishment. Clark and

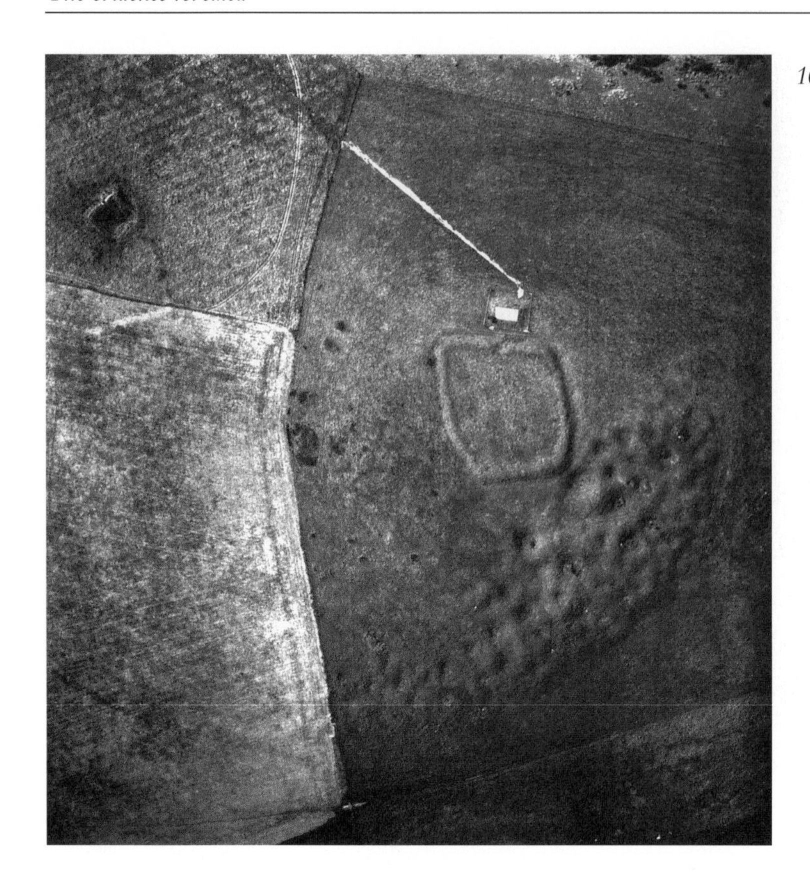

10 Harrow Hill from the air in October 1980. The flint mines are visible as a broad sweep of hollows disappearing into the ploughed field to the left (south) of the photograph. The small, Later Bronze Age, earthwork enclosure overlies and obscures the upper (western) fringes of the mine group. NMR 1846/076. English Heritage © Crown Copyright

Piggott, for example, in their 1933 article defending a Neolithic origin for flint mining in Britain, commented that, in respect of the Blackpatch excavations, 'we cannot recommend a recent publication on this important site', for whilst significant discoveries had been made, the evidence 'is presented so unscientifically that we cannot utilise it'.

Following their investigation of Shaft 21 at Harrow Hill, the Curwens moved to examine a series of irregular hollows along the north-western side of Church Hill opposite Tolmere Pond, presumably looking for an area of prehistoric mining, as yet unclaimed by Pull. The Tolmere pits proved disappointing however, and the excavations came to an abrupt end. Work at Harrow Hill was restarted by George Holleyman on behalf of the Worthing Archaeological Society in 1936 (**11**). Holleyman was keen to ascertain the date of the small rectangular enclosure that crowned the hill, as well as to determine the position of settlements relating to the mining phase. Three shafts, numbered I, II and III, were investigated by the 1936 team, two of the shafts lying beneath the ramparts of the Early Iron Age enclosure (**12**). The results were published the following year in the *Sussex Archaeological Collections*.

Even without the obvious health and safety considerations of working below ground, the clearing and recording of basal galleries in the 1920s and '30s could prove laborious, dangerous and time consuming, especially if the gallery in question was choked with rubble. A vivid depiction of the restricted space available to the modern excavators was later provided by Edmond Venables, who, in an article written for the *West Sussex Gazette*

11 (above) The Harrow Hill excavation team enjoying breakfast at Leigh Farm in 1936. George Holleyman is seated at the far right of the photograph. © Worthing Museum and Art Gallery

12 (right) A break from recording the main gallery of Shaft III at Harrow Hill in 1936. © Worthing Museum and Art Gallery

in 1960, describes a visit to one of the mines opened by John Pull. 'I entered the . . . tunnel' Venables noted,

> which was so narrow that my shoulders rubbed against the walls on either side, while the roof was so low that I could not proceed on hands and knees but was forced to crawl along on my chest. Behind me came a doctor on holiday from India, and behind him came Frazer Hearne. The gallery ran for 60 feet into the hillside, and at the far end was a tiny round room, just large enough for me to turn round but not for my companions to do so. Therefore, they had to wriggle out backwards, and, while I do not suffer from claustrophobia, I was scared pink that they might become wedged in the confined space. When wearing an ordinary jacket, it is one thing to go forward, but quite another thing to go backwards. I was particularly apprehensive about Frazer Hearne, for he was the most burly of the trio and he was wearing a rough tweed plus-four suit, and I had horrible forebodings that his jacket would ruckle up from the hem and that he would be trapped in the narrow tunnel.

A similar feeling of the difficulties experienced by those examining the basal galleries, as well as the exhilaration associated with being the first to explore the subterranean workings, was provided by Elliot Curwen in his book *Prehistoric Sussex* published in 1930. 'A long dark tunnel stretches before us', Curwen observed;

> Slowly and with awe, one of the excavators creeps into the gallery, candle in hand, noticing everything, and careful to disturb nothing. He is acutely conscious that he is the first human being to enter this underground workshop for some four thousand years. Suddenly he catches sight of a row of holes cleanly punched in the chalk wall . . . while on the floor close by is a pick made from the antler of a red deer . . . the holes look as if they had only been made yesterday, fresh and clean-cut, with the chalk burred a little at the lip by the pressure of the pick. Progress along the gallery is far from easy. One must crawl on elbows and stomach, trailing useless legs over hard and angular pieces of chalk, one's fingers spluttered with candle grease. It is warm, and the silence is intensified by the tiny, far-away song of the mosquitoes who have found their way through the chinks in the chalk to this subterranean place of repose.

After finishing with Blackpatch, Pull moved his centre of investigation to Church Hill, excavation of the flint mines here commencing in December of 1932. Work continued intermittently until the outbreak of war in 1939, with detailed excavation summaries appearing regularly in the *Sussex County Magazine*. In November 1945, following the removal of the army from Church Hill, Pull returned, this time being joined by his son-in-law Arthur Voice. Excavation commenced in 1946 with the opening of the 'Great Shaft' (Shaft 4) and continued, with a minor break in 1949 to investigate the site at Tolmere, until 1952. Six shafts (1, 2, 4, 5a, 6 and 7), three pits (A, B and C), fifteen flint working floors and ten round barrows were examined at Church Hill during this time.

13 John Pull emerging from a gallery within Shaft 27 at Cissbury. © Worthing Museum and Art Gallery

In 1947 Pull was persuaded to rejoin the Worthing Archaeological Society. The following year he became a member of the Committee and in 1952 he was elected President. In the same year Pull mobilised the Society to restart a programme of excavation at Cissbury (**13**). Until 1956, work concentrated upon the group of mines to the south-west of the Iron Age enclosure. Two shafts, 24 and 27, and three flint working floors were fully opened at this time, whilst another two shafts, 18 and 23, were partially sampled. Unlike his work at Blackpatch and Church Hill, Pull did not publish summaries of the Cissbury excavations within the popular press. It would appear, however, from the nature of reports preserved in Worthing Museum, that a detailed publication was being seriously considered. Unfortunately, Pull's untimely death prevented this. In November 1960, whilst working as a security guard in the Durrington branch of Lloyds Bank, he was shot during an armed raid. His killer was one of the last people to be hanged in England.

To the end of the twentieth century

Investigation of further flint mine sites in southern Britain continued throughout the 1950s and '60s, but on a smaller scale than that previously conducted by Peake, Armstrong, Holleyman and Pull. Between 1954 and 1955, Barbara and James Watson excavated a shaft at Martin's Clump in Hampshire on behalf of J.F.S. Stone. Unfortunately Stone died before a full report on the site could be made, though a short note appeared later in the *Proceedings of the Hampshire Field Club*. At Long Down in West Sussex, a single shaft and two working floors were examined by E.F. Salisbury between 1955 and 1958, a brief report appearing in the *Sussex Archaeological Collections* for 1961. At Durrington in Wiltshire, two small flint mine shafts (numbered 4 and 5) and three shallow surface workings were examined following their unexpected exposure in the edge of a sewage trench cut in 1952. A short note, by A. St J. Booth and J.F.S. Stone, appeared in the *Wiltshire Archaeological and Natural History Magazine* the same year.

Of all the Neolithic mine shafts excavated in Britain, only two, Pits 1 and 15 at Grimes Graves, had remained clear for regular public access throughout the post-war years. In 1970, the Department of the Environment closed access to Pit 15 following concerns regarding public safety. A decision was then made to open a new shaft, primarily for display purposes, but also in the hope of resolving issues regarding the chronology and past environmental conditions of the Grimes Graves site.

A shaft at the north-eastern margins of the site was duly excavated by Roger Mercer in 1971, the upper fills of the second shaft to the immediate east being examined the following year. For the first time in the history of flint mine investigation, considerable provision was made during the course of the project regarding the health and safety of the excavation team. A fixed gantry provided a secure point of access into the shaft and a platform from which soil could be swiftly moved to waiting dumper trucks via a petrol-driven conveyor belt. Hard hats and field telephones were standard issue for those working below ground level, whilst an electricity generator provided an additional source of light. The 1971 shaft, though contributing much to the debate on Neolithic flint mines, was ultimately deemed unsuitable for display purposes due to the limited nature of subterranean gallery systems, and was not kept open. Instead, attention focussed on Pit I, first opened by Peake in 1914, which, through the provision of secure access and cover, new internal wall supports (**14**) and a series of locked iron grilles designed to limit access to the galleries (**colour plate 15**), was made safe for continued public access and enjoyment.

Following the work of Mercer and the Department of the Environment, examination of mines at Grimes Graves continued under the aegis of the British Museum. The British Museum's programme, directed by Gale Sieveking and conducted by the Prehistoric Flint Mines Working Group of the Dutch Geological Society (Limburg Section), ran from 1972-76 (**15**). The main objective of the programme was to re-examine a number of shafts that had been explored in the nineteenth and early twentieth centuries, and survey them to modern standards. By employing the skills of the Dutch Flint Mines Working Group, it was also hoped that prehistoric extraction techniques could be interpreted through the eyes of a group of modern professional miners. Part of the programme was, in addition, dedicated to the recovery of antler material for radiocarbon dating analysis, the first time that modern dating procedures had been used in the interpretation of Neolithic mines.

Five shafts were re-explored during the 1972-6 programme, namely Greenwell's Pit of 1870, Peake's Pit 2, and Armstrong's Pits II, III and 15. During the course of the excavations, the Dutch team also partially examined the fills and subterranean galleries of a further nineteen shafts (numbered 3a, 11a, 11b, 11d-h, 15a-k), as well as a number of shallow quarries and flint working floors. Resurvey of the shafts revealed a number of inconsistencies in the original published gallery plans (*see* **4**), something which is perhaps

14 A Department of the Environment foreman at work in 1973 rebuilding an internal section of Pit 1 in order to make it both safe and secure for continued public access. © The British Museum

15 Members of the Dutch mining team photographed in 1973. P.J. Felder is seated fourth from left. © The British Museum

not too surprising considering the extreme difficulties faced by the earlier teams in accurately plotting subterranean features. The new surveys also demonstrated the level of damage caused by unsupervised public access to the galleries of Shaft 15, which had been left open following the completion of Armstrong's work in 1939. In some cases visitor damage, which had significantly enlarged gallery systems, had penetrated areas beyond those originally exposed by Armstrong, doing untold damage to previously undisturbed archaeological deposits.

The termination of the British Museum's work at Grimes Graves in 1976 marked the end of the last major phase of intensive excavation into Neolithic flint mines in Britain. Minor investigation of shafts has since been conducted by Fred Aldsworth at Nore Down, West Sussex in 1982, and by David Ride at Martin's Clump in 1984. In 1982, as part of the Fourth International Flint Symposium, P.J. Felder excavated Shaft 13 at Harrow Hill on behalf of Gale Sieveking, further investigations being carried out by Greg Bell two years later. A combination of trial excavation, fieldwalking and geophysical survey at Church Hill, Harrow Hill, Long Down and Stoke Down, conducted by Robin Holgate between 1984-86 on behalf of English Heritage, has better indicated the nature of Neolithic extraction at these sites, as well as the extent of agricultural damage sustained in recent years. The results of limited work at other sites, namely Slonk Hill and Windover Hill in East Sussex, Compton Down in West Sussex, Hambledon Hill in Dorset, Fareham and Little Somborne in Hampshire, East Horsely in Surrey, Pitstone Hill in Buckinghamshire, Dunstable Downs in Bedfordshire, Riddlesdown in Greater London, and Liddington in Wiltshire, has unfortunately proved more difficult to quantify. In most of these latter examples, a Neolithic date looks most unlikely.

Up until the 1990s, the vast majority of archaeological investigation into Neolithic flint extraction had been undertaken upon sites recorded from the chalklands of southern England. Since 1991, however, work by the Archaeology Department of National Museums of Scotland has revealed evidence for a series of Neolithic extraction pits cut into the Buchan Ridge Gravels of Grampian in north-east Scotland. At Den of Boddam, Alan Saville detected the surface remains of pits covering an area of around 12 hectares (30 acres). Excavations conducted between 1991 and 1993 demonstrated that a series of bell-shaped, ungalleried pits had been cut into the Gravels in order to extract rounded flint cobbles. A similar series of pits, largely obscured by later ploughing, were archaeologically examined by Saville to the west of the Den of Boddam, at Skelmuir Hill in 1994.

The investigation of flint mines in the final years of the twentieth century has been characterised by the analysis of the last substantial pieces of unpublished excavation data relating to the Norfolk and Sussex mine series (Grimes Graves by the British Museum and the Sussex John Pull archive by the present author), and the first systematic investigation of all known surface areas of Neolithic mining activity. This latter survey, conducted by the Royal Commission on the Historical Monuments of England between 1994 and 1997, and forming part of the 'Neolithic Industry and Enclosure Project', comprehensively investigated all potential areas of mining in England, compiling detailed plans of every known site. The results of the survey, published by English Heritage in 1999, have revolutionised the perception of Neolithic flint extraction, demonstrating just how extensive, and indeed how well preserved, the mine sites really are.

2 Hoax!

The early history of flint mine exploration is littered with a somewhat surprising quantity of fraudulent data, faked artefacts and suspected hoaxes. This may be due, at least in part, to the way in which some of the first mines were archaeologically investigated, by teams of paid labourers working under supervision. Sometimes this supervision was not close, the relevant antiquarian involved in the work being somewhere else entirely. Labourers were, in some early instances, paid by the finds that they made, something which could conceivably have generated the desire to create more interesting, and financially rewarding, discoveries.

The first flint mines were furthermore being explored at a time when understanding of the full nature and diversity of the prehistoric past was still in its infancy. The concepts of Palaeolithic and Neolithic in terms of artefacts and features were poorly defined and could be easily manipulated. To complicate matters, the deposits found at the base of the flint mines were extremely well preserved and survived in great quantity. Here antiquarians could, for the first time, crawl where the ancient Britons had crawled, see what they had seen and experience the same, sometimes claustrophobic, sense of working underground. Here there was no feeling of a site being disturbed by treasure hunters, developers or farmers in the interim. The tools, impressions and markings made by prehistoric people were as fresh as if made only yesterday. The link to the past was not only tangible, but hugely exhilarating. Here there was potential, if one were so minded, to make data fit the theories and to do so in conclusive fashion. Even the smallest of finds could change the perception of what the shafts were and how they had originally been used. The problem that we face today is that, by modern standards, the amount of on-site recording conducted was minimal. Attempting to positively identify a fraud, even if highly suspected, can prove extremely difficult.

Greenwell's stone axe

The first doubts regarding the authenticity of specific finds from Grimes Graves came at the very end of the nineteenth century, when concerns were being raised about the date of the Norfolk site. Arguments for a Palaeolithic origin could be made for almost all of the artefacts recovered from the site, especially as understanding of the terms Palaeolithic and Neolithic were at this time ill-defined. The ground axe that Canon Greenwell had recovered from his 1868-70 excavation (**16**), proved a notable impediment for those advocating a Palaeolithic date for the mine however, as it was a classic type-find of the Neolithic period. Greenwell, in his paper of 1870, mentions the object in a fairly casual

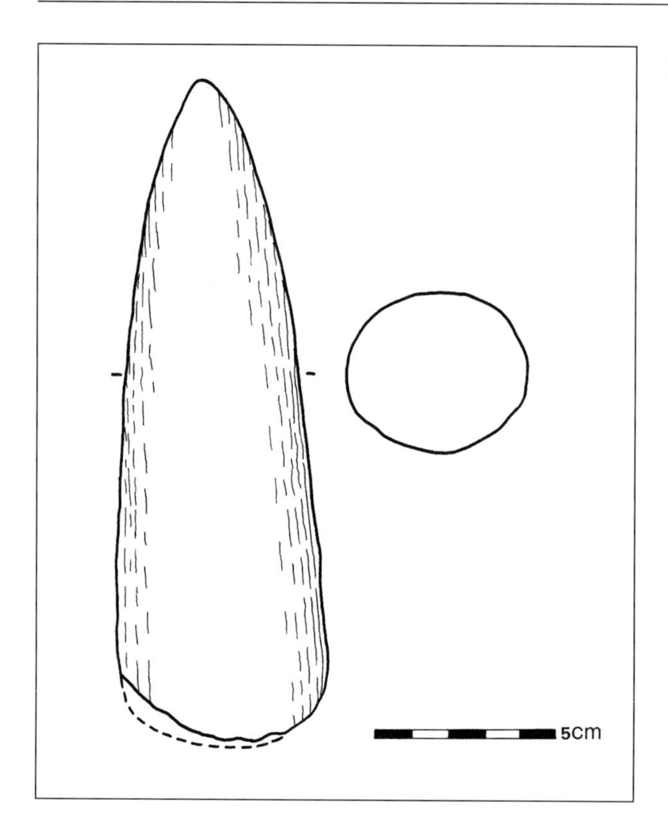

16 The stone axe recovered from Greenwell's Shaft at Grimes Graves in 1869: a notable stumbling block for those advocating a Palaeolithic date for flint mining. Redrawn from Clark and Piggott 1933

manner, noting that the walls of the first gallery in his shaft had been originally cut with a stone 'hatchet', an example of which 'was found in the first gallery, four feet from the entrance'. This axe was, as Greenwell noted, a somewhat unusual find, though its presence in the mine helped to establish a Neolithic date 'when metal was unknown, but when the grinding and polishing of stone was understood'.

Although only a single artefact, the discovery of such an axe from a primary context in a mine, could effectively destroy the whole argument concerning a Palaeolithic origin for flint extraction. It is hardly surprising, therefore, that rumours surrounding the validity of the find were soon rife within certain antiquarian circles. The axe, it was said, was a clever modern forgery. It had not been found in such a primary position within the mine. It had even perhaps been 'surreptitiously introduced into the workings by modern workmen'. In 1908, with the artefact having been increasingly excluded from archaeological debate, W. Allen Sturge decided to resolve the issue once and for all. First, in the hope of discovering the origin of the rumours, Sturge interviewed those archaeologists who had accepted the find to be a hoax. In the course of these interviews, no evidence to substantiate the idea of deliberate fraud could be ascertained. In fact Sturge noted that the only real doubts concerning the authenticity of the find had been from those who believed that, as the mines were Palaeolithic, the axe 'ought not to have been found there'. Only later did this somewhat circular argument become formalised into a story of dishonest workmen trying to deceive Greenwell.

Next Sturge wrote to Greenwell, asking for a more definitive account concerning the finding of the axe. Greenwell replied that, though it was true that he had not been present at the moment of first discovery, he had been called to the spot by a workman who believed the find to be bone. At that point Greenwell had personally overseen the removal of the axe from the chalk rubble. The context of artefact was not, in any case, a significant issue, Greenwell reiterating that long before its discovery, the presence of just such a stone tool had been indicated by marks relating to the original cutting of the mine, preserved upon the walls of the gallery. On examining the axe head, Greenwell discovered that 'with a blunted cutting edge, and with a small piece broken off one corner', the object exactly matched the marks recorded from the gallery wall. This was clearly the very axe that had been used to cut this particular part of the subterranean workface. Sturge then interviewed the son of one of the principal workmen employed during the 1868-70 excavation, concluding that 'there can be no possible question of the authenticity of the axe'.

Of course the establishment of a secure context for the stone axe did not eradicate suggestions that the Grimes Graves mines were Palaeolithic in origin. Four years after Sturge's rebuttal of the suspected hoax, Reginald Smith, Keeper of the British and Medieval Antiquities at the British Museum, was firmly advocating that the mines predated the Neolithic on the basis that certain flint tools recovered from the site matched known Palaeolithic examples. Though Smith accepted that the ground axe head was not fraudulent, he argued that it was still a unique find, whilst discoveries made in Norway and elsewhere had then recently suggested that the grinding and polishing of stone could have occurred long before the Neolithic. Smith's arguments appear, from a modern perspective, to be unnecessarily complex. The evidence was building up against the Palaeolithic hypothesis, especially as the distinct palaeoforms that Smith and others referred to were increasingly being seen, not as finished artefacts, but as an intermediary stage in the manufacture of Neolithic axes. What the proponents of the Old Stone Age hypothesis needed was a type-find of their own — something that would clearly link Grimes Graves to an early period in human development. In 1916 they got what they were looking for.

The 'flint crust' engravings

The examination of flint working floor 16 at Grimes Graves by Peake, Armstrong and Mr and Mrs E.T. Lingwood in 1916, produced a number of interesting artefacts, reported upon the following year by Peake in his presidential address to the Prehistoric Society of East Anglia. The bulk of the material was, as one would expect, represented by struck flint, most of which was classified as being Palaeolithic. There was, however, one particular find of quite unusual nature: a single piece of 'flint crust' with lines cut directly into the cortex. The exact context and potential significance of the piece was not commented on by Peake in the published report, though he did observe that the piece had originally been found by Armstrong. More pieces of engraved flint cortex were found, apparently by Peake, in 1920, this time from the area of floor 75. One piece bore 'an engraved outline suggesting portions of the human figure'. Following this discovery Armstrong made sure that 'every fragment of flint crust' unearthed during the course of his excavations was duly carefully examined. Sure enough, in the days that followed, more startling discoveries were made.

The investigation of floor 85c produced a piece of mined floorstone, 'embedded about 2in deep in the red sand', which had been carved with a 'naturalistic representation' of an elk or red deer. A second cortex engraving, found in the upper layers of the floor, only 1.2m from the first, portrayed the head and upper torso of a horse with 'an impaling arrow or lance' apparently penetrating its neck. The depictions were crude, though the material upon which they had been carved was exceedingly tough, Armstrong observing that 'considerable skill . . . must have been necessary' to complete the imagery. Favourable comparisons were immediately made between the new discoveries and examples of Old Stone Age art from the south of France. Those who had long argued that the British flint mines predated the Neolithic now had just the evidence they needed. In his conclusion to the year's interim statement, published in the *Proceedings of the Prehistoric Society of East Anglia* for 1922, Armstrong observed that the floor 85c engravings strongly implied that 'Grimes Graves was in occupation by Palaeolithic man'.

Armstrong continued the examination of floor 85c, and of associated features, with his colleague Dr Favell in August 1921. One of the working floors, identified as floor c, produced a large number of incised blocks of floorstone, four of which possessed further representational depictions. The first, found by Armstrong, was of an 'elk or hind', its head raised as if 'browsing from an overhanging branch'. The fainter outline of a 'calf-like creature' and two horned animals identified as ox were also noticed from this first piece. The second engraving, also found by Armstrong, depicted 'three animal heads, two of which have horns'. These were interpreted as being deer and ox. The last two major pieces were found by Favell, one with an unidentified animal, the other with a 'triple parallel line engraving'. The lines potentially linked the flint crust engravings with the linear incisions noted by Peake and others from the basal workings of Pits 1 and 2 at Grimes Graves and those opened by Lane Fox and Harrison at Cissbury in the late 1870s. Again Armstrong noted that 'the art of engraving on stone and bone has long been looked upon as a distinctive feature of Late Palaeolithic times', therefore the finding of such material from working floors associated with the mines was 'of more than ordinary importance'. The evidence gathered by Armstrong suggested to him that, though several periods of extraction activity were demonstrated at Grimes Graves, the earliest phases in all probability dated to the end of the Old Stone Age.

The pieces of engraved cortex were shown to many eminent scholars, amongst whom was L'Abbe Henri Breuil, Professor au College de France and acknowledged expert of Palaeolithic art. Breuil, a talented artist in his own right, had been copying and recording examples of recently discovered cave art since 1900. In his life he spent, by his own reckoning, well over 700 days in the caves of France and Spain, painstakingly tracing prehistoric images for posterity. Breuil appears to have been satisfied over the authenticity and nature of the pieces from Grimes Graves, commenting that the first to be found from floor 85c was likely to represent a red deer (*Cervus elaphus*). It is a shame that Breuil did not have time to analyse the pieces further. If he had, he may well have recognised them, for both of the floor 85c 'discoveries' are almost exact copies of Palaeolithic engravings that he had already observed from a number of cave sites in southern France and northern Spain.

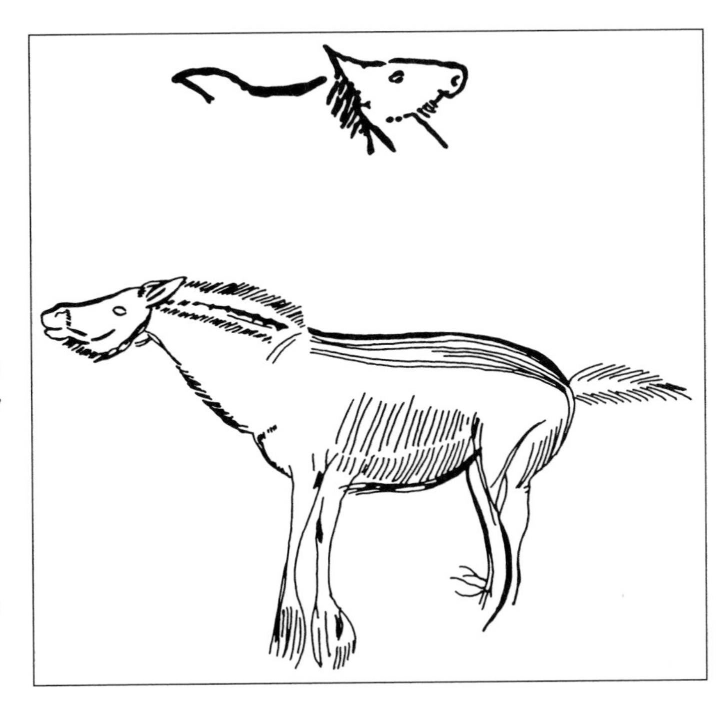

17 Inspiration for the flint crust engravings?: The horse engraving found by Armstrong on flint from floor 85c at Grimes Graves (top) compared with a genuine Palaeolithic example (bottom), recorded by Breuil from Trois Freres in the early years of the twentieth century. Neither to scale. Top redrawn from Armstrong 1922. Bottom redrawn from Bahn and Vertut 1988

The horse from floor 85c is a particularly fine copy of a Breuil original, in this instance a horse from the site of Trois Freres made by the abbe in the early years of the twentieth century (**17**). The extended nature of the horses head, the position and shape of the eyes, ears, nose and mouth in both examples are too close as to be coincidental. Even the hairs on the underside of the horses head, as well as the nature of its tail, mirror the original from France. All the copier has done to alter the basic format, so as to suggest dissimilarity, is shorten the dimensions of the horse and invert the whole image so that the Grimes Graves copy faces right, not left as in the original. Something similar has happened with the Grimes Graves red deer and, although no direct comparison can be seen in the Trois Freres assemblage, sufficient parallels exist within Breuil's portfolio, most notably perhaps the ibex recorded from the Spanish cave site of Castillo (**18**). As with the horse, the most significant difference between the Grimes Graves 'original' and that from a genuine Palaeolithic context is that the Norfolk example again faces in a different direction. The other pieces recovered from floors 16, 85c and c may also be closely paralleled with examples of engraved Palaeolithic art recorded from the south of France.

This all, of course, leaves us with the question of responsibility. Who, within the excavation team at Grimes Graves, was so keen to establish a Palaeolithic date for flint extraction on the site that they were prepared to fabricate the evidence? Suspicion must obviously fall upon those who first proposed an early date and those who later defended it vigorously. Whoever the culprit was, and there may have been more than one person responsible, they would need to be sure that the hoax would not be detected. Any faked artefact would need to be plausible and its context and means of discovery would all have to be accepted without question. It would need to be comparable with definite pieces of Palaeolithic archaeology recovered from secure contexts elsewhere in Europe, but it must

18 *Inspiration for the flint crust engravings?: The Grimes Graves red deer (top) found by Armstrong, compared with a Palaeolithic ibex (bottom), recorded by Breuil from Castillo. Neither to scale. Top redrawn from Armstrong 1922. Bottom redrawn from Bahn and Vertut 1988*

not be so comparable that suspicions would be raised regarding authenticity. The fraud would further require a direct link to a significant phase of mining, so that it could not be easily dismissed. What better in this respect than an engraved piece of mined floorstone?

Given the range of finds, as well as the five-year period over which they were all found, we may plausibly assume that the hoaxer was present at all times. Whoever they were, they would need to ensure that the frauds were all securely and plausibly placed. They would also need to guarantee that all examples of their handiwork were recovered. As suspicion would certainly have been aroused if only one person had discovered every single engraving, the hoaxer would need to make sure that the pieces were set down where they may reasonably be 'found' by other members of the team. If this failed, leaving the hoaxer no option but to 'discover' the artefacts his or herself, then they would need to ensure that a sufficient number of independent witnesses were present to verify the authenticity of the find.

Suspicion could fall, as it had with Greenwell's axe in 1870, upon any workman employed to move spoil. Interestingly, no extra workmen appear to have been used in the exploration of working floors at Grimes Graves between 1916 and 1922, as no major features were then being opened. In fact Peake specifically notes that 'no workmen were available' in 1916, all work being carried out by himself, Armstrong and the Lingwoods. In 1921, the second batch of engravings were found during work conducted by Armstrong, B.W.J. Kent and J.B. Sidebotham. The final set of carvings were discovered the same year in an excavation staffed only by Armstrong and Dr R.V. Favell. It would appear that throughout all these discoveries there was only one constant: A. Leslie Armstrong. It was Armstrong who found the very first piece of engraved floorstone, as Peake notes in the 1917 paper. It was he who found the first 'animalistic' carvings from Floor 85c, although he is very careful to note that both Kent and Sidebotham were present when the discoveries were made. It was he who was first able to identify the animals engraved, noting that they were 'so faintly drawn as to be unnoticeable unless deliberately looked for'. It was he who first connected the pieces to Palaeolithic examples recovered only a few years previously from cave sites in France and Spain. It was he who, perhaps rather cheekily, even demonstrated how the engravings had originally been made, using a flint blade on a piece to scratch a series of lines and his monogram 'ALA'.

The only pieces of engraved flint not directly found by Armstrong were those discovered by Peake in September 1920, Armstrong making it very clear that the examples were found 'a few days prior' to his own visit to the site (therefore clearing him of potential responsibility), and those found by Favell in 1921. The first pieces could easily have been planted by anyone for Peake to find, providing that they knew where he was likely to be working. Of the latter group of four pieces, only two were actually found by Favell, Armstrong being in close proximity at all times. The last piece to be found by Favell was located, in Armstrong's words, 'within half an hour of abandoning the site!', and it is likely that, had Favell not found the piece by the end of the day, the forger would have had to step forward to 'find' it for him.

The balance of probability is therefore that the forger of the Palaeolithic-like engravings at Grimes Graves was Armstrong himself. Armstrong was a highly capable and talented archaeologist, but he may have felt that, at Grimes Graves, his theories were coming under increasing, and thoroughly unwarranted, attack. Mining in Norfolk had, in his mind, clearly begun in the Palaeolithic. All that he needed was more conclusive proof, and the engravings certainly provided this. The urgency with which Armstrong later defended the Palaeolithic origins for the Norfolk site, and the passion with which he attacked those, such as Clark and Piggott, who doubted him, may perhaps now be viewed in a new light. Increased criticism of his theories in the latter half of the 1930s may have driven Armstrong to greater efforts in order to discover new evidence to support the now rather beleaguered Palaeolithic hypothesis. In July 1939, whether coincidence or not, just such a piece of evidence was found.

The Venus of Grimes Graves

The arguments surrounding the possible Palaeolithic or Neolithic origin of flint mining rumbled well on into the 1930s. Armstrong, though initially an ardent supporter of an early date for the mines, formulating his own evolutionary concept for flint extraction, may, by the late 1930s, have been harbouring significant doubts concerning his former beliefs. Gillian Varndell of the British Museum has noted that, in an unfinished draft concerning the final season at Grimes Graves, Armstrong had observed that the Palaeolithic axe forms, which had been used for so long to support an early date for flint extraction, may represent no more than a particular technique of flint knapping, one which was employed throughout the Neolithic period. If Armstrong was having doubts concerning his original interpretation of the mines, then these may have been communicated to his workforce. It is certainly interesting that, at a time when the chronology of the Norfolk mine series finally appeared to be nearing resolution, another explosive find almost dragged the whole debate back to square one.

On 6 July 1939, less than two months before Britain's declaration of war against Germany, the final layers of fill were removed from the base of Pit 15, the last shaft to be excavated by Armstrong at Grimes Graves. No detailed account of what happened on that or any subsequent day has survived. Armstrong's site notebook unfortunately does not cover this particular phase of work, possibly because the pressures of completing the examination of the shaft proved too great. It is clear, however, that the discoveries made during these last days were unlike anything yet recorded from a British flint mine. On the south-western edge of the pit, standing on a chalk plinth to the immediate right of gallery 7, stood a 10.2cm high carved chalk figure of 'a pregnant woman kneeling, with arms extended upon the thighs and prominent breasts' (**19**). In front of the figurine, on the floor of the shaft, lay 'an ogive shaped platform' of densely packed flint, the apex of which pointed towards the carved figure, almost in the way of a directional arrow (**20**). Seven

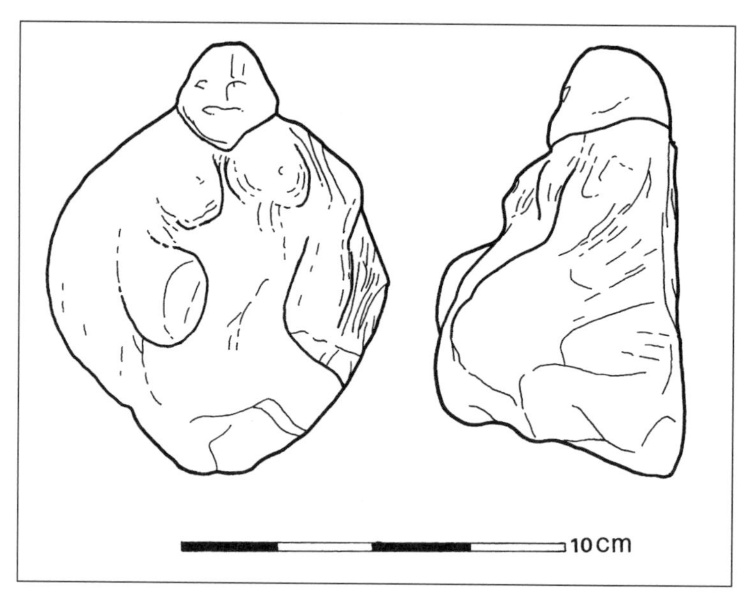

19 The Grimes Graves chalk goddess figurine from Pit 15: front and side. Redrawn from Longworth and Varndell 1996

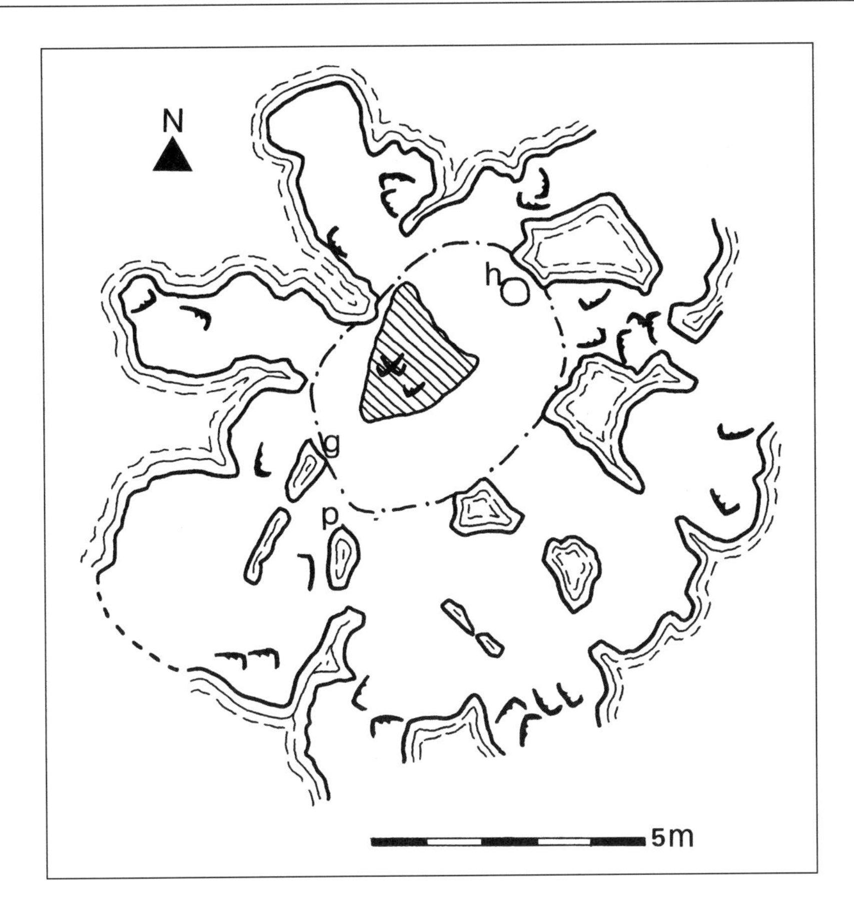

20 *The gallery plan of Pit 15 at Grimes Graves as recorded by Armstrong in 1939 but never published by him. The positions of antler picks and the so-called 'ritual group' are all marked: g = goddess figurine; h = hearth; p = phallus. Compare the gallery plan here with the 1972-6 resurvey by the British Museum (figure* **33***). Redrawn from Longworth and Varndell 1996*

antler picks were observed lying over the platform, whilst a small 'chalk vessel' was found at the base of the pedestal supporting the figurine. Behind the platform, on the opposite edge of the shaft from the figurine, Armstrong noted the presence of charcoal and wood ash which he interpreted as a hearth which had 'probably played some part in the ritual performed there'. A carved chalk phallus (**21**) was recovered from an area of the shaft floor to the south-east of the female figure, whilst a discrete cluster of three flint nodules 'arranged in the form of a phallus' as well as a large oval nodule, were found 'in the central area' of the entrance to gallery 7.

The carved female figure has, since its discovery, represented the crowning discovery from the Grimes Graves site, appearing on the cover to the first series of official guidebooks, as well as being reproduced in countless publications and taking pride of place for many years in the British Museum's prehistoric gallery. As one would expect, many attempts were made to interpret the piece, though the official view, as noted in the

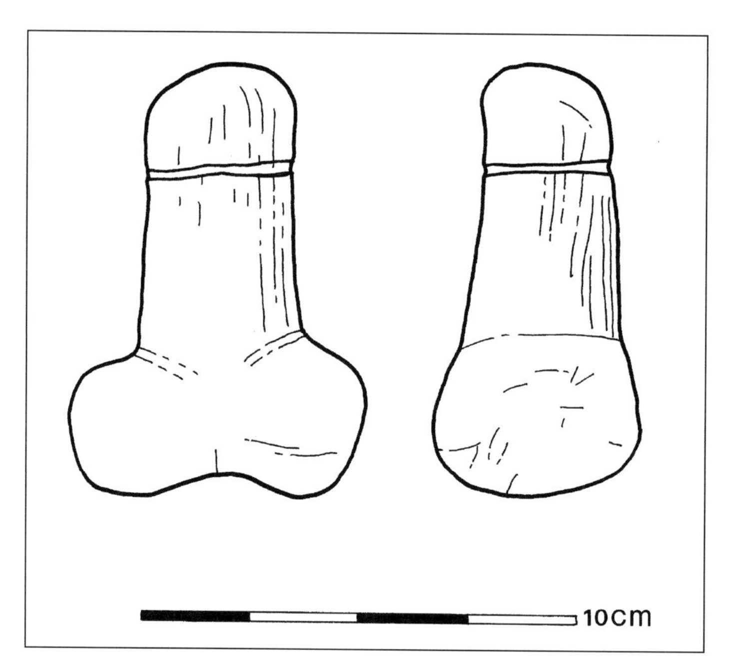

21 The carved chalk phallus from Pit 15 at Grimes Graves. Redrawn from Longworth and Varndell 1996

1963 guide, was that it represented 'an earth goddess' which, in combination with the other recorded finds, had been designed as an 'appeal for more abundant or better quality flint in the next pit'. Quite what Armstrong thought of the assemblage is not known, though he repeatedly used the term 'goddess' when describing the figurine.

As a piece of Neolithic representational art, the female figure is unique. Examples of carved chalk body parts, most noticeably male genitalia, have been recorded from a variety of other Neolithic sites in southern Britain, but none approach the full body form of the Grimes Graves example. Parallels may be drawn, however, with an earlier form of prehistoric carving, namely the so-called 'Venus' figurines occasionally found in mainland European Palaeolithic contexts. The term 'Venus' first appears to have been applied to these carved female figurines in the early 1860s. Comparatively few examples of this type of Palaeolithic representational art are known, but their dramatic form, with pendulous breasts, bulging thighs and enlarged bellies, is undeniably striking. Dating the figurines has proved difficult — few come from well stratified contexts and fewer still are found in close association with datable material, though the current assumption is that the more developed pieces were being manufactured around 30,000 BC.

Unlike the floor 85c and C engravings at Grimes Graves, the Pit 15 figurine possesses no direct parallel from Europe, though the basic similarity of form, swelling breasts and ample belly, is clear enough. No mention is made of any such comparison by Armstrong or any other commentator on the mines at the time of discovery, presumably because the debate over the origins of the mines was effectively coming to an end. The pit from which the figure was retrieved was also not one of Armstrong's so-called 'primitive pits', which he had earlier suggested represented the first shafts cut at the Norfolk site. The implication of the find would however have been obvious, especially after Smith's paper of 1912, in which he argued that a carved chalk penis found by Greenwell in the course of the 1868-70 excavations was more likely to be of Palaeolithic date as 'Neolithic man has so far given no evidence of artistic capacity at all comparable to that of the Palaeolithic troglodytes'.

It is the nature of discovery that, perhaps above all else, gives rise to serious doubts concerning the authenticity of the Pit 15 assemblage. In 1984, Ethel Rudkin, a close friend of Armstrong, retold the events of 1939 to Kevin Leahy of Scunthorpe Museum, a story that was later related to Gillian Varndell of the British Museum. Rudkin remembered that, on the day of the discovery, Armstrong had been behaving in a strange way and had not permitted her access to the excavation area. This seemed somewhat bizarre, as Rudkin was an experienced excavator, apparently the only other one on site that day, and had accompanied Armstrong on a number of previous expeditions. Nevertheless, Rudkin accepted Armstrong's judgement and waited patiently at the surface in her car. At some point Armstrong emerged from Shaft 15, carrying both the figurine and the phallus, both of which he left in Rudkin's care. Presumably quite bored by this time, Rudkin made a copy of the figurine with a flint blade from a piece of waste chalk rubble. When Armstrong returned again, he reacted with fury to the duplication of his prized artefact. Their friendship ended that day.

Perhaps Armstrong was enraged because he felt that Rudkin was not treating the find with the seriousness it deserved. Rudkin later confessed that the duplicate and original were, on the day of the discovery, being passed around, swapped and replaced by members of the excavation team, something which may well have hurt Armstrong deeply. A mischievous streak certainly appears to have permeated the work team at Grimes Graves, as demonstrated by a carved chalk head of an Egyptian sphinx residing in the British Museum's Armstrong collection.

Two possibilities present themselves regarding the origin of the female figurine. Firstly that Armstrong was himself implicated in the manufacture of the piece, as he clearly was in the flint crust engravings found some seventeen years previously. In this scenario, his desire to exclude Rudkin from the work face could be explained by his need to fabricate the evidence in peace. Armstrong's anger at Rudkin over her duplication of the 'original' artefact would therefore be understandable, for she had just demonstrated how quick and easy it was to make a plausible modern copy. It is not fully clear what Armstrong's motive in such a hoax would have been however, especially if he was already beginning to argue that the 'Palaeolithic tool forms' discovered at Grimes Graves were not necessarily Palaeolithic at all. Pit 15 was not, as noted above, in any case a Primitive Pit of the sort that Armstrong had earlier advocated were of pre-Neolithic date.

A second possibility is that Armstrong was not part of the hoax. Given his involvement in the earlier frauds, however, he may well have suspected something was amiss. In this scenario the hoaxer could have been someone who either remained adamant that the mines were of Palaeolithic date, or maybe they just wished to enliven a somewhat dull excavation. If Armstrong possessed doubts regarding the authenticity of the piece, and did not know for sure who had been responsible for its fabrication, then his reasons for excluding experienced members of the team, such as Rudkin, may have had more to do with a desire to understand what he was actually dealing with and to work out just who the major suspects for the hoax were likely to have been. Returning to the surface to find that Rudkin had copied the first figurine could, in this particular scenario, have upset him as it appeared to closely implicate her in the deception.

Stuart Piggott, writing in 1986, remembered that rumours were circulating at the time of discovery that the whole assemblage had been faked in order to deceive Armstrong. Unfortunately, given the pedigree of rumours that similarly circulated around the discovery of Greenwell's stone axe in 1870, such whisperings must be treated with caution. Nevertheless, it is true that the Pit 15 figurine would have been comparatively easy to manufacture and duplicate, and, as it had been made by someone using a flint blade, it is almost impossible to date conclusively. The similarity to Palaeolithic forms (especially given the more obvious 'flint crust' frauds of 1916-21), its uniqueness in the British Neolithic, anomalous position in the mine, relative ease of manufacture, evidence of duplication and strange circumstances of discovery and removal, without detailed record, must all argue against the piece being authentic. It is perhaps unlikely, given Armstrong's revised ideas of the Palaeolithic origin for the mines, that he was himself ultimately part of the hoax, for it is unclear what he would have had to gain from it. It is of course possible that the perpetrator, or perpetrators, of the fraud were hoping to re-establish the Palaeolithic debate by creating something that was out of place in the context of the British Neolithic. If so, then it is arguable that they could perhaps have planned their fraud with more care and attention to detail.

Alternatively, as noted above, the fraud may have been intended as a way of enlivening the final days of the 1939 season. If the placing of the pieces at the base of the shaft was intended either to add sensation to the dig, or as a practical joke to temporarily deceive Armstrong, then it is likely that the joke seriously backfired. Whoever had been responsible for the placement within the mine would have been unwilling to confess once the finds had been accepted and their discovery notified to a number of prominent specialists without being made to look foolish. Perhaps Armstrong himself suspected something, or heard the rumours to which Piggott alluded, and as a consequence did not have the heart to continue the debate surrounding the piece, or felt he could not write a definitive version of the discovery in 1939 without himself being implicated.

If the 'Grimes Graves Goddess' is, in all likelihood, no older than the third decade of the twentieth century AD, how does this affect our understanding of the remaining parts of the Pit 15 assemblage? The chalk phallus is, in intent at least, mirrored by similar pieces from elsewhere in the British Neolithic, though none are quite as accomplished as the Grimes Graves example. The flint platform may be genuine, since similar platforms of mined flint were recorded from the Blackpatch site in Sussex (most notably in Barrow 3). It is possible, even if the other artefacts from the base of Pit 15 were faked, that the platform was itself genuine, perhaps providing the inspiration for the hoax in the first place. Given that the platform appears to have been shaped so that it is orientated towards the pedestal and figurine, significant doubts regarding its authenticity must be raised. It may of course have been genuine, having been only modified by the hoaxers, or it could well have been entirely generated by them for Armstrong to find. Given the controversy that surrounds the chalk finds from Pit 15, as well as a number of discoveries from elsewhere at Grimes Graves, all finds recorded from the base of this, the last pre-war shaft to be excavated, must of necessity be treated with extreme caution and suspicion.

The anomalous bronze axe head

In the course of the partial re-examination, in 1921, of the basal galleries in Shaft 1 at Grimes Graves, Armstrong discovered a Later Bronze Age socketed bronze axe. The position of such an artefact, so deeply embedded in the lower fills of a mineshaft, was clearly anomalous. Roger Mercer, writing in 1981, noted the find, commenting that its presence here probably indicated some on-site mischief-making. Unlike the Palaeolithic deception from the flint cortex however, the purpose of such mischief would seem unclear. Why would Armstrong, who appears to have been working with only one other excavator, B.W.J. Kent, at this time, wish to propagate a Bronze Age date for the flint extraction, when he had so strongly advocated a Palaeolithic date in other quarters? It is possible that someone, including perhaps Armstrong and Kent, wished to suggest that mining had an extensive life span, continuing well past the introduction of metal to the British Isles. It is possible that some other interested party wished to dispense with the Palaeolithic/Neolithic debate and restart the argument that the mines of Grimes Graves were essentially Bronze Age.

It is perhaps more plausible that the bronze axe was not an intentional fraud, as others had suggested for the stone axe recovered by Greenwell's team in 1870. Armstrong had already noted, prior to his reinvestigation of Pit 1, that 'considerable spadework was necessary' because a large quantity of debris (some 2.5m), had formed in the base of the shaft, following the weathering of the exposed shaft walls. Such erosion, leading to the gradual enlargement of the weathering cone of the pit, could easily have dislocated spoil from the surface area of the shaft mouth. Instances such as this, as Armstrong himself noted in 1922, could have ensured that material relating to the later use of the site, the axe included, would have fallen from the upper sandy layer and into the still open basal levels of the pit. As other forms of Later Bronze Age metalwork have indeed been found around the mouths of flint mines, this remains a distinct possibility. The chance that the bronze axe head indicates an intentional piece of foul play is, here at least, rather slim.

Ancient writing from Cissbury

Engravings set within the very walls of mine shafts had been noted at Cissbury since the mid-1870s and at Grimes Graves since the excavations of 1914. J. Park Harrison had become particularly interested in the discovery of carvings from the Cissbury pits, recording a diverse series of markings between 1875 and 1878. Most of the recorded pieces appeared genuine enough, since having been paralleled by markings at other mine sites such as Harrow Hill and Long Down, but some did arouse a certain degree of concern regarding their authenticity. At the entrance to the northern gallery at the base of Willett's pit, for example, Harrison observed two markings 'resembling the figure 16'. The pieces were not copied in detail, but Harrison's later comments suggest that both clearly compared with the Arabic numbering system. Both had been cut with a flint, Harrison noting that 'no difference could be detected in the tone or colour of the incisions and that of the old chalk surface'.

Harrison became increasingly obsessed with the markings from Cissbury, discovering a range of similar pieces from Tindall's 1874 shaft and more from Willett's earlier investigations and those overseen by Lane Fox. Some of these pieces were in situ, but most appeared on loose blocks of chalk. Their apparent regular setting and organisation suggested to Harrison that they might indicate an early form of writing. Others were not so impressed. Lane Fox, after Harrison had delivered his first paper on the subject to the Royal Anthropological Institute, noted that 'I cannot bring myself to feel the same confidence in their antiquity that he does', drawing attention to the fact that the shafts in question had long open to the public after excavation and that the marks could easily be modern. 'Nothing could be more natural', Lane Fox went on 'for an individual . . . to immortalise himself by scoring his name, especially upon any object or monument of antiquity', adding that, both he and his workmen had done exactly that, following their exploration of the deeper pits, with the date of the excavation 'as a record for future generations'.

Some of the incisions recorded by Harrison were very likely to be genuine, Lane Fox observing that a number had actually been revealed in his presence, but probably not all were of similar antiquity. Particular doubt was cast on those figures that more closely resembled numbers or a form of writing. 'I had myself been on the look out for such marks', Lane Fox observed in 1877, 'but for obvious reasons did not tell the men.' This implies that Lane Fox was well aware that workmen employed to excavate the flint mines may, in their willingness to please the director of operations, have found items that they believed would impress him. Though not doubting the integrity of his own team, Lane Fox observed dryly that 'one might infer' from the number of inscriptions found after Harrison's first discovery, 'that the marks were not made until after the attention of the workmen had been drawn to the occurrence of said features'. Then again one often does not find a particular form of evidence until one knows what one is looking for and it is possible that so many engravings were only recorded after Harrisons's first discovery, simply because no one had previously been aware of their existence.

Harrison remained convinced of the authenticity of the markings, reiterating, in the discussion that followed the presentation of his paper in 1877, that none of the engravings appeared to have been of recent origin. A number of new carvings had been observed in Willett's pit, most noticeably one by a certain 'William Penfold' who had gained access to the shaft in 1875. These particular impressions 'at once caught the eye, owing to the fresh appearance of the letters', whereas the other pieces possessed the 'warmer tint of the old chalk surfaces'. The debate continued, especially after further engravings were recorded by Harrison at Cissbury, but never appears to have attained resolution. It is a pity, in this respect, that a detailed record of the more unusual forms was not taken at the time, for it is now almost impossible to decide upon the authenticity of all pieces. Certainly unusual carvings did not prove to be unique to Harrison's explorations, other forms later being noted by Pull from Cissbury and Church Hill. Unfortunately the absence of a more detailed record for the pieces found in 1875-8, when combined with the observation that the shafts from which the marks were found had not been sealed to prevent public access, means that the argument concerning origin, meaning and authenticity cannot be taken further at this stage.

The Cissbury fish

Disturbance of subterranean working areas by unauthorised visitors to the mines was something that particularly worried John Pull during his later investigation of shafts at Cissbury between 1952 and 1956. It was only during the investigation of Shaft 27, however, that doubts regarding the contamination of the workface became very real. In May 1953, a human skeleton was partially uncovered at the entrance to one of the gallery systems and, whilst there is no doubt as to the authenticity of the skeleton itself, one find in particular caused Pull some concern.

On the 2 June, following the removal of the majority of the skeleton, excavation of gallery fill revealed a number of finger and toe bones that had been overlooked. While this material was being carefully removed, a curious piece of carved and polished bone in the shape of a fish was recovered (**22**). Pull, in a letter to the British Museum, noted that the find had been made 'near the left hand' of the skeleton, the implication perhaps being that the individual concerned had been carrying the piece at the time of the roof collapse. Since its discovery, however, there has been some considerable doubt over the genuineness of the fish, especially as it compares extremely well with a number of post-Medieval gaming counters noted elsewhere across Sussex.

It is possible that the find represents something dropped by an illicit visitor to Shaft 27, though security to this feature appears to have been sound. Alternatively, the artefact may have been placed within the gallery as part of a prank intended to temporarily deceive Pull. It is certainly clear throughout the letters and notes surviving in Worthing Museum that the atmosphere amongst the volunteer team at Cissbury was lively, Pull himself being noted for 'a certain impish humour'. Given the seriousness in which the mine excavation work was taken, however, it would seem unlikely that Pull himself would have been responsible for such a prank, especially, as with Armstrong in Pit 15 at Grimes Graves, he would appear to have had nothing to gain from such a deception. Earlier in his career Pull had been accused, by an anonymous critic, of hoaxing a particular find, in this case an 'engraved' flint. Pull retorted angrily that his critic was 'absurdly mistaken in supposing

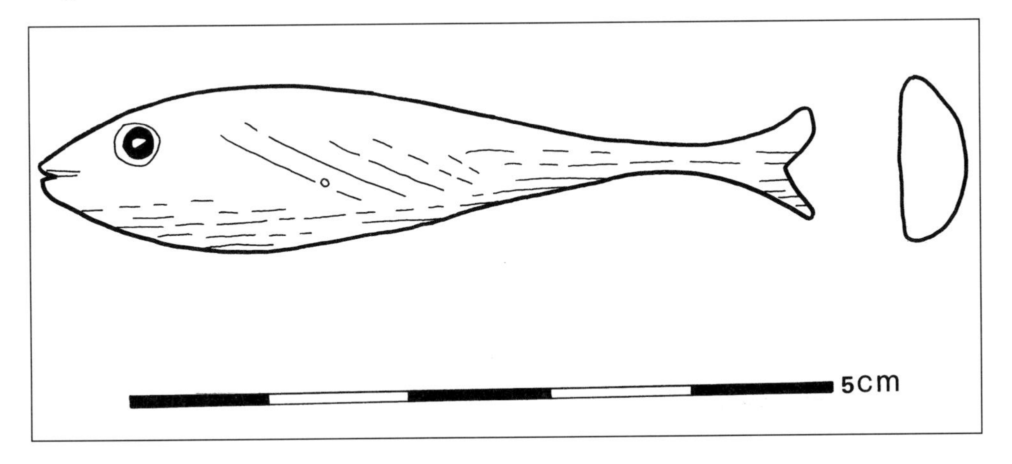

22 The carved and polished bone fish from Shaft 27 at Cissbury. Redrawn from Russell 2000

that the excavators have removed and examined well over 100 tons of debris at Blackpatch for the purpose of perpetrating jokes upon scientific authorities or the general public. Nor have the excavators done this with the object of recording jokes which may have been played upon them.'

If the fish is modern, as seems likely, its placing in the gallery being intended as part of a practical joke by persons unknown, then as with the Grimes Graves figurine, it is probable that whoever was responsible would have been unwilling to confess once the find had been made public. Pull may well have entertained some doubts concerning the authenticity of the find, but, when writing to the British Museum, he goes to some length to convince the Keeper, and perhaps by implication convince himself, that forgery was unlikely, commenting that as the shaft was securely fenced 'there is little chance of any planting by any intruder'.

The Cissbury deer

The discovery of the so-called 'ivory fish' and the acknowledgement that it is not a genuine Neolithic piece may give credence to the view that a series of carvings later recorded from the walls of galleries radiating from Shaft 27, one of which appeared to be fish-like, may similarly be fraudulent. These carvings, discovered between November 1953 and August 1954, consist of the heads of two red deer, a short horned bull, a possible fish and a more enigmatic 'star sign'. Given that the animal engravings discovered at Grimes Graves were obvious forgeries, doubt must further surround the authenticity of the Cissbury pieces, especially as there are certain similarities between the Cissbury pieces and examples of Palaeolithic cave art such as the famous 'swimming deer' of Lascaux in France. It is unlikely, if the Cissbury heads were fakes, that they had been intended to reopen the debate concerning a Palaeolithic origin for the British flint mines, as the Grimes Graves examples may have been intended to do. There was never any doubt that the Cissbury mines were Neolithic, and certainly by the mid-1950s all discussion of Palaeolithic flint extraction in Britain had effectively ceased.

Alternatively, bearing in mind the possibility of unauthorised access to the subterranean working area, something that had earlier bothered both Lane Fox and Harrison, the carvings could have been made by a visiting member of the public. Pull, however, went to some length to secure the basal levels of opened shafts, and seems convinced that these areas could not have been reached by the public without there being obvious signs of forced entry. Notice of the fraudulent ivory fish, found within the entrance of gallery 1, may however suggest that the deer carvings were part of a similar style of prank, perpetrated by one member of the team who was able to make the markings appear genuine. Engravings into chalk are just as inherently undatable as chalk objects, especially if their creation has been via an obviously non-modern implement such as a flint blade. In such circumstances, the possibilities for hoaxing are considerable. The fact that the Shaft 27 engravings appeared stained with age, being filled with 'redeposited (fluffy) carbonate', and were only revealed once the excavators were in the process of clearing the galleries of rubble, would however appear to indicate that they were not the product of a single modern practical joker.

It is further important to note that the markings were found by different people working at various times over a period of a nine months. Suspicion would certainly have been aroused if one person were implicated in the discovery or identification of all the markings. Deliberate markings, albeit of a different, more abstract, kind, had already been identified within a number of excavated mines at Cissbury, and, given the present evidence, the presumption must be in favour of the Shaft 27 engravings being authentic. That is to say they were contemporary with the original use of the mines.

The Lavant Caves

Perhaps the most daring of all hoaxes associated with the study of Neolithic flint mines is that which was perpetrated in the early 1890s at a site near Chichester, in West Sussex, known as the Lavant Caves. The flint mine or 'cave' at Lavant was apparently discovered in around 1890 by a shepherd who lost two hurdles he had been carrying through an opening in the roof of the buried feature. Realising the potential significance of the find, the landowner, the Duke of Richmond, having first constructed a brick stairway into the caves, commissioned a full investigation of the feature. In 1893 a paper was delivered to a meeting of the Sussex Archaeological Society by the director designate of the excavations, duly reported in the *Sussex Daily News*, but a full publication was unfortunately never forthcoming.

Hadrian Allcroft managed to piece some of the detail surrounding the excavations over twenty years later in 1916, noting that the cave had consisted of 'a number of domed chambers of irregular size and plan connected by galleries or passages' (**23**). The height of the galleries was between 1.2 and 1.5m and, although the full dimensions of the chambers was not recorded, a visitor to the excavations observed that she could stand upright in at least one of them. Five galleries and three chambers were partially cleared during the course of the 1893 season, though the original point of entrance into the cave was never found. Following the clearance of the basal levels, the imminent collapse of the roof structure ensured that no further examination was possible. Some time shortly after 1909 the caves appear to have fallen in and the entrance sealed.

Up to 1.5m of chalk debris was observed at the base of the Lavant cave. Finds within this deposit included Roman pottery, bronzeware and mosaic tesserae, some sixteenth-century metalwork, a Georgian halfpenny, a few animal bones, at least one human tooth, some worked flint, a chalk cup, and a red deer antler. The artefacts suggested to Allcroft that the feature was in all probability part of a flint mine similar perhaps to those recorded from Cissbury. Unlike the Cissbury mines however, the Lavant Cave would appear from the finds assemblage to have remained open throughout the Roman period and well into the sixteenth century. This interpretation was later supported by Elliot Curwen who further observed that the surface area around the cave was covered in hollows that were suggestive of backfilled mine shafts. Surface examination of the Lavant site by the Royal Commission on the Historical Monuments of England in 1995 has, however, indicated that the morphology of site is perhaps more comparable with known areas of post-

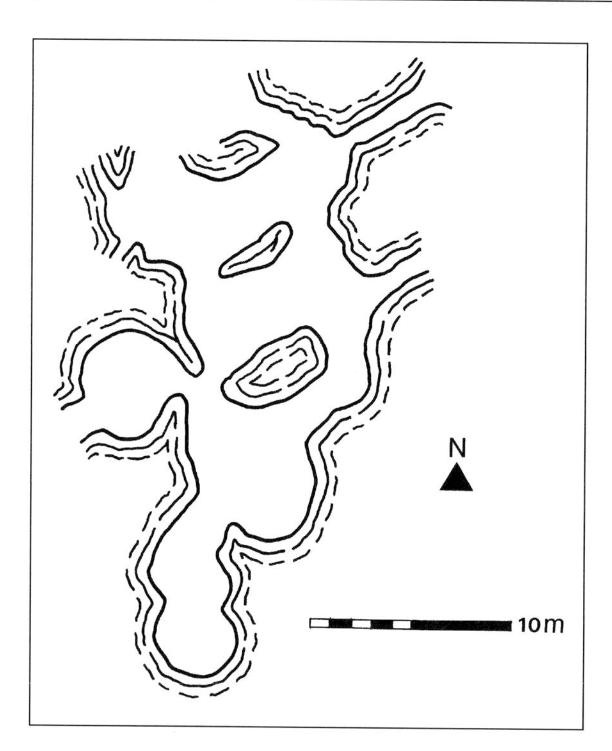

23 The apparent floor plan of the Lavant Caves, exposed by Dawson in 1893. This plan was pieced together by Allcroft some twenty years later using the memories of those who had originally visited the site. Note that the original point of entrance into the subterranean system does not appear to have been found by Dawson, access being gained through a collapse in the roof structure. Redrawn from Allcroft 1916

Medieval chalk quarrying, rather than with prehistoric flint extraction.

A major problem with interpreting the Lavant site is the lack of any clear context or stratigraphic sequence for the diverse range of finds, something not helped by the absence of both a detailed report and of the artefacts themselves. Generally speaking, when the site is referred to, interpretation follows the model outlined by Allcroft and Curwen of a Neolithic flint mine significantly reused in later periods. One factor that is not usually discussed however, is contribution of the chief excavator, one Charles Dawson.

Dawson, a solicitor with an appetite for antiquarian pursuits, is a man already well known to history, for it was he, together with Arthur Woodward and Pierre Teilhard de Chardin, who in 1912 uncovered the first traces of an entirely new species of pre-human: the Piltdown Man. Since the revelation that the 'fossil' remains recovered from Piltdown in Sussex were faked, several candidates for the deception have been put forward. These have included the original excavation team, as well as the writer Conan Doyle, the anatomist Arthur Keith, zoologist Martin Hinton, museum curator William Butterfield, neurologist Grafton Elliot Smith, palaeontologist William Solas, jeweller Lewis Abbott and chemists John Hewitt and Samuel Woodhead. None of these individuals, however, would appear to fit the bill quite as well as Dawson.

Dawson is implicated in a number of archaeological, geological and anthropological deceptions, some daring, some surprisingly low-key, but each with a definite target in mind, usually a fellow antiquarian, museum official or other influential scientist. In 1893, for example, he presented the British Museum with a Roman statuette that provided the earliest example of cast iron found in the world. It was later shown to be a modern replica. In 1907 he presented the director of the Pevensey Castle excavations with a Roman tile stamped with the letters HON AUG ANDRIA (translated as 'Honorius Augustus Anderida'), something which indicated the latest phase of official building work in Roman Britain in the late fourth or early fifth century AD. A thermoluminescence test conducted on the tile in 1972 indicated that the piece was no more than seventy years old, that is to say it had been manufactured at the time of the 1906-7 excavations. Investigation into Dawson's other discoveries reveals further spurious finds including a tooth of a new species of dinosaur (named *Plagiaulax dawsoni* in his honour), a strangely complete prehistoric hafted axe, a well-preserved prehistoric boat and a unique form of Roman horseshoe. Given this pedigree, all of Dawson's finds, theories and publications must now, of necessity, be viewed with the deepest suspicion.

Whilst there can be no doubt that the Lavant Caves actually existed (it is likely that they represent part of a post-Medieval chalk quarry), there must, given Dawson's antiquarian background, be significant doubt with regard to the finds that he claimed to have made there. The list of artefacts contains a wide diversity of forms including, somewhat surprisingly, tesserae from a Roman mosaic floor. The worked flints, chalk cup and red deer antler from the Cave all helped to establish a Neolithic date for the site, placing it with the discoveries made less than twenty years before by Canon Greenwell at Grimes Graves and Colonel Lane Fox at Cissbury. Other artefacts, including the tesserae, pottery and metalwork, provided finer chronological detail, demonstrating that Dawson's flint mine possessed greater currency than those investigated elsewhere, having been reutilized in the Roman period and again in the sixteenth century. Unfortunately there was no independent verification as to the context of the finds and, interestingly enough, all the artefacts had mysteriously disappeared by the beginning of the twentieth century. Allcroft, writing in 1916, observed that no further details regarding the site could be obtained, noting that he 'found the greatest difficulty in ascertaining something of the facts after the lapse of no more than twenty years'. Neither could the site itself be re-examined, having been considered too dangerous to keep open.

Dawson's reticence in publishing the details of his work at the Lavant Caves can perhaps now be understood. The site was just one of many archaeological discoveries made by the Lewes solicitor in the later years of the nineteenth century which helped to establish him as an antiquarian of some repute. This was recognised in 1895, two years after delivering a verbal report on the Caves to the Sussex Archaeological Society, when he was finally elected as a fellow of the Society of Antiquaries. Given this and other academic rewards later heaped upon him, Dawson's motives for generating fraudulent artefacts can be clearly understood. What is surprising however, considering the widespread publicity given to the Piltdown and Pevensey frauds, is that the authenticity of the Lavant Caves has never come under suspicion, the site continuing to be referred to by some as a potential Neolithic flint mine. It is unlikely that even Dawson himself could have guessed that this particular deception would still be fooling people over a century after its initial 'discovery'.

3 Flint mines: date and distribution

Where are the flint mines?

Over seventy sites in Britain have at some stage been referred to as Neolithic flint mines. Of this group, only fourteen sites may really be classed as possessing definite Neolithic characteristics, where extensive periods of excavation and survey have revealed a considerable amount of data (*see* **1**). These sites comprise Blackpatch, Church Hill, Cissbury, Harrow Hill, Long Down and Stoke Down in West Sussex, Durrington and Easton Down in Wiltshire, Martin's Clump in Hampshire, Grimes Graves in Norfolk, and Den of Boddam and Skelmuir Hill in Grampian. There are three further sites, at Tolmere and Nore Down in West Sussex and Buckenham Toft in Norfolk, where Neolithic flint extraction is probable, if not conclusively proven. Sites where Neolithic mining remains a possibility comprise the plough-disrupted sites of High Salvington, Mount Carvey, Myrtlegrove, West Stoke and Roger's Farm in West Sussex, Brading Down on the Isle of Wight and Ringland in Norfolk.

In addition to this list, there are a considerable number of sites where Neolithic mining has at some time been claimed, but where resurvey, most notably by the Royal Commission on the Historical Monuments of England, have shown the evidence to be questionable. Sites viewed as possessing doubtful Neolithic associations comprise Madehurst and Slonk Hill in West Sussex, Clanfield and Little Somborne in Hampshire, East Horsley and Woodmansterne in Surrey, Bacton, Cranwich, Easton, Eaton, Great Massingham, Great Melton, Lynford, Markshall, Stanhoe and Whitlinham in Norfolk, Hackpen Hill in Wiltshire, Peppard Hill in Oxfordshire, and High Wycombe in Buckinghamshire.

At Slonk Hill the mouth of a large pit has been partially investigated, but as yet there is no evidence of date or function. At Bacton, Clanfield, Cranwich, East Horsley, Easton, Eaton, Great Massingham, Great Melton, Little Somborne, Lynford, Madehurst, Markshall, Peppard Common, Stanhoe, Whitlingham and Woodmansterne, a number of Neolithic surface finds, possibly related to flint working, have been recorded, but no conclusive evidence for the existence of actual mines has yet been found. The evidence recovered from Lynford is further complicated by the disruption caused by eighteenth-century gunflint pits and areas of gravel extraction. A shaft at High Wycombe was revealed during the construction of a railway, though insufficient archaeological examination was conducted to either confirm or deny a Neolithic origin. The affiliations of Hackpen Hill remain uncertain, though they could represent natural features.

Shafts or surface pits where a Neolithic date was originally conferred but which, through excavation or surface examination, may now be safely removed from the discussion, comprise Bexley Plantation, Bow Hill, Chanctonbury Hill, Compton Down, Goodwood, Highdown Hill and Lavant Down in West Sussex, Wilmington Hill and Windover Hill in East Sussex, Riddlesdown in Greater London, Badgerdell Wood in Hertfordshire, Liddlington in Wiltshire, Ashtead in Surrey, Hambledon Hill in Dorset, Grimsditch Wood in Essex, Crayford, St Peter's and Wye in Kent, Norwich and Weybourne in Norfolk, Wanborough and Warlingham in Surrey, Dunstable Down and Whipsnade Zoo in Bedfordshire, Pitstone Hill in Buckinghamshire and Fareham in Hampshire.

The surface indentations upon Ashtead appear to be Iron Age or Roman, those on Bow Hill, Crayford, Grimsditch Wood, Hambledon Hill, Highdown, Pitstone Hill, Riddlesdown, Warlingham, Wilmington Hill, Windover Hill and Wye are almost certainly Medieval or post-Medieval quarries, whilst those at Bexley Plantation, Goodwood and Liddlington are likely to belong to the nineteenth century. Compton Down and St Peter's may be reinterpreted as single post-prehistoric marl pits. The complex subterranean workings recorded from a site at Lavant Down site in around 1890, would appear to represent the remains of a Medieval or later chalk quarry within which certain finds were deliberately planted in order to suggest a Neolithic date. The site claimed at Norwich is extremely difficult to assess, lying as it does beneath two modern roads (namely Coslany Street and Westwick Street), but the density of medieval and later stone quarries in this area suggests caution with regard to applying a Neolithic date.

When does mining begin?

In an attempt to better place the Neolithic flint mines of Norfolk and Sussex within a national and chronological framework, samples of antler used in the initial extraction process were submitted to the British Museum for radiocarbon determination in the late 1960s. Unfortunately much of the early radiocarbon dating was conducted prior to establishment of a detailed sampling programme and, though a huge number of dates have now been generated, especially during the course of the British Museum's work between 1972-6 at Grimes Graves, serious doubts have recently been raised as to the validity of the exercise. Much of the material sampled was only loosely stratified or provenanced, and is useful only in the most general of senses. It has been noted that much of the material used would not be considered today as suitable for radiocarbon dating. A revised programme of analysis is, however, underway, though the results are not yet available.

The lack of a clear sampling strategy for the pieces examined to date, when combined with the poverty of accompanying contextual data means that it is not possible to provide any secure statements about when large scale flint extraction began and ended. The artefactual and stratigraphic data from Grimes Graves, when combined with the existing radiocarbon chronology, flawed though it seems, suggests that mining began and ended here in the third millennium BC. Data recovered from Easton Down would, on present evidence, suggest a similar developmental sequence. Radiocarbon dates from the Sussex sites would, on face value, suggest that mining began on the South Downs at the end of the fifth millennium BC, possibly as early as 4200BC, and continued on to the end of the fourth millennium.

The stratigraphic and artefactual observations gathered from John Pull's excavations at Blackpatch, Church Hill and Cissbury, however, imply that flint extraction continued at these sites for a longer period than is currently accepted. At Blackpatch there are a series of clear stratigraphic relationships linking features containing collared urns and Beaker pottery with areas of large-scale flint digging. Similar observations may also be made for Barrow sites 1, 3, 5, 6, 7 and 9 at Blackpatch where freshly mined, unweathered and apparently unutilised floorstone flint appear to be integral to the final phases of activity. In Barrow 9, one such deposit emphatically sealed layers containing disarticulated human bone and Beaker pottery. The type of flint material described and recorded by Pull and Sainsbury in such circumstances can only have been derived from freshly excavated shafts and cannot be related to mere reuse of earlier waste dumps and spoil heaps. At Church Hill the evidence from flint working floor 2 and the ditch of Hut Site 1 provides a similar story, albeit on a smaller scale, of flint extraction continuing into the Later Neolithic. No such evidence has yet been located at Cissbury, where the only material of post Early Neolithic date would appear to be the Beakers retrieved from nearby barrow mounds by antiquarian excavators.

That the majority of chipping floors are broadly contemporary with the main period of mining is something that seems reasonably certain, though the date of 'chipping' activity itself cannot adequately be resolved without a detailed radiocarbon dating programme. Artefacts other than flint associated with the floors are rare, though Beaker pottery was recovered from beneath floor 2 at the eastern margins of Shaft 2 at Blackpatch. The pottery was associated with cremated bone and so presumably represents part of a formal burial deposit. How this deposit relates to the floor itself, however, is uncertain. Pull seemed convinced that the pot was sealed by the floor, and is therefore earlier than the deposition of the flint. Certainly this is the impression given by the recorded section drawing, but it is of course conceivable that either the pot was intrusive, or that the floor had slumped over the burial at a considerably later date, effectively reversing the stratigraphic relationship. Pull strenuously argued against the likelihood of either possibility, noting that here 'we are faced with the fact that the cremated interment is undoubtedly of the same date as the flint mines'.

In other words it is clear that significant phases of Later Neolithic activity were being conducted at Blackpatch and, to a lesser degree, at Church Hill during times of major phases of flint extraction. Whether such extraction involved the cutting of deep shafts similar to those of earlier periods, or whether flint was being extracted in lesser quarries or in open cast pits is as yet unknown, especially as no clear examples of Later Neolithic shafts have yet been archaeologically examined, but the supposition that the extraction of deep seated flint in Sussex had ended by 3500BC would appear untenable.

Flint mines and other monuments

Neolithic flint mines were dug in a landscape being increasingly dominated by other forms of monumental structure, namely the enclosure and the linear mound. Linear mounds, or long barrows, are characterised by a rectangular pile of earth with flanking ditches (**24; colour plates 14, 15**). Most contain a variety of artefacts and structured deposits, which sometimes include human bone. Enclosures are represented by an area of land surrounded by a ditch and earthen rampart (**25; colour plates 16, 17**). The discontinuous nature of the ditch circuit in this class of monument has led to the application of the term 'causewayed enclosure'.

The meaning of Neolithic long mounds has proved difficult to explain, though plausible comparisons have been made between the long houses recorded from Neolithic sites in central and Atlantic Europe. If long mounds were based upon the form of continental long houses, then perhaps the mounds could represent a type of 'house tomb', in which the bodies of a particular community were placed. Unfortunately this theory is somewhat hindered by the lack of any meaningful quantity of human bone from the majority of earthen long mounds. Sometimes it would appear that the importance of the mound lay more within its construction, composition and location, than with any association with the human dead. The stone-cambered long mounds of Western Britain have produced more considerable quantities of human bone, though these are usually

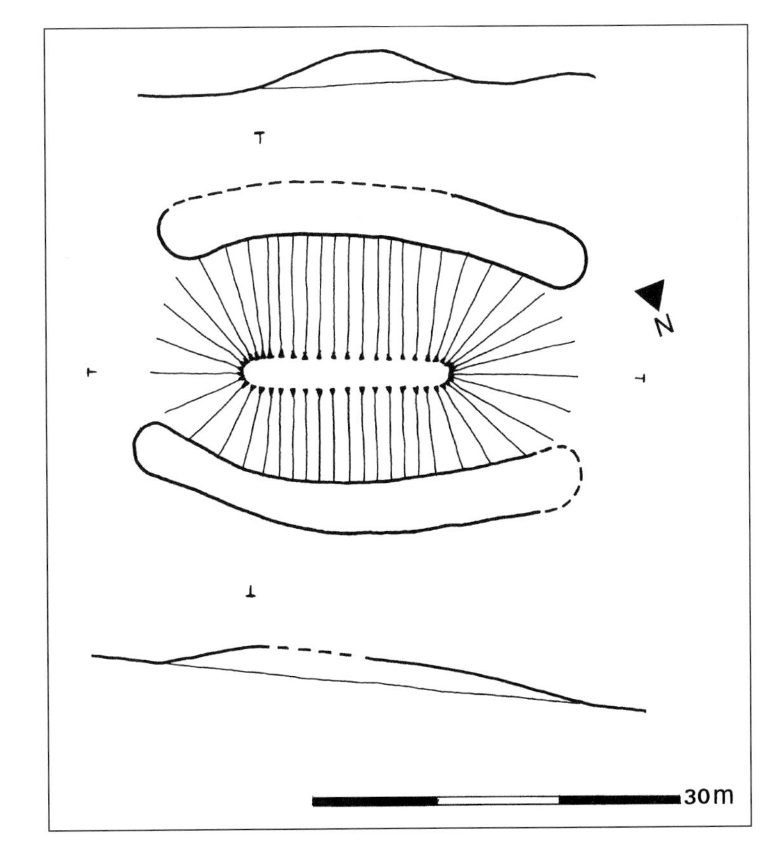

24 Plan and profiles of the Camel's Humps Neolithic long mound on Cliffe Hill, near Lewes, East Sussex. Redrawn from Toms 1922

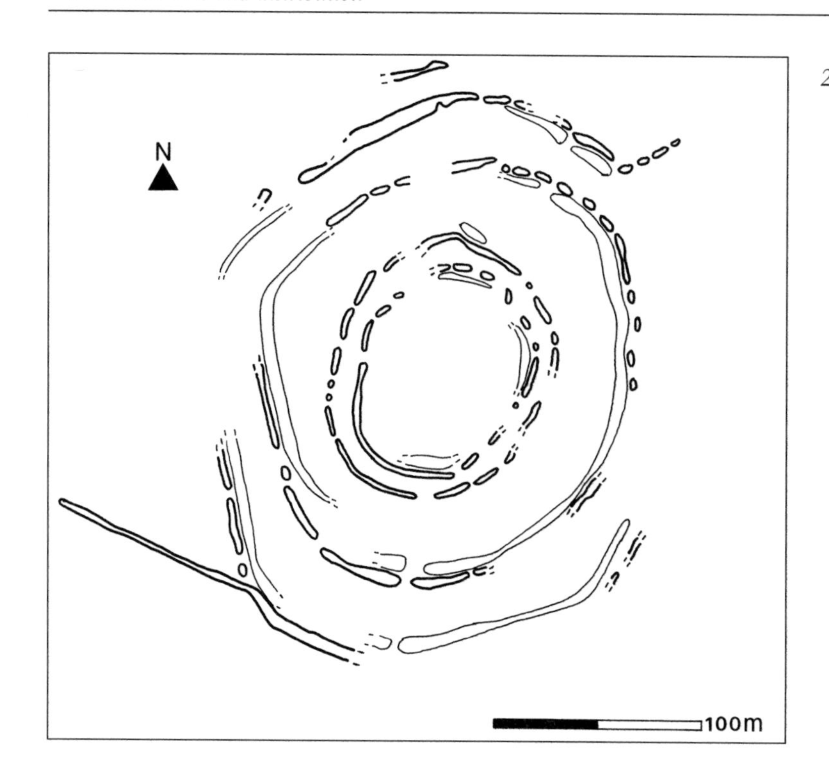

25 Plan of the multi-phase Neolithic enclosure recorded from Whitehawk Hill in Brighton, East Sussex. Redrawn from Russell and Rudling 1996

confined to a small part of one end of the mound. Occasionally the recorded chambers can be shown to represent a secondary element to the mound, something which further suggests that the disposal of human remains did not provide the motivating force behind the building of these structures.

Long mounds were probably designed as a form of symbolic house structure, containing a range of objects specific to the social group that constructed them. These community markers could be represented by the accumulation of different soils or geologies common to a particular area or through the deposition of artefacts made by a specific human group. Alternatively they may contain the remains of animals that lived, or had been killed, within a particular territory. Only occasionally was human bone incorporated into the mound, presumably as a representative sample of the community. Other materials of an organic nature such as drink, food, wood, textiles or leather, could also have played their part.

Long mounds were built at specific points in the landscape for a variety of reasons. It may be tempting, however, to view them as structures which were designed to lay claim over an area of land. Such claims need not be political in nature for there may have been a greater desire to dedicate aspects social identity to a local deity in order to ensure the long-term good will of supernatural forces. The deposition of cultural markers, such as pottery, flint and bone could have been designed as a way of taming a wild space by seeding it with the identity of a particular human group. The desire for increased soil fertility, ample food stuffs, game and the provision of subterranean flint may also have been important, something that could explain the similar range of artefacts deposited within and around backfilled Neolithic flint mines.

Archaeologists have, in the past, had difficulty in interpreting the first enclosures of the Neolithic, though the evidence would seem to imply that these sites were intended to act as areas of clearly demarcated, seasonal settlement. Enclosures would seem to represent a defined space where particular human groups could return to at semi-regular intervals in order to interact, engage in trade, corral livestock, reaffirm allegiances, and, perhaps more importantly, re-establish patterns of temporary settlement. At such times, any number of different social groups could have reaffirmed their own identity by remodelling enclosure ramparts or by depositing markers specific to their community, such as pottery and human bone, within the backfilling segments of ditch (**colour plates 19, 20**).

Some enclosures, such as Whitehawk, Windmill Hill, the Trundle and Briar Hill, were continually redeveloped over time, with new circuits of bank and ditch being added. Other enclosures seem to have been built, used and allowed to decay without any significant modification. The progressive expansion of certain enclosures may have been in order to increase social standing, as the sites in question increasingly began to dominate the skyline. Some sites, with heavily embellished ramparts and entrances, may have gradually formed the basis for more substantial and permanent forms of settlement.

4 The morphology of flint mines

Excavation and survey at Neolithic flint mine sites across Britain have revealed a mass of data relating to the nature and extent of prehistoric extraction. Given the quantity of information recorded, the observations that follow are set out under site specific headings, rather than as a continuous narrative. For the purposes of clarity, only those sites previously noted as possessing positive Neolithic characteristics are described.

Blackpatch

At least 100 shafts are known to have existed over an area of 1.5 hectares (4 acres) at Blackpatch. Few of the features are visible on the surface today, however, the site having been bulldozed flat in the 1950s. The majority of recorded shafts appear to concentrate upon the western slopes of the hill, possibly within the initial area of flint outcrop.

A variety of extraction techniques have been recorded from the Blackpatch site. Shafts 5 and 6 and the central cut of Barrow 2, located at the northern and eastern limits of the mining area, are best viewed as adit mines or quarry pits, descending no deeper than 1, 1.8 and 1.3m respectively. Within Shaft 5, a series of shallow workings had removed part of a subterranean flint layer. Only two of these workings could really be described as galleries, though neither extended more than 1.6m from the quarry wall. The only evidence of flint extraction in Shaft 6, beyond that located during the actual cutting of the pit itself, was a slight undercutting of the southern wall. The central cut within the Barrow 2 pit did not appear to have exploited a significant quantity of flint, although a further area of excavation through the floor of the feature may indicate an abortive attempt to reach deeper seams. The possible failure of this speculative shaft to locate an adequate flint seam, perhaps due to constraints on time or labour, or because subterranean seams here were inconsequential, may have prompted its sudden abandonment and backfill with special deposits, which, in this instance, included human body parts. A similar argument for the abandonment and backfill could be forwarded to explain the positioning of a Late Neolithic round mound (Barrow 3) over Shaft 5 if this pit had also been considered unsuccessful in its attempts to extract good quality subterranean flint.

Shafts 1, 2, 4 and 7 at Blackpatch descended to depths of no more than 3.3m (**26**), exploiting what appears to have been the first major seam of flint encountered during their excavation. Seven short galleries extended from Shaft 1, one of which connected with the gallery of a mine to the north-east (**27**). The nature of cutting and later filling of these interconnecting galleries probably indicates that both shafts had been open at

26 Shaft 1 at Blackpatch, showing the full area examined by John Pull and the Worthing Archaeological Society in 1922. The entrances to galleries vi and vii are visible at the base of the shaft. © The Sussex Archaeological Society

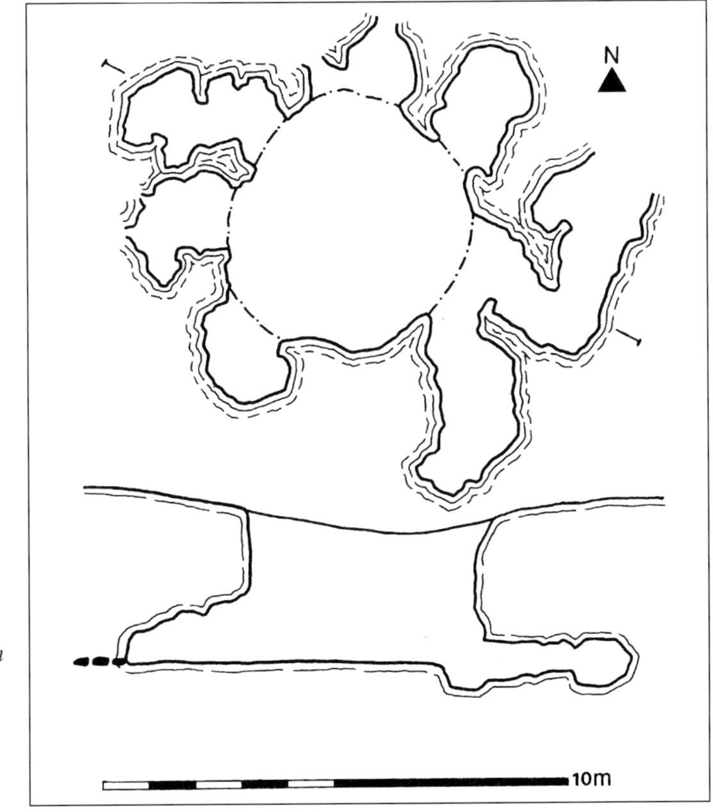

27 Blackpatch: gallery plan and profile of Shaft 1 as excavated in 1922. Redrawn from Goodman, Frost, Curwen and Curwen 1924

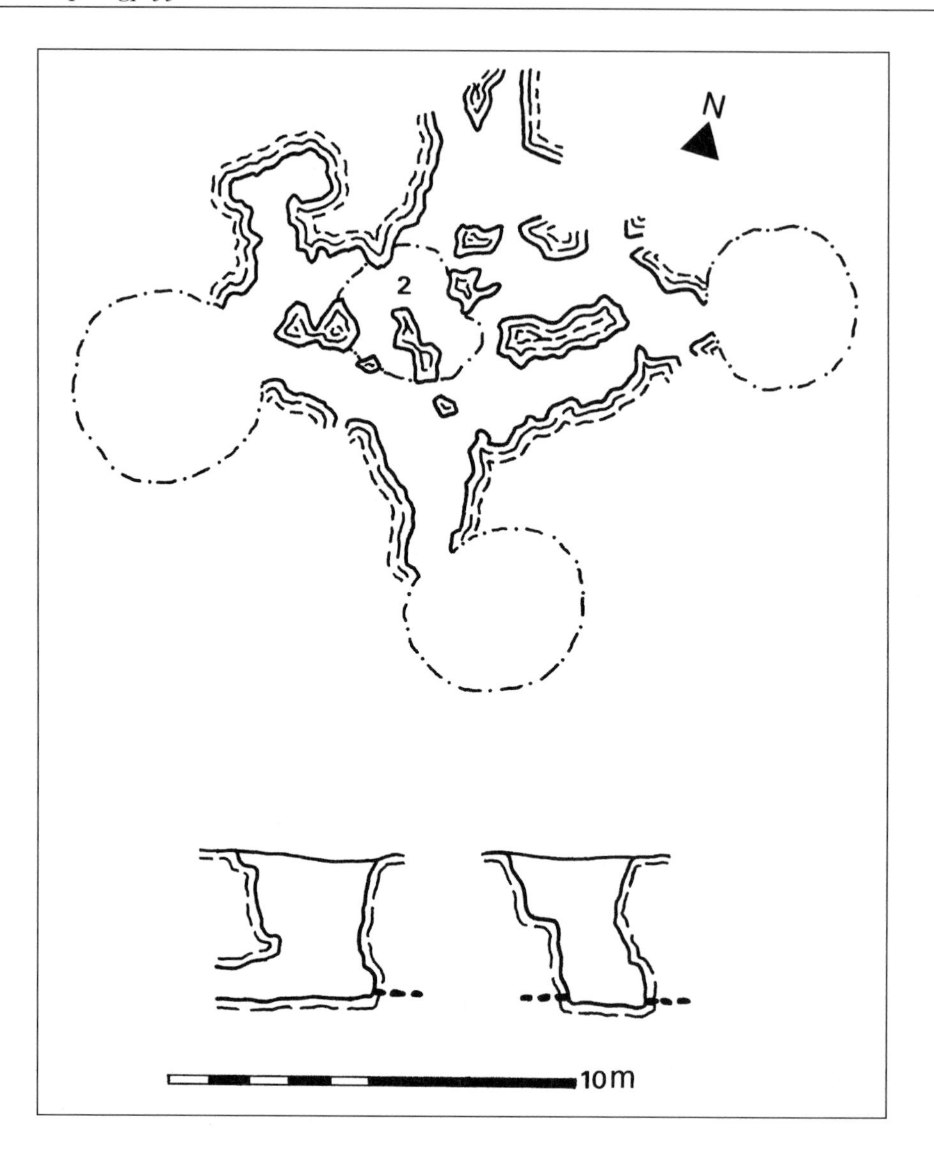

28 Blackpatch: gallery plan and profiles of Shaft 2. Redrawn from Russell 2000

the same time. A complex of galleries extended from the lowest levels of Shaft 2, connecting it with at least three other shafts to the east, south and west (**28**). Initial extraction within these basal galleries had been sufficiently extensive as to seriously destabilise the overlying chalk rock. Little is known of the nature of workings within Shaft 4, though Shaft 7 possessed nine galleries connecting it to at least four other shafts (**29**) in a manner reminiscent of some of the more complex basal gallery systems recorded at Cissbury.

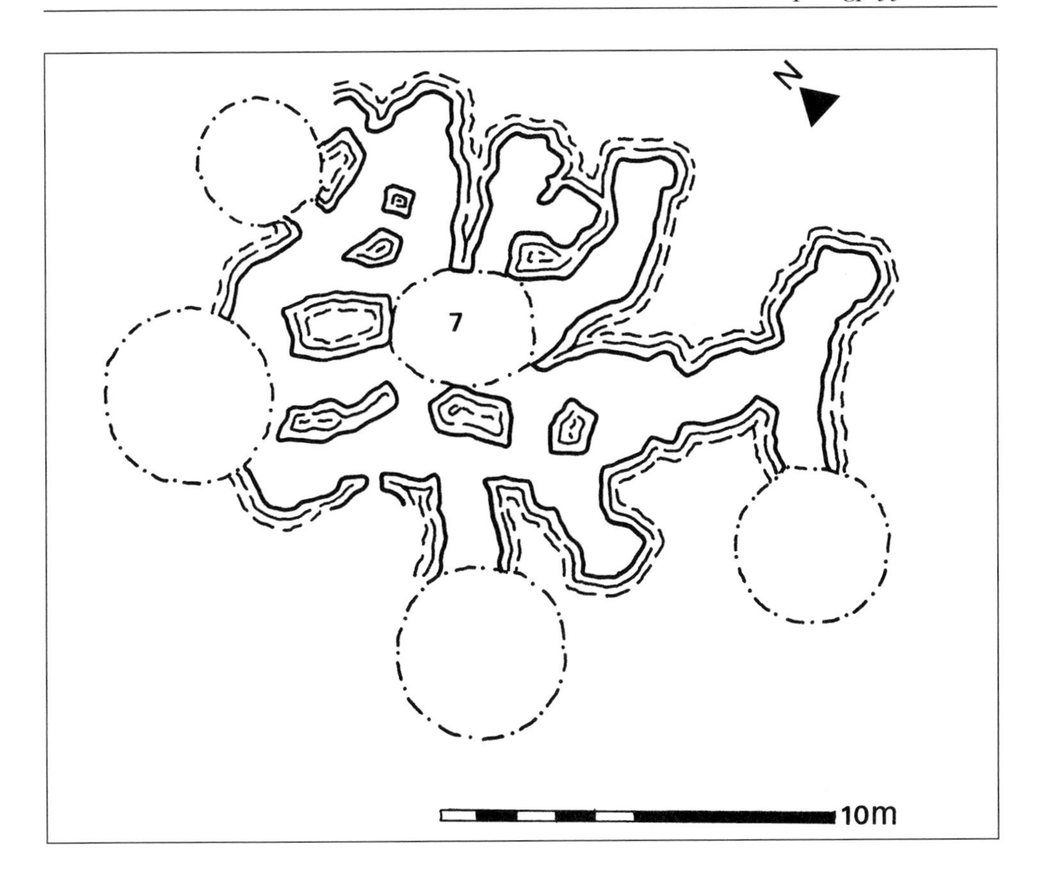

29 Blackpatch: gallery plan of Shaft 7. Redrawn from Russell 2000

Church Hill

At least 26 shafts have been recorded from the Church Hill mine site, although given the amount of plough damage across the hill, it is likely that more originally existed. David Field has suggested that mining probably began on the steeper eastern slopes of the hill, where the flint may first have outcropped, and gradually moved towards the summit.

Shafts 1, 2, 4, 5a, 6 and 7, examined by Pull, exploited seams of flint at depths of 4.9, 3, 5, 3.6, 5.8 and 4.9m respectively. With the exception of Shaft 2, the details of which unfortunately remain vague, all shafts appeared to have exploited seams beneath the first to be encountered. Shafts 1 and 2 did not possess basal galleries, though a series of small headings had been cut at the north, west and southern sides of Shaft 1, perhaps in an attempt to remove a greater quantity of flint from the fourth seam. Pull and Voice noted that within Shaft 4, substantial cuttings had been made into the third seam to be encountered (**30**). Their recorded section drawing seems in addition to indicate that some attempt had also been made to remove the primary seam which lay close to the surface. As with Shaft 1, however, it was the fourth seam that was the target of the Neolithic miners with five galleries, one connecting with Shaft 5, extending out from the basal

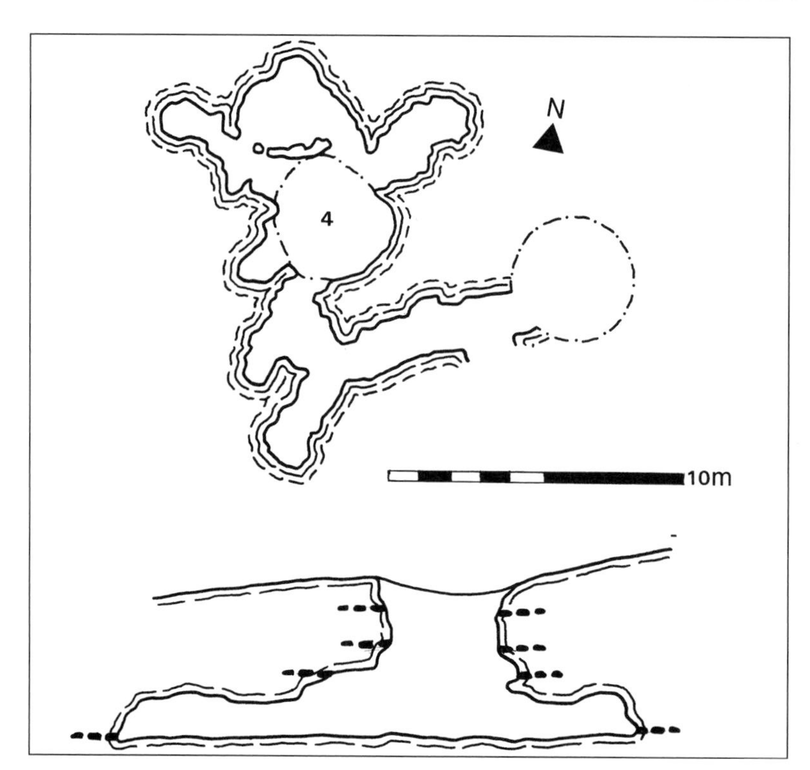

30 Church Hill: gallery plan and profile of Shaft 4. Redrawn from Russell 2000

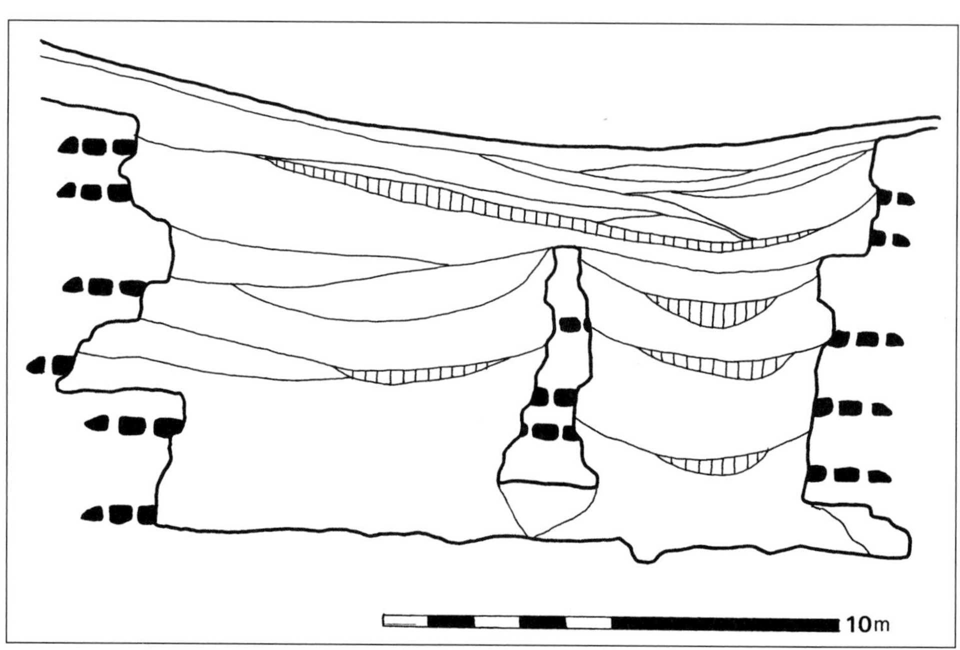

31 Church Hill: paired Shafts 6 and 7 in section. Both pits would appear to have been originally cut and worked together, the only true gallery recorded from either being the single one that joined them. Hachured layers indicate areas of flint knapping. Redrawn from Russell 2000

levels. The fourth seam had also been extensively worked within Shaft 5a, with two galleries connecting it directly with Shaft 5.

The nature of these linking galleries when combined with the non-appearance of Shaft 5a from the modern ground surface, may suggest that 5a was originally a satellite to Shaft 5 and therefore similar in this respect to the lesser shafts recorded around Shaft 13 at Harrow Hill. Some attempt had been made within Shaft 5a to exploit the third seam to be encountered, whilst a deepening within the floor of the pit had partially exposed a fifth seam. Shafts 6 and 7 at Church Hill probably represent paired shafts (**31**), originally being cut, worked and remaining open at the same time. Both pits had passed through five seams of flint before terminating at the sixth, with headings being driven into the fourth, fifth and sixth seams. The only true gallery defined within the basal levels of either shaft was that which connected the two.

No definite evidence of lesser flint extraction pits or drift mines, such as noted at Blackpatch, were identified at Church Hill, with Pit A, a 2.4m deep cut passing through but not exploiting a seam of surface flint, perhaps indicating the most promising of potential candidates. The other pits recorded from Church Hill, Pits B and C, are almost certainly Iron Age in date and presumably relate to a later period of occupation on the site.

Cissbury

Cissbury represents the largest single area of flint extraction on the South Downs, with at least 270 shafts having been recorded (**32, 33**). Mining probably began along the north-western edges of the hill, where the flint may first have outcropped.

Evidence for flint extraction at Cissbury is both extensive and diverse, with at least 20 shafts having been archaeologically examined between 1873 and 1956. Of the late nineteenth-century excavations for which we possess detailed records, it may be seen that the shafts investigated varied considerably in depth, No. 1 Escarp and No.1 Counterscarp bottoming at 2m and 2.2m, Willett's Shaft 1 at 4.3m, Willett's Shaft 2, the Cave Pit and Shaft V at around 6.1m, Shaft VI at 9.1m and Tindall's Shaft at 12m. The Large Pit lived up to its name, possessing an overall diameter of 20m and descending to at least 12.8m, at which point the sudden and unexpected collapse of the standing section forced an end to the investigation.

The nature of subsurface workings exposed during the nineteenth-century examination of the Cissbury shafts was also varied. As at Harrow Hill and Church Hill, occasional attempts seem to have been made to extract primary and secondary seams encountered during the sinking of deep shafts. Nowhere is this clearer than within the Large Pit. This particular shaft cut through six seams of flint, the two uppermost layers being exploited by a series of terraces, all flint having been totally removed from the floors of these cuttings. The first terrace, at a depth of 2.7m, was only 0.3m wide along its northern edge, broadening to around 2.4m along the western and southern faces of the shaft. The second terrace, at a depth of 5.5m, extended to a maximum width of 3m along the west and south-western walls. The flint seam had been further extracted by the digging of small undercuts along the southern and western shaft wall, one of which,

32 Cissbury from the air in October 1977. The flint mines dominate the western slopes of the hill (at the bottom of the photograph), extending southwards, beyond the line of the Iron Age enclosure. The Iron Age ramparts obscure much of the outer margins of the mine site, whilst agricultural activity within the enclosure itself has levelled a number of shafts. A small, roughly rectangular enclosure, of possible Neolithic date, investigated by Lane Fox in 1867, may be seen in the top left of the photograph, within the area defined by the Iron Age ramparts.
NMR 1193/09. English Heritage © Crown Copyright

measuring 2.4m in length, may be more plausibly interpreted as a gallery. A further four seams were cut through as the shaft descended below the second terrace, the shaft itself narrowing to around 4.3m at its lowest traceable point. Unfortunately, as the Large Pit was not bottomed, the full nature and extent of basal workings could not be determined. Lane Fox speculated that the sheer scale of the shaft may have been due to the fact that it represented a number of open quarry pits and surface workings which had been joined together to become the first terrace and from which deeper cuttings were later made.

Terrace cuts observed within additional shafts at Cissbury, most notably Willett's Shaft 2, the Cave Pit, and Shaft V, may relate to similar attempts to quarry material from multiple seams. In the absence of a clearly defined flint layer, however, an alternative

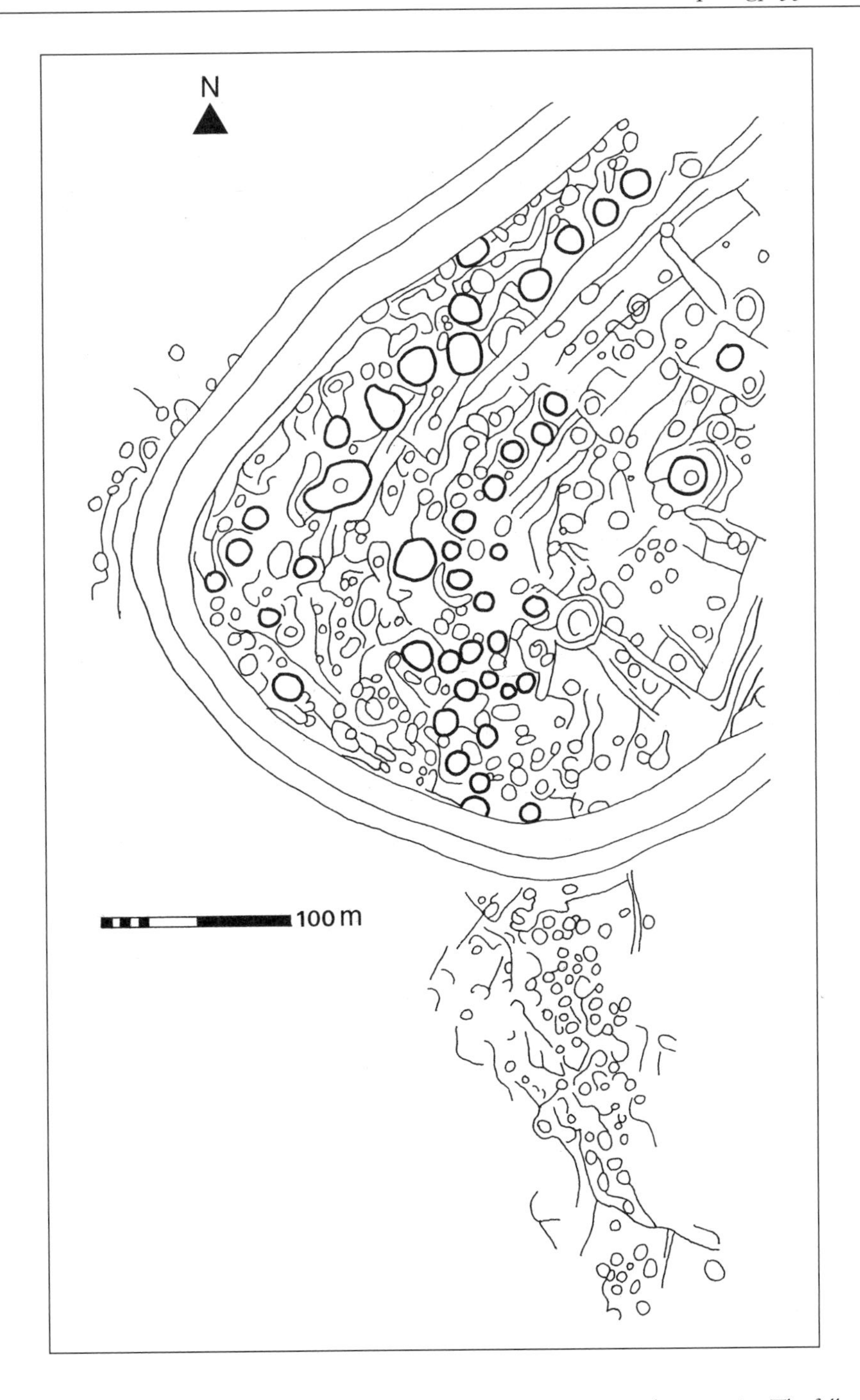

33 Cissbury: simplified surface plan of the earthwork features that constitute the mine site. The full extent of flint extraction here remains unclear due to the dramatic nature of the Iron Age rampart circuit, though it is apparent that a number of mine shafts extend beyond the later enclosure at the north-western margins of the site. The line of shafts that extend to the south of the hill fort include those features examined by Pull between 1952 and 1956. Redrawn from Barber, Field and Topping 1999

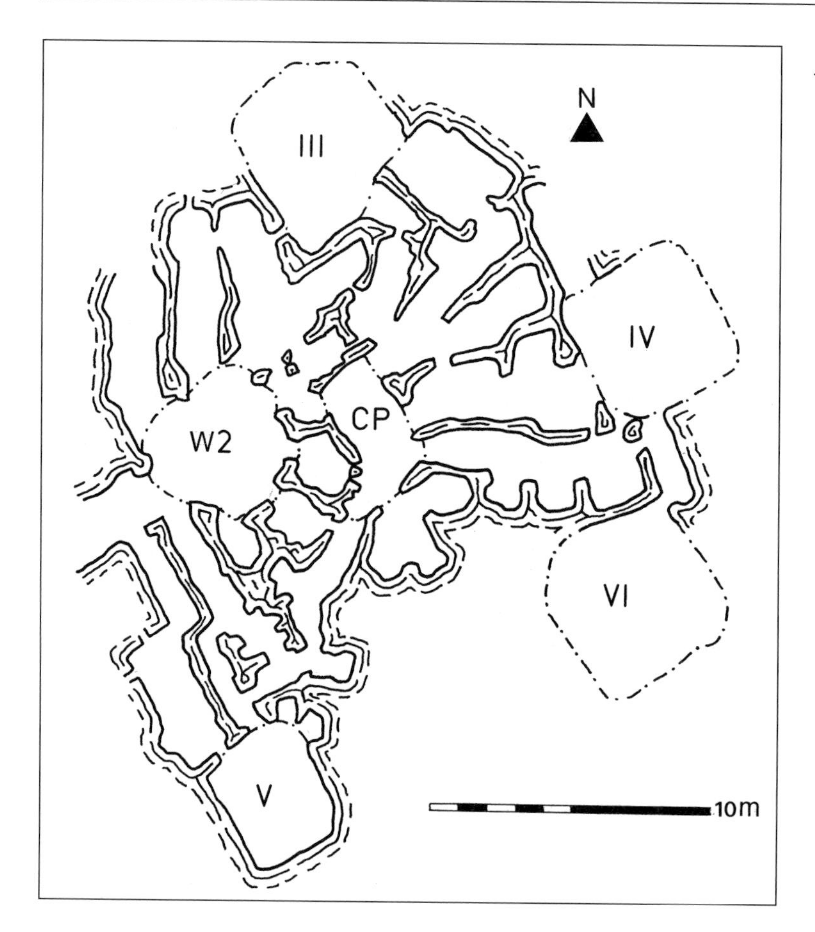

34 Cissbury: gallery plan of Shafts III, IV, V, VI, Willett's Pit and the Cave Pit. Redrawn from Harrison 1878

explanation may be that these shelves represent an attempt to lessen the excavation workload by narrowing the area of the shaft, thus reducing the quantity of material being brought to the surface. A third explanation may relate to the modification of shaft walls during the initial excavation of spoil, in order to create a series of discrete platforms from which ladders could be firmly embedded. Similar narrowing of shaft walls may be seen in Shaft 2 at Blackpatch, Shafts 5a and 6 at Church Hill and Shafts III and IV at Grimes Graves. A cut in the central floor of Willett's Shaft 2 was interpreted at the time as a speculative hole dug to ascertain the depth of the next flint layer, though it may alternatively be viewed as a form of sump.

Galleries and lesser undercuts into the shaft wall, were recorded from a number of the shafts examined in the nineteenth century (**34**), though the level of recorded detail is variable. The base of Willett's Shaft 1 was punctured by a series of interconnecting chambers or galleries, which Willett noted were around 1.5m in diameter. A total of 8 galleries, measuring between 0.9 and 1.5m in width, were recorded from the basal levels of Willett's second shaft. All appeared to have filled to within at least 0.6m of their roofs with chalk rubble. Three galleries (2, 3a and 6) were cleared by Willett to almost their full lengths, gallery 2 extending for some 5m before ending in a rounded terminal, possibly linked, via a window, to a shaft to the immediate north. Two galleries and two headings were identified at the base of Shaft V, four galleries were identified at the base of No. 1 Counterscarp Shaft, No. 2 Counterscarp Shaft and the Skeleton Shaft, five from No. 1 Escarp Shaft, No. 2 Escarp Shaft and Shaft VI, whilst seven were observed at the base of the Cave Pit. Many of these galleries were accompanied by additional areas of limited undercutting of the shaft wall.

Certain galleries, such as the northern gallery in No. 1 Escarp Shaft, possessed internal chambers which widened the working area considerably, whilst others, most notably the southern branch of gallery E in the Cave Pit, terminated in a domed chamber. The entranceways into galleries E and F within the Cave Pit appear to have been deliberately sealed by the insertion of two large blocks of chalk which had to be broken apart in situ by the excavation team before exploration of the gallery could commence.

No undercuttings or galleries appear to have been observed within the shaft opened by Tindall in 1874, though Harrison later comments that a basin-shaped hollow was recorded at in the floor of the feature. Harrison deduced from this that the shaft was probably a well and had not been cut primarily for the extraction of flint. That Tindall's feature was Neolithic in date seems, on the basis of the artefactual assemblage, clear enough and it remains possible that either the cut represents an exploratory or unfinished mine shaft, or that galleries were originally set within the feature, but were overlooked during the investigation or remained uncommented upon following Tindall's death the following year.

Shafts 24 and 27 cleared by Pull at Cissbury bottomed at a depth of 4.5 and 5.8m respectively. Shaft 24 exploited the second seam of flint encountered through a series of six galleries, two of which connected with other shafts, whilst Shaft 27 extracted flint from the third and fourth seams through a series of galleries connecting the feature with at least four other shafts. A series of 'animalistic' carvings were recorded from the basal levels of Shaft 27, whilst a human skeleton was found blocking the entrance to gallery 1 (**35**). The plans produced by Pull for the excavation of Shafts 24 and 27 appear to show a complicated system of subterranean galleries similar to those explored within Shafts I, III, IV, and VI to the north within the area now encircled by the Iron Age enclosure, and to the series of galleries recorded from Shaft 7 at Blackpatch. Galleries within Shaft 27 appear to have been further linked by the repeated use of windows.

Easton Down

The flint mines at Easton Down cluster at one end of a narrow chalk valley or coombe, and cover an overall area of around 16 hectares. The upper flint seam, or topstone, lies in some places just below the present ground surface. Flint seams are irregular but appear to be inclining in a slight southerly direction. At least 90 shafts and their associated spoil heaps have been recorded from surface indications, though more may well have been obscured by later field systems.

Six shafts, B1, B1a, B19, B45, B49 and B67, have been archaeologically examined at Easton Down, bottoming at depths of 4.4, 1.8, 0.6, 5, 5.1 and 2.7m respectively (**36**). Four of the three shafts, namely B1a, B19, B45 and B67, may have been abandoned by the

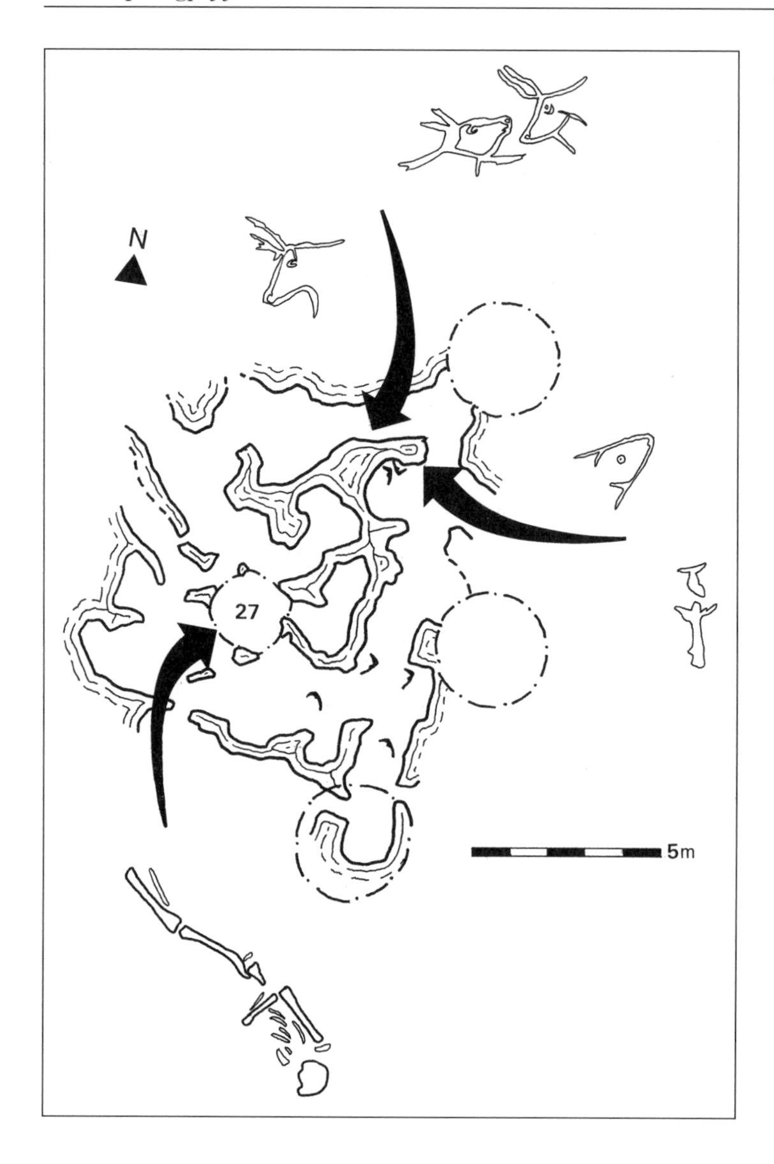

35 Cissbury: gallery plan of Shaft 27 as recorded by Pull between 1952 and 1954, showing the location of the incised deer, bull, fish head and 'miner's symbol' (not to scale), discarded antler picks and the extended female skeleton blocking the entrance to gallery 1. Redrawn from Russell 2000

Neolithic miners prior to the discovery of flint seams. Such a disproportionate number of unfinished shafts from a single area may appear somewhat strange, though our understanding of how flint seams were originally detected and followed in the Neolithic is, however, unclear. It is possible that mine sites elsewhere in Britain similarly contained a high number of abortive shafts, as the prospective miners attempted to locate a good source of subterranean flint. The apparently unfinished pits recorded from Blackpatch (Barrow 2) and Tolmere may, in this instance, provide a parallel. Alternatively, it is possible that pits B1a, B19, B45 and B67 at Easton Down were not originally intended as places of flint extraction and may have served some other purpose, perhaps linking the communities that dug them with the spirits of the underworld.

Pit B1 descended to a maximum depth of 4.4m, four seams of flint being cut through in the process: the topstone, lying only 0.3m below the ground surface, floorstone and two

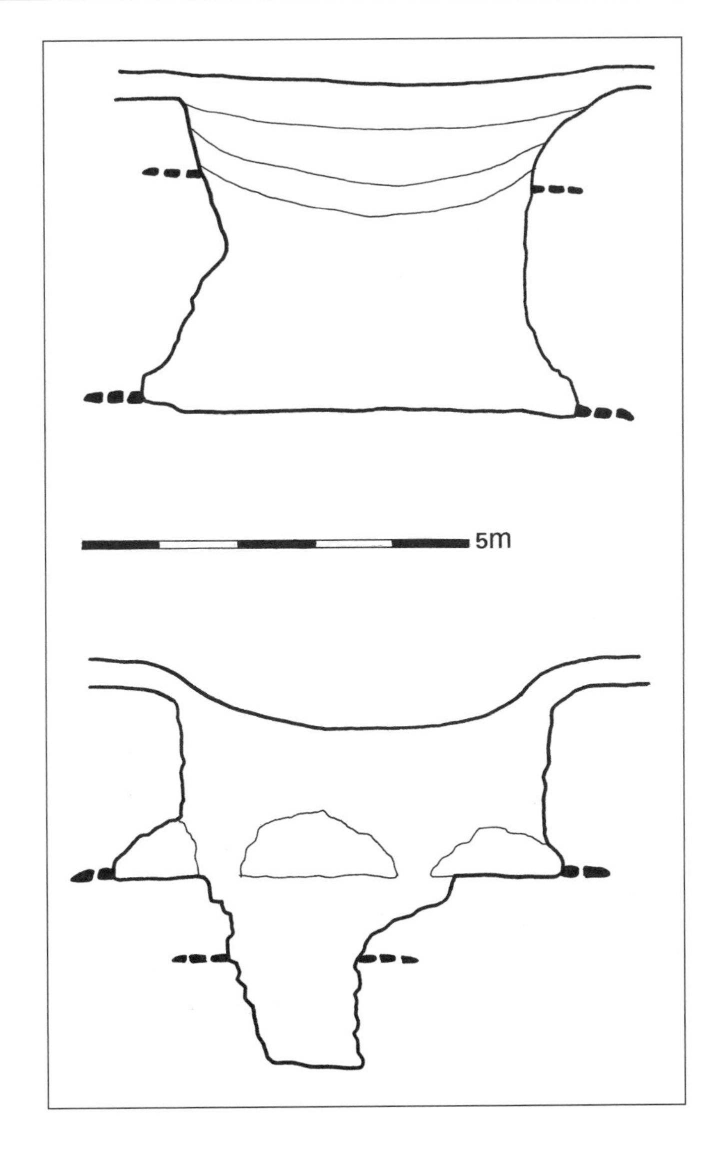

36 Easton Down: section of Pit B1 (top) and profile of Pit B49 (bottom). Note the enlarged undercuts, or 'proto-galleries', extracting flint from the second seam within Pit B49. Top redrawn from Stone 1932; bottom redrawn from Stone 1935

layers of tabular flint, one lying only 0.15m above the basal deposits. Both the floorstone and the overlying layer of tabular flint had been extracted by undercutting the shaft wall. Pit B49 descended to a maximum depth of around 5.1m, cutting through three layers of tabular flint in the process. Four enlarged undercuttings, or proto-galleries, penetrated the shaft wall at a depth of 2.4m, in order to extract the second seam. It may be that this second layer originally represented the desired flint source, and only afterwards was an attempt made to reach deeper seams by cutting a second pit through the floor of the first. Alternatively the original intention may have been to dig a substantial shaft, and only after the third seam was reached, at a depth of 3.5m, was a decision made to more fully exploit the second.

Grimes Graves

Grimes Graves represents the largest single area of deep Neolithic flint extraction yet recorded from Britain, with at least 433 shafts covering an area of around 7.6 hectares (19 acres) (**37; colour plate 5**). The mines are situated along the north-facing margins of a shallow, south-east to north-west aligned, dry valley. Shallow pits appear to cluster along the western, north-western and south-western periphery of the site with the larger shafts concentrated in the south and east. The disparate nature of shaft morphology at Grimes Graves, which includes paired shafts, open cast and linear quarries, prospection pits, pit-quarries and adit mines, may imply that extraction was not conducted on an organised or systematic basis. As with Cissbury, the evidence for mining at Grimes Graves is extensive and diverse, at least 35 shafts having been archaeologically examined to basal levels between 1868 and 1976. Unfortunately the records covering a significant proportion of the earliest features to be explored are incomplete, therefore much discussion has, of necessity, been centred around those shafts that have been well published or recently reassessed.

Greenwell's Shaft descended to a maximum depth of 12.2m, three layers of flint being cut through in the process. Four main galleries, each further enlarged by means of additional cuttings or niches driven into their walls, extended from the north-western to southern edges of the shaft wall. Two further gallery systems, extending from unexcavated shafts C and D, pierced the eastern wall of Greenwell's feature. Pits 1 and 2, opened by Peake in 1914, descended to depths of 9.1 and 9.5m respectively, three seams of flint being cut through in both. Ten galleries were found at the base of Pit 1, one of which (gallery VIII) appeared to have been originally cut from an adjoining shaft. At least six galleries had been dug from the base of Shaft 2, linking it with galleries extending from other shafts to the immediate north, south-east and west. Armstrong claims to have found an additional two galleries at the northern at western edges of the shaft wall when the feature was re-explored in 1920, but the details of these have been lost.

Shaft III descended to a maximum depth of 4.06m, some 0.3m beneath the floorstone deposit, which may indicate the desire to extract the basal flint by undercutting it (**38**). A 1.2m square 'platform' had been left along the western edge of the shaft wall, at a height of 1.37m above the floor of cut. Armstrong interpreted this as an aid to entering the shaft, noting that a series of steps had apparently been cut in an upwards direction from the platform, along the south-western wall. Later reinterpretation of Shaft III has suggested that the feature did in fact belong to two distinct phases. In phase one, the pit had been dug to the level of the wallstone, a depth of around 2m. A second cut had then been made along the north-eastern edge in order to reach the floorstone. A series of undercuttings along the southern wall had further removed the flint from this basal level. A second shaft, Pit 3a, was later explored 1.5m to the south east of Pit III. This displayed a similar extractive sequence to that revealed in Pit III, in that the wallstone had first been exploited through the cutting of niches, before a deeper cut was made to reach the floorstone, at a depth of 4.75m. Niches were the main way of extracting the floorstone within the 3.2m deep Pit 14.

Pits IV, V and VI measured 3.8, 3.9 and 4m in depth respectively. In all three shafts, the

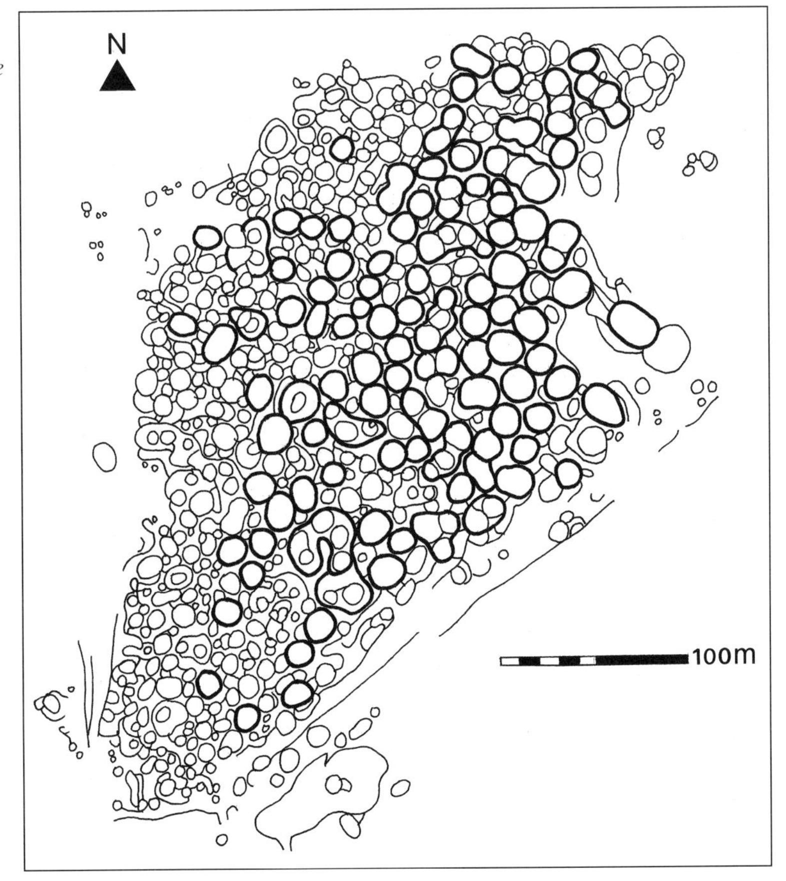

37 Grimes Graves: simplified surface plan of the earthwork features that constitute the mine site. The linear quarries and twin shafts appear to cluster at the eastern margins of the extraction area. Redrawn from Barber, Field and Topping 1999

floorstone had been exploited from the shaft wall, by means of undercuts, an undercutting from Pit IV breaching the basal level of Pit VI. A rough series of steps appear to have been cut along the eastern wall of the Pit IV, whilst a series of steps, descending to a short platform at a height of 1.2m from the floor, appear to have been recorded from Pit V. Elongated Pits 9, 10 and the interconnected Pits 8, 8a and 8b had all exploited a disturbed layer of floorstone nodules, lying at a depth of between 2.1 and 2.9m, by the cutting of niches into the shaft wall.

Pit 11 descended to a maximum depth of 4.3m, galleries connecting it with at least seven shafts of smaller dimensions (11a, b, d, e, f, g and h) to the north and south (**39**). Pit 12 was 5.5m deep, at least five galleries being discovered on the northern, western and southern sides. The eastern edge unfortunately remained unexplored by the excavators. The partially examined Pit 13 measured 4.6m in depth, one gallery and three niches exploiting the floorstone seam. Nine galleries radiated out into the floorstone at the base of Pit 15 (**40**), connecting the shaft to at least a further six shafts (15A, 15B, 15D, 15E, 15F and 15H). A series of lesser niches, extending to a maximum of 0.9m, had also been cut at a depth of 4.1m in order to exploit areas of the wallstone. Armstrong believed that these features were secondary to the initial cutting of the pit, having been cut only after the feature had partially backfilled. The shaft exposed in 1971 measured 12.1m in depth,

38 Grimes Graves: Pits III (foreground) and 3a as exposed by the British Museum in 1976. Note the two levels of working in Pit III, the central deeper cut being made to extract the floorstone. © The British Museum

39 Grimes Graves: Shaft 11f as photographed in 1973. © The British Museum

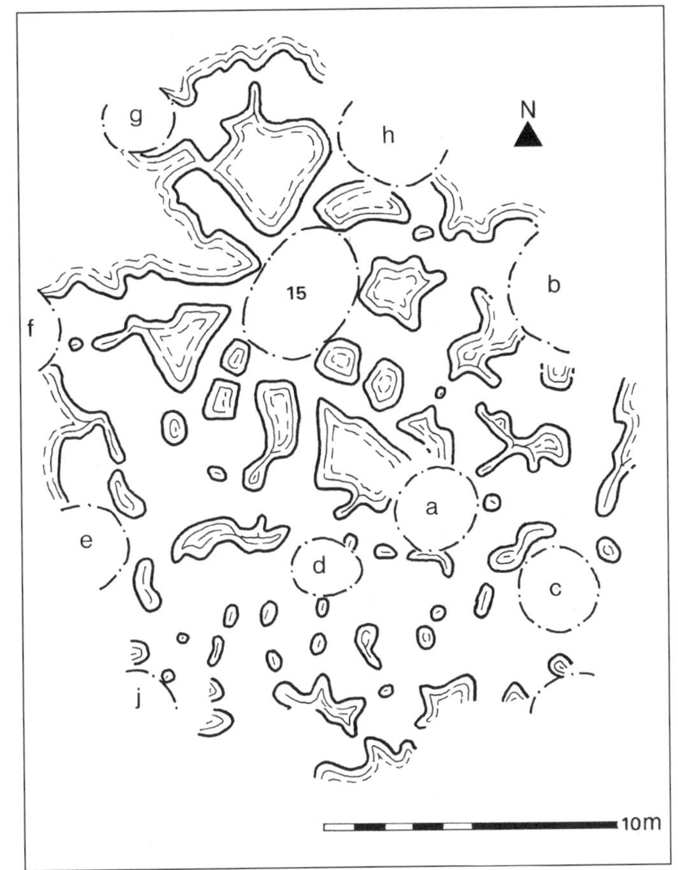

*40 Grimes Graves: gallery plan of Shaft 15 and 15a-h as recorded by the British Museum between 1972 and 1976. Compare this with the original plan of the Pit 15 galleries as drawn by Armstrong (figure **33**). Part of the disparity between gallery form and dimensions as recorded in these two drawings may be due to inaccuracies in the original plan, though significant visitor disturbance to the subterranean levels following the completion of Armstrong's work in 1939 has undoubtedly enlarged a number of the galleries, niches and chambers. Redrawn from Longworth and Varndell 1996*

cutting through three layers of flint in the process. The floorstone was exploited through the cutting of three galleries, one of which broke into a gallery extending from an unexcavated shaft to the immediate north-east. The remaining two galleries were not extensive, extending no more than 2.6m from the shaft wall.

Harrow Hill

Around 160 shafts have been recorded from the eastern and north-eastern slopes of Harrow Hill (**41; colour plate 6**), the subterranean flint seams tilting in a north to south direction, in contrast to the actual slope of the ground surface. Here flint appears to have been extracted primarily by means of open cast quarries at the point of initial outcrop, and, as the seam descended into the hill, access to the flint necessitated the cutting of increasingly deeper pits, until a second high level outcrop was finally detected. Such a methodology may explain the seemingly diverse nature of the Neolithic land cuts at Harrow Hill, Shafts I, III and 13 descending to 3m, 2.6m and 3.2m respectively, whilst Shafts II and 21 descended to 4m and 6.8m (**42, 43**). In some cases more than one seam of flint was exploited within any given shaft. The cutting of Shaft 21, for example,

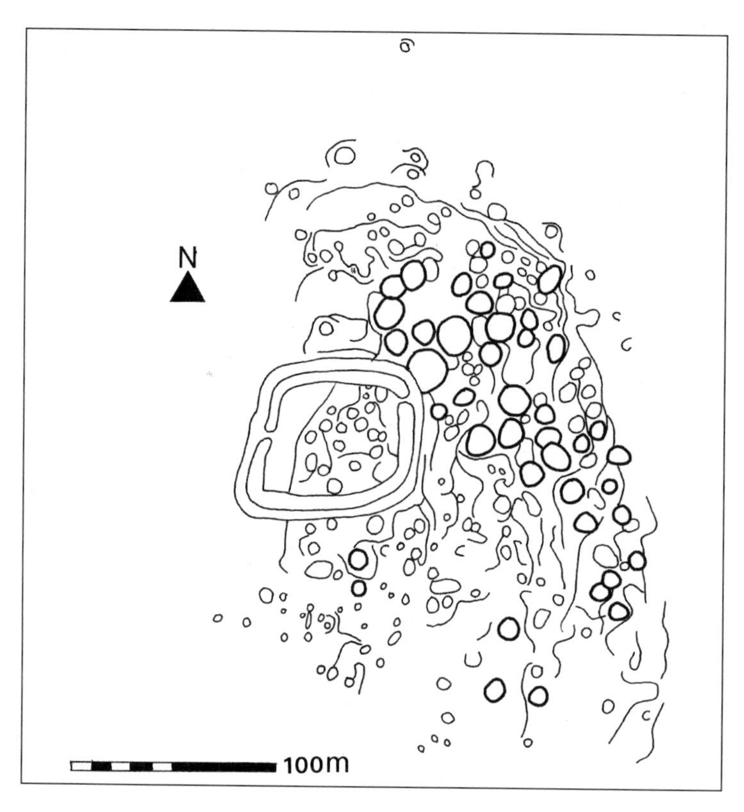

41 Harrow Hill: simplified surface plan of the earthwork features that constitute the mine site. Note how the Later Bronze Age enclosure overlies and obscures a significant number of shafts at the western margins of the site. Redrawn from Barber, Field and Topping 1999

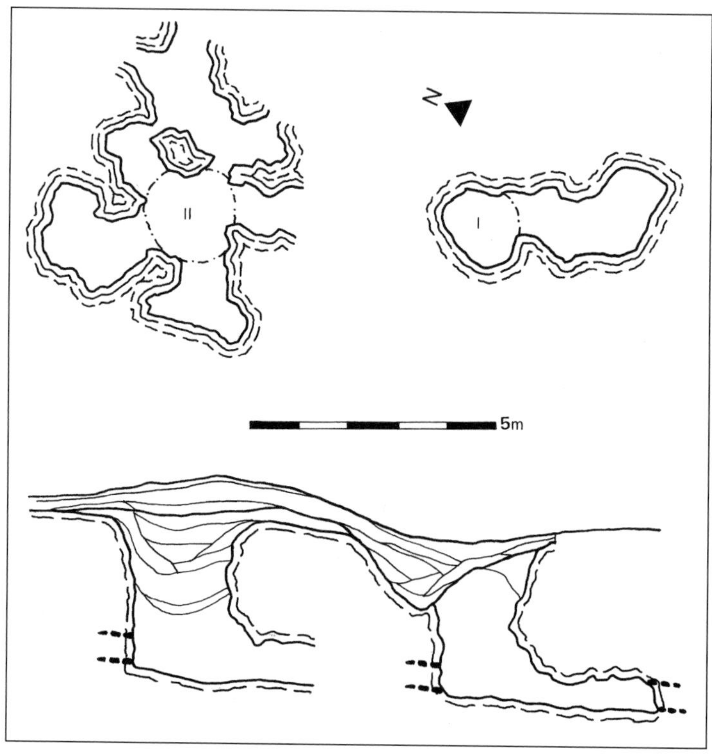

42 Harrow Hill: gallery plan and sections of Shafts I and II. Note how the earthen rampart of the Later Bronze Age enclosure seals the backfill of Shaft II, whilst the northern edge of Shaft I has been cut into by the external ditch. Redrawn from Holleyman 1937

43 Harrow Hill: looking from the ground surface into the main gallery of Shaft I as excavated in 1936. © Worthing Museum and Art Gallery

involved the removal of flint from the first, second and third seams, the second and third being removed through the excavation of galleries.

At times it was clear that at Harrow Hill the open-cast quarrying of surface flint was followed by the cutting of a deeper pit, the earlier area of extraction acting as a working platform to aid in the removal of flint. This is particularly clear in Shaft 21 where the first seam to be encountered had been partially removed by cutting a small recess into the wall of the pit (**44, 45**). A series of adit mines to the immediate north-east of Shaft 21 appear to have further exploited this first layer of flint. From such excavated evidence it is apparent that the difference between the exploitation of seams close to the surface through open cast or drift mines and the cutting of deeper pits with subterranean galleries, is not always a chronological one.

Basal galleries at Harrow Hill do not extend very far from the shaft wall, perhaps due to the close proximity of the shafts to one another and perhaps also in a deliberate attempt to ensure that the maximum quantity of flint was removed during extraction

44 Harrow Hill: the 'upper east gallery' of Shaft 21 in 1924, photographed shortly before its collapse. The gallery was cut in order to exploit the second seam of subterranean flint encountered within the shaft, at a depth of 3.7m. The main area of extraction focussed upon the third seam of flint, located within the shaft at a depth of 6.7m.

without having to sacrifice large amounts to the unexcavated gallery walls and roof supports. Excavations at Harrow Hill in 1982 revealed that Shaft 13 had been surrounded by a series of smaller shafts or satellites (**46**), most of which had not been observed at the surface. In areas where the chalk overburden was not extensive, prehistoric miners seemed to have dug shafts in pairs in order to exploit the desired layer of flint. This is particularly clear within Shafts 4 and 5, 9 and 12, 24 and 25. By pairing shafts, access, lighting and ventilation within the basal working areas may have been substantially improved.

45 Harrow Hill: Shaft 21 under excavation in 1925. The entrances to four basal galleries, numbered IV, III, II and I, may be seen at the bottom of the picture, gallery IV lying to the immediate left of the modern ladder. All four galleries exploited the third seam of flint encountered within the shaft. The line of the second seam may be seen behind the ladder, at the point of the tenth rung down. Also pictured at this level is the entrance to the 'upper west gallery', which partially exploited the second seam encountered within the shaft. Traces of less substantial surface flint extraction may be seen above and to the right of this gallery. © The Sussex Archaeological Society

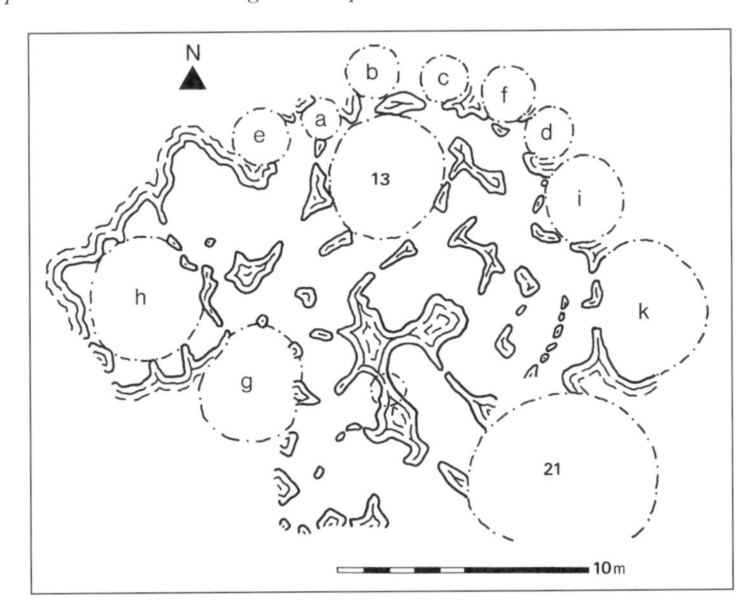

46 Harrow Hill: gallery plan of Shaft 13, satellite Shafts 13a-k and Shaft 21. Redrawn from McNabb, Felder, Kinnes and Sieveking 1996

Other Mine Sites

At Tolmere, of a series of 45 shallow features extending along the western face of the chalk ridge, only two excavated examples, Pits 38 and 40, cut to a depth of 1 and 1.9m respectively, are likely to be Neolithic in date. It is possible that these features represent the remains of abortive shafts or part of a larger system of pits searching for a flint seam to exploit. Unfortunately, as archaeological investigation at this site has to date been limited, caution must be emphasised regarding the exact interpretation of these features.

Four pits have been investigated to basal levels at the Den of Boddam. The features, which descended to depths of 2.7, 3, 4.1 and 4.4m, were cut in order to extract rounded flint cobbles from the Buchan Ridge Gravels. All appeared to have originally been bell-shaped, being slightly larger at the base than at the surface, subsequent edge collapse having obscuring this design. At Skelmuir Hill two similar pits were examined, descending to depths of 2 and 3m below the modern ground surface. Survey across the Den of Boddam by the Royal Commission on the Ancient and Historical Monuments of Scotland has indicated that the original zone of extraction may have been as large as 12

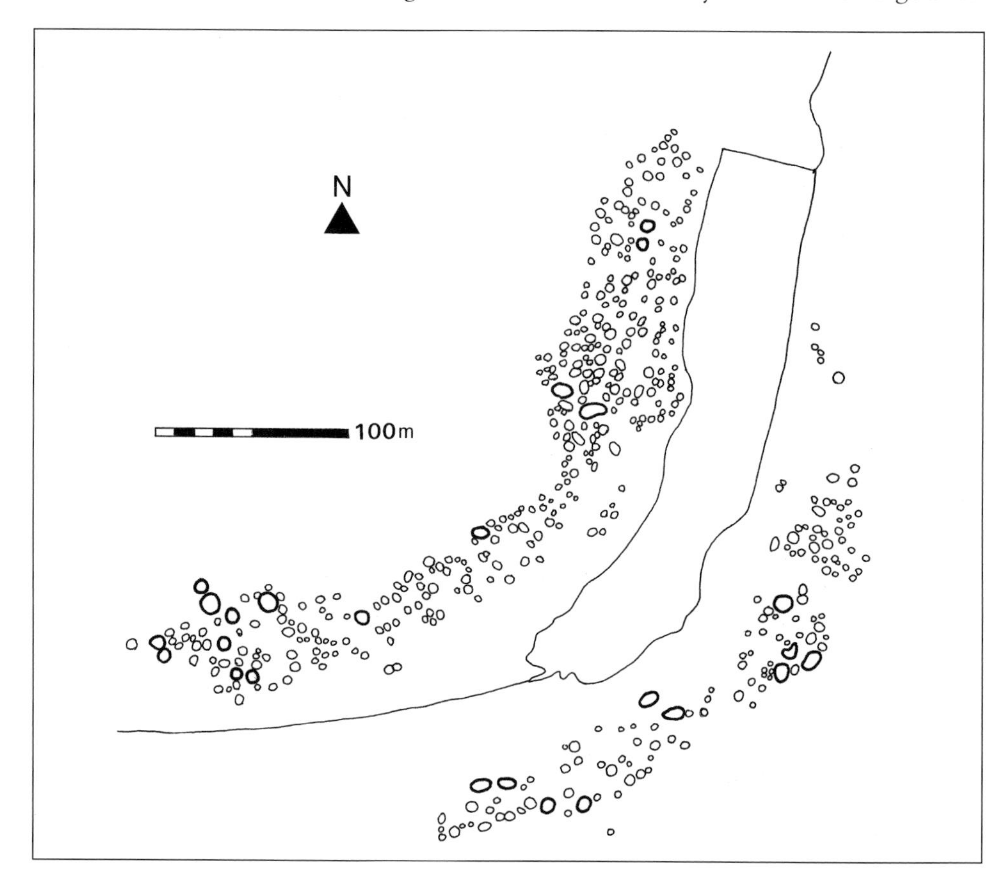

47 Den of Boddam: simplified surface plan of the flint extraction site, which today extends on both sides of a nineteenth-century reservoir. Redrawn from Saville 1995

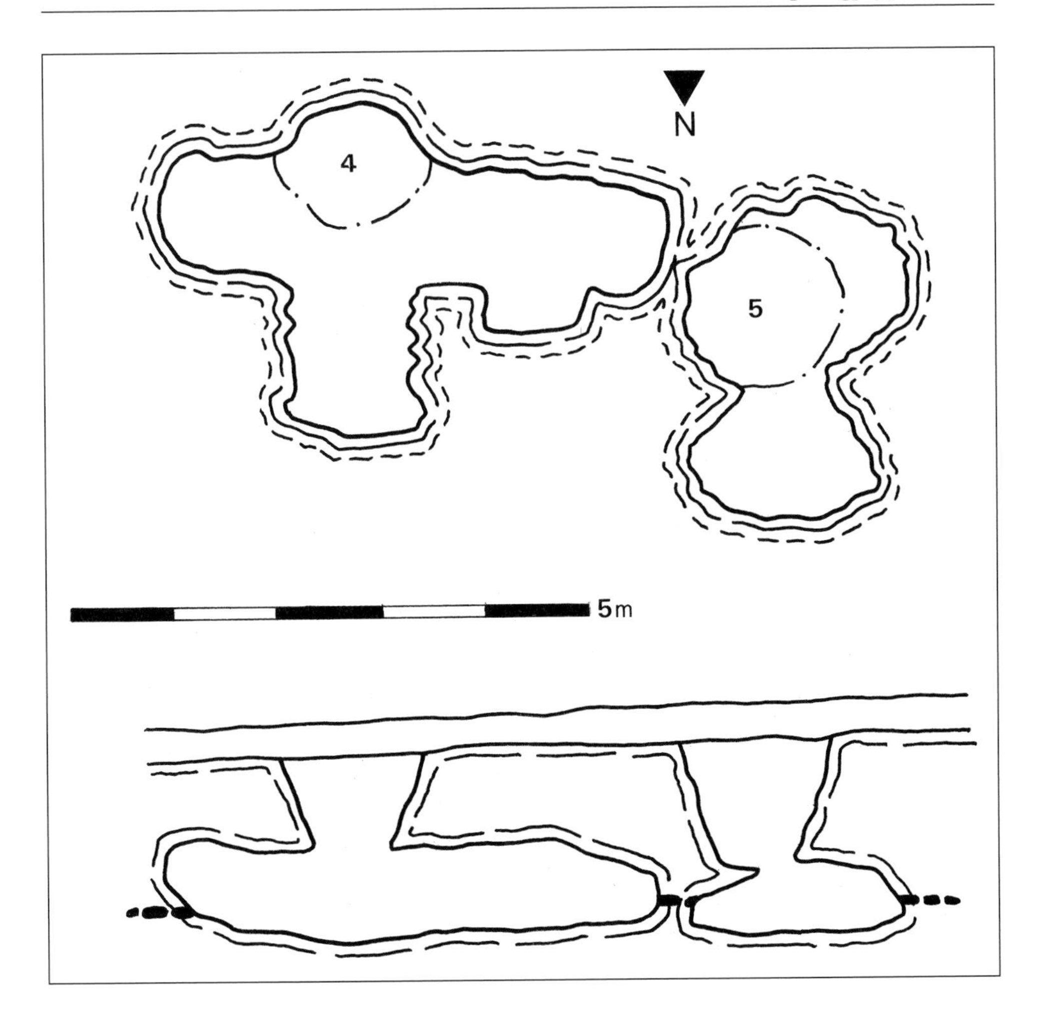

48 Durrington: gallery plan and sections of Pits 4 and 5. Much of Pit 4, with the exception of the northern (lower) gallery is speculative, full examination of the feature proving impossible in 1952. Redrawn from Booth and Stone 1952

hectares, comprising perhaps as many as 1000 separate pits (**47**). The full extent of the Skelmuir Hill site is more difficult to assess, ploughing having largely obliterated all trace of surface features, though 25 pits were noted in 1918, in a strip of land around 180m in length.

At Durrington, two 'pit-shafts', numbered 4 and 5 (**48**), and three lesser areas of flint extraction, identified as Pits 1-3, have been archaeologically examined. Pits 1-3 were little more than surface workings, descending to a maximum depth of 0.61m in order to exploit a poor quality seam of tabular flint. Shaft 4 was recorded to an overall depth of 2.1m. At least three galleries extended out from the base of the cut, the longest estimated to have run for around 2.4m, exploiting a discontinuous seam of tabular flint. Shaft 5 was represented by two discrete pits, separated by a distance of no more than 0.36m, and

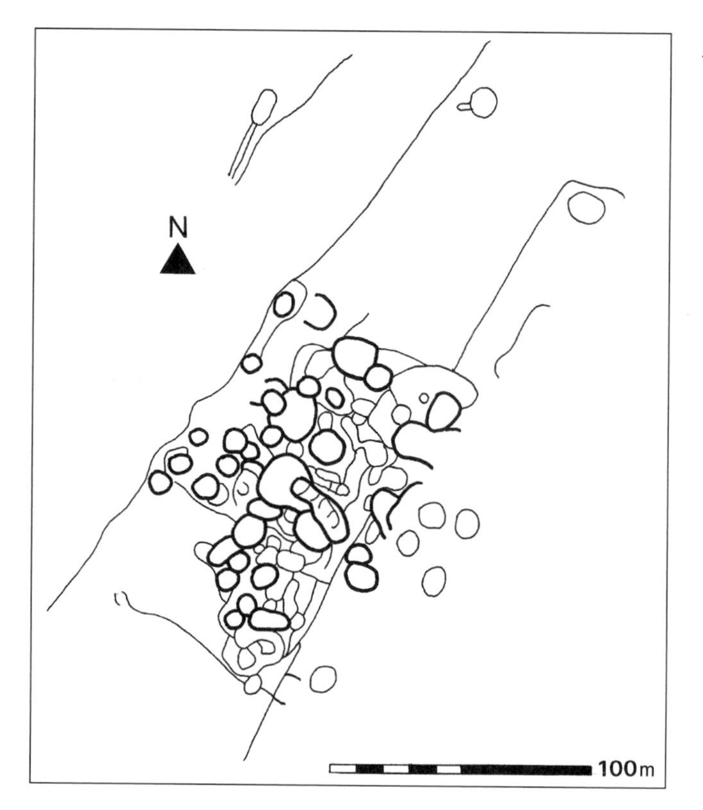

49 Long Down: simplified surface plan of the earthwork features that constitute the mine site. The elongated pit quarries cut into the upper, eastern slopes of the hill. Redrawn from Barber, Field and Topping 1999

linked by a single short gallery at a depth of just over 2.1m. This double pit exploited the same layer of tabular flint as that found in Shaft 4.

Only single shafts have been fully examined at the sites of Long Down and Martin's Clump. The Long Down example measured over 4.6m in depth, cutting through four seams of flint. The lower levels of the shaft did not appear to contain galleries or evidence of undercutting, though a narrowing of the walls in two places close to the base, may indicate part of a platform intended to aid in the extraction process. Surface investigation by the Royal Commission on the Historical Monuments of England suggests that the Long Down shafts, which today number in excess of 50 (**49**), were originally arranged in tiers along the line of contour, with a series of linear, open-pit quarries cutting into the upper slopes (**colour plate 13**).

At Martin's Clump the single excavated shaft descended to a maximum depth of 3m. It is not known how many flint seams were originally encountered within this feature, though a single undercutting appears to have extracted flint to a distance of 0.9m from the shaft wall. Martin's Clump itself may potentially represent the largest area of Neolithic flint mining in Britain, for the site today would seem to cover at least 8 hectares, possibly with as many as 1000 separate shafts and lesser pits. Unfortunately, extensive amounts of recent ploughing and landscaping activities have obscured much of the central part of the site.

Galleries do not appear to have played a feature in any of the three shafts examined at Stoke Down, though Shafts 1 and 3 possessed a limited number of undercuttings, demonstrating that in at least three areas the flint seam had been followed into the shaft wall. The shafts, numbered 1, 2 and 3, were bottomed at depths of 4.6, 2.9 and 4.2m respectively. Aerial photographs held in the National Monuments Record in Swindon, and transcribed by the Royal Commission on the Historical Monuments of England, suggest that the original area of extraction at Stoke Down comprised at least 70 shafts, cut in a linear strip along the chalk ridge for a distance of more than 750m.

In contrast to Stoke Down, the site at Nore Down is minute, with only 9 shafts (**colour plate 14**), covering an area of around 0.5 hectares (1.25 acres), recorded to date. Although none of the features at Nore Down have been fully examined, surface indications appear to suggest that the shafts, grouped into two sets of four with a single outlier, were all probably all open at the same time.

5 Working underground

Artefacts and artefactual assemblages

Evidence of the type and range of durable tools originally employed in the flint mines has been observed from a number of shafts and gallery floors (**50**). Such finds, which often include picks, rakes, punches and mallets made from antler, ox scapulae and stone axes, possess the appearance of having been freshly discarded (**51**), usually in significant numbers (**52**). The abandonment of equipment within galleries seems curious from a modern perspective, as digging or building tools are today often jealously guarded by their owners (**53**). The discovery of useable cutting and digging tools within backfilled shafts may of course indicate that instability within the rock face of certain mines caused a sudden abandonment, miners being subsequently unable or unwilling, to retrieve lost possessions.

Antler and bone could alternatively represent a resource which could easily be replenished, shed antler being available at the very end of the winter and cut antler being available at a time of deer kill. This may have made tools formed from such material an almost disposable commodity, especially if they were regularly becoming blunted through use. The presence of abandoned tools within the galleries of the mines may be taken as indicating that these objects were being deliberately left, either because they had become in some way contaminated by use within the galleries, so that they could not be safely used anywhere outside of the mine without risking a form of spiritual pollution. It is also possible that the tools were intended as an offering or thank you to the deity or sprit residing within this particular area of the landscape, or as a way of imprinting the ground with the cultural attributes of the social group engaged in the flint extraction.

From the numbers of tools recovered within the mines, as well as from marks left upon the walls of excavated galleries, it would appear that the antlers of red deer (*Cervus elaphus*) represented the primary tool used during the extraction of the flint seam (**54, 55**). Estimates of the numbers of antlers required for use in the cutting of each shaft and the subsequent extraction of flint have varied between 100-150 and 400, these calculations being dependent upon how many people are thought to have worked in each mine and how long a period each pit is supposed to have been open. Whatever the exact figure, it is clear that the majority of antlers used in the mines had been naturally shed, cut examples from slain deer being rare, though examples have been recorded from Cissbury and Grimes Graves. This would imply a degree of deer herd management or control by those engaged in mining. Antler was a highly prized and valuable resource in the Neolithic and Bronze Age, and the systematic gathering and preparation of shed examples for use in digging must have represented a major aspect of the daily routine of life. So important was

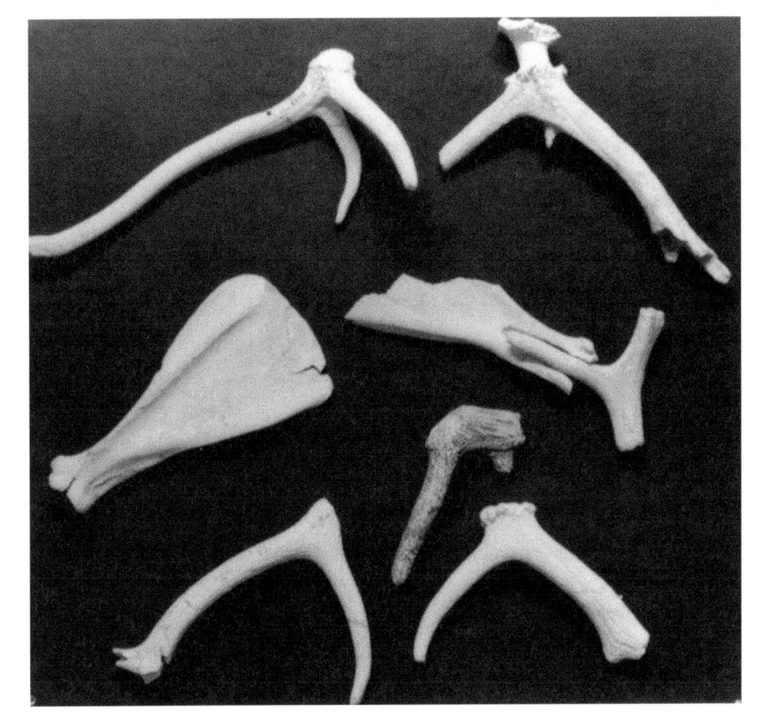

50 Harrow Hill: examples of the bone and antler tools recovered during the excavation of Shaft 21. Note that a piece of cut antler from the mine has here been fitted to a fragment of scapula in the belief that it was originally intended to act as a handle, 'the beam forming a most comfortable grip'. © Worthing Museum and Art Gallery

51 Grimes Graves: gallery 16 in Pit 15 showing three antler picks as recorded in 1973. © The British Museum

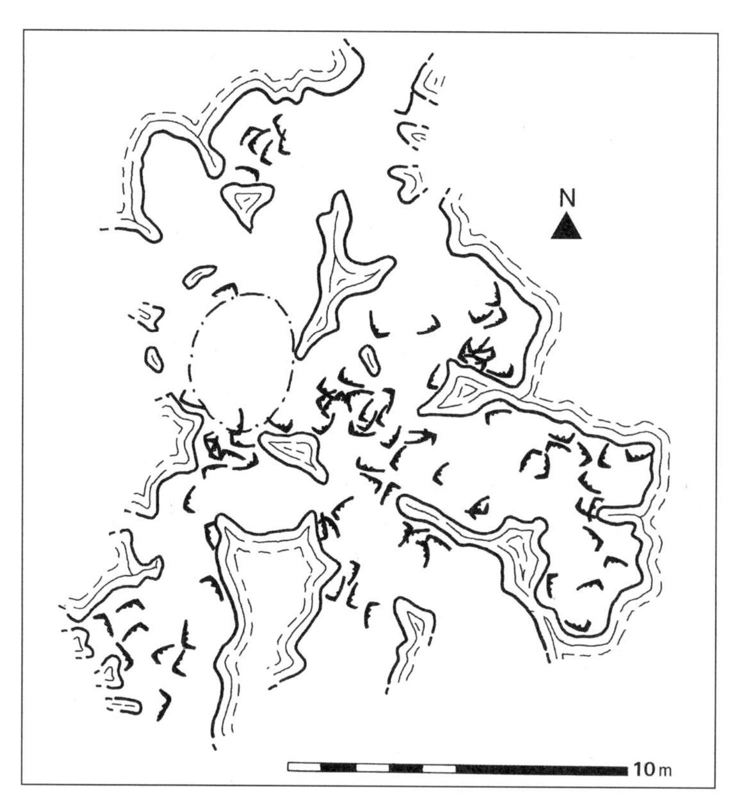

52 *Grimes Graves: plan of the main galleries extending from Greenwell's Pit, as recorded by the British Museum between 1972 and 1976, showing the positions of antler picks not disturbed or removed by Greenwell. Redrawn from Longworth and Varndell 1996*

53 *A parallel for Neolithic tool discard? An abandoned Department of the Environment rake as discovered in the 'eastern' gallery of Pit 1 by the British Museum team in 1973. © The British Museum*

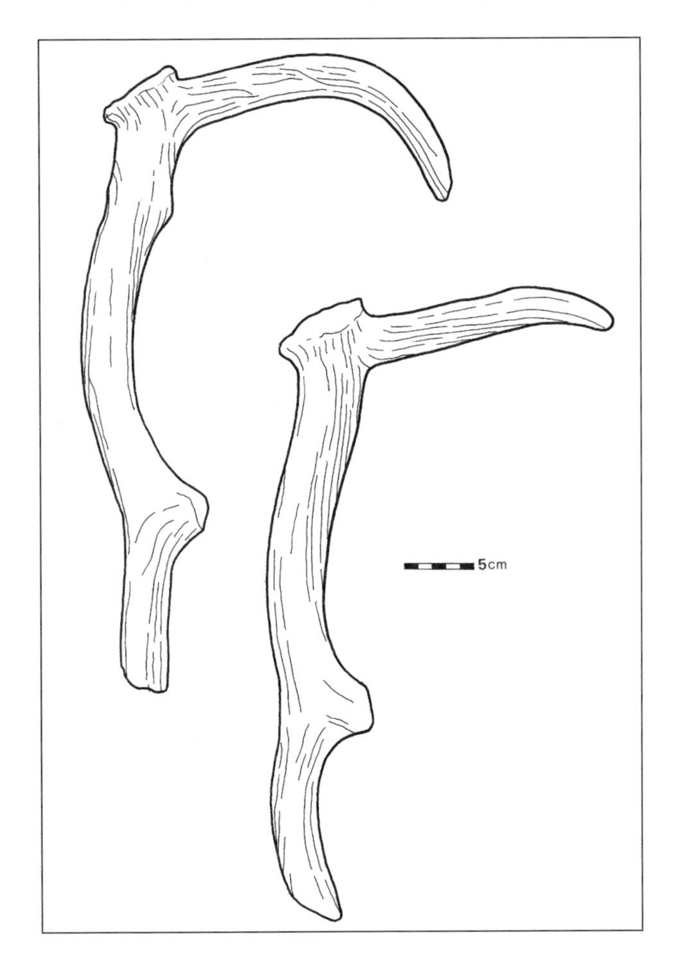

54 Two antler picks recovered from Greenwell's Pit at Grimes Graves between 1868 and 1870. Redrawn from Clutton-Brock 1984

this natural resource to the Neolithic miners, that Juliet Clutton-Brock, in her 1984 analysis of antler picks from Grimes Graves, has suggested that red deer may well have been protected by human groups and not predated on for food.

Antler, with its sharply pointed brow tine, formed the perfect digging tool and could be successfully used to pick away at the natural joints or fissures in the chalk face. By gradually removing blocks of chalk from above a flint seam, a worker in the mine could expose a sufficient mass of flint before levering and breaking it up. The chalk directly overlying a flint seam seems to have been preferred as it tended to be softer than that encountered elsewhere, the impervious nature of the flint below having halted the downward percolation of surface water. Evidence surviving in the walls of galleries and niches suggests that the usual method of removing this softer chalk layer was to pick away at the chalk wall, creating a series of parallel holes which could later be worked into a deep horizontal groove. The point of the antler was useful in 'hooking-out' loose chalk rubble from the workface and, when reversed, the back of the antler shaft could be used as a hammer to break flint up into more manageable pieces.

Hand and fingerprint impressions preserved in the chalk silt on the handles of some antlers recovered from Grimes Graves, clearly demonstrated how the picks had originally

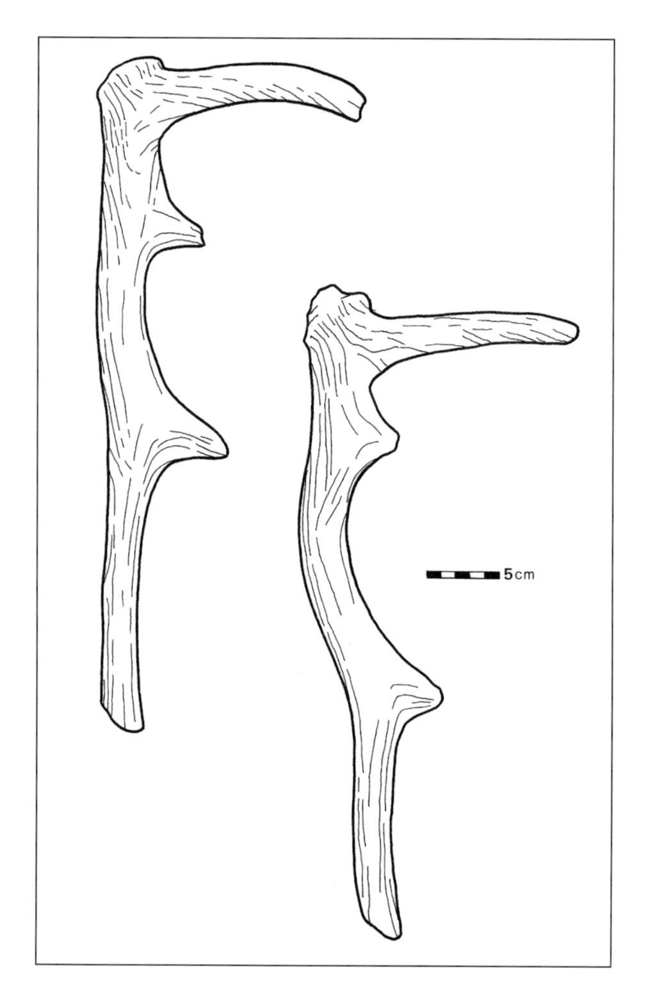

55 *Two antler picks recovered from Greenwell's Pit at Grimes Graves between 1868 and 1870. Redrawn from Clutton-Brock 1984*

been held and used, the main point of grip being halfway down the beam or shaft of the pick (**56**). Unfortunately, the discovery of five and six thousand year old fingerprints on such tools, though an undoubtedly spectacular link to the people of the mines, has told us little of their average age, sex and lifestyle. The build up of chalk silt on the handles of picks could perhaps be explained as a natural process, whereby the dust generated by extraction adhered to the antlers in the damp and sweaty atmosphere of the mine. Alternatively wads of chalk silt may have been deliberately used by those engaged in extraction, in an attempt to limit the wear of antler on hand, though it is difficult to see how this would have aided a firm grip.

In one of the earliest recorded pieces of experimental archaeology, Lane Fox tested the effectiveness of the antler pick during the course of his 1875 excavation season at Cissbury. Having first trimmed the pick into shape using a flint blade, Lane Fox and a member of his work team dug into an undisturbed area of chalk bedrock, noting that 'we had made an excavation 3 feet square and 3 feet deep in an hour and a half'. To dig out a gallery similar to the longest recorded from Cissbury, which at that time was 27ft (8.2m), Lane Fox calculated would have taken at least twelve hours.

56 P.J. Felder demonstrating how to wield an antler pick at Grimes Graves in 1976. © The British Museum

The pick does not appear to have been the primary tool for flint extraction in all mines however. At Blackpatch, in the galleries of Shafts 1 and 7, Pull noticed that a variety of punches had originally been hammered into natural lines of cleavage in the chalk so as to dislodge blocks which could then be levered up and away from the workface. In gallery I of Blackpatch Shaft 1 and gallery III of Shaft 21 at Harrow Hill, a series of holes, apparently formed by the systematic hammering of punches into fissures in the chalk face, were recorded set in two parallel rows (**57**). The intention here seems to have been to 'wedge out the intervening block of chalk' though this had, for some reason, never happened. Many examples of the punch, cut from antler tines, and the hammer, formed from the crown of an antler, were found in the Blackpatch mines, other examples also being found, less frequently, from Church Hill, Cissbury and Grimes Graves. Experiments to assess the validity of using wedges, punches and hammers in order to detach large blocks of chalk were successfully conducted by Lane Fox at Cissbury in 1875.

That other types of digging tool were probably being utilised in the mines is demonstrated by evidence from Shafts 4 and 7 at Church Hill where a series of deep and regular impressions implied the use of large wooden bars or mauls. At Grimes Graves, in Greenwell's Pit and in Pits 1 and 2, clear evidence, in the form of marks in the chalk wall, suggest that stone axes or adzes were at times used in the excavation process. Such tools appear, more often, to have been employed to shave back and enlarge gallery entrances, remove awkward projections in the chalk wall or break up the more stubborn flint seams.

57 *Pick or wedge marks left on the wall of gallery III, Shaft 21 at Harrow Hill. The holes appear to have been arranged in parallel rows with the intention of 'wedging out the intervening block of chalk'.* © *The Sussex Archaeological Society*

Occasionally the hafted bone, usually the radius or metatarsal of an ox, may have been used to break up chalk in favour of the antler pick or stone axe. It is possible that such bones could have been mounted onto the brow tine of an antler pick, perhaps to extend the life of a pick that had already been blunted by overuse.

Whilst antler picks seem to have been used to dislocate flint through the removal of the surrounding chalk, ox scapulae and rakes, made from the crown tine of antlers, appear to have been employed in the movement of chalk rubble from specific working areas (**58**). The ox scapula, or shoulder blade, is a fairly common find from the Sussex mines, though it is found less frequently in Norfolk. When first encountered it was thought to represent a primitive form of shovel. As with the antler pick, Lane Fox conducted experiments into the use of such scapulae in earth moving, concluding that 'I could fill a wheelbarrow with it in five minutes, but with the hands I could do so in four minutes'. The ox scapula did

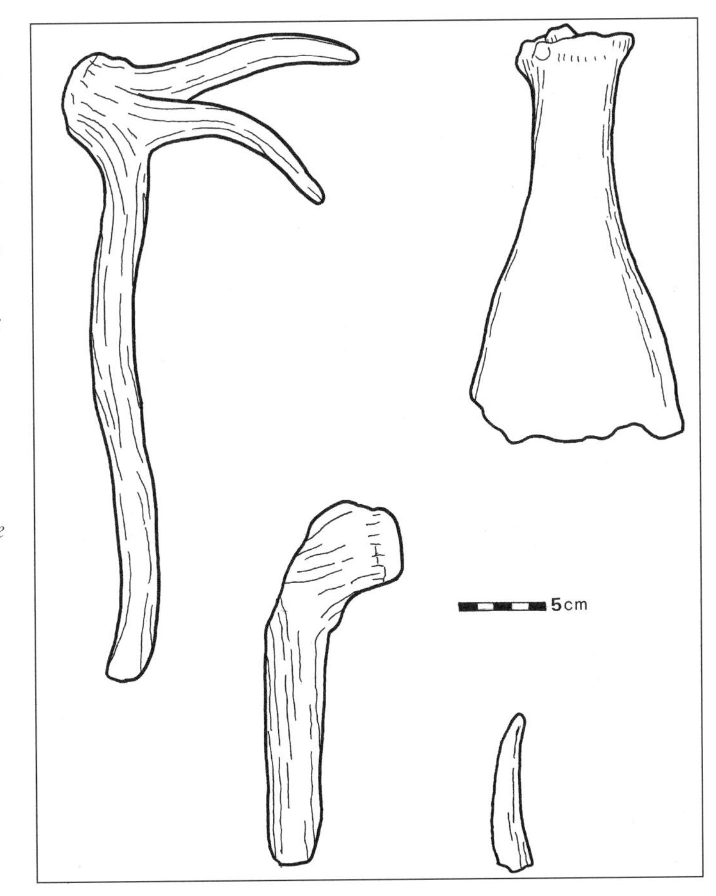

58 Other Neolithic digging tools recovered from flint mines. Clockwise from left: an antler rake from Harrow Hill, Shaft 21; an ox scapula from Harrow Hill, Shaft 21; an antler tine from Shaft 4 at Church Hill; an antler hammer from Shaft 21 at Harrow Hill. The tine is redrawn from Russell 2000 whilst the rake, hammer and scapula are redrawn from Curwen and Curwen 1926

not appear therefore to be terribly effective if used as a shovel, something later confirmed in experiments conducted by E. Cecil Curwen at Harrow Hill.

Lane Fox suggested that scapulae may have been as a way of saving the hands from excessive wear, though the sharp rear edge of the bone 'injured the hand whilst shoving it into the rubble, and would certainly make a sore place in time'. Only when fitted to a handle 'and properly prepared' did the ox scapulae attain a degree of efficiency, Lane Fox then being able to fill his wheelbarrow in the quicker time of two minutes. Though none of the bones recorded at this time appeared to have been hafted, the Curwens suggested that at least two scapulae derived from their excavation at Harrow Hill could originally have been modified by the addition of handles. Two pieces of cut antler beam, recovered from the investigation of Shaft 21, fitted snugly into scapulae sockets, one piece, with a long tine set at a right angle to the shaft, even forming 'a most comfortable T-grip'.

Whether shovels and rakes would actually have been necessary during the mining and extraction process is debatable. Chalk rubble discovered from the basal workings of certain mines at Grimes Graves would appear to indicate that it had all been moved and dumped by hand. Long distance transportation of rubble could safely be conducted by placing the rubble in baskets and hauling these out and away from the workface using ropes. Perhaps, as suggested after earthmoving tests conducted in the 1960s during the Overton Down experimental earthwork programme, scapulae were not used primarily for shifting rubble, but for scraping up areas of highly fragmented chalk from the working floor.

The extraction process

The process of flint exploitation in the lowest levels of Neolithic mines has been well documented from Cissbury, Grimes Graves, Church Hill, Harrow Hill and Blackpatch, but only at Grimes Graves and Harrow Hill has there been an attempt made to reconstruct the sequence of extraction. This is partly due to the research strategy devised by the British Museum to record the mechanics of flint mining, but also because the team of people employed to investigate the Norfolk mine series between 1972 and 1976 and the Harrow Hill site in 1982, included Dutch mining engineers and ex-miners, who, it was hoped, would be able to provide a level of experience unknown to the average archaeologist.

The galleries re-explored by the Dutch miners at Grimes Graves and Harrow Hill appear to have followed a relatively clear and orderly method of cutting and flint exploitation. First the gallery would be cut to its full intended length, all flint being removed from the floor of the tunnel at this stage (**59**). Flint extracted from the floor at this point is taken to the surface, whilst all loose chalk rubble is removed from the working area (**60**) and dumped elsewhere in the shaft (**61**), either in recently abandoned adjacent galleries (**62**), or upon the floor of the shaft itself. Stage two in the extraction process appears to have been characterised by removal of more floorstone through the successive cutting of alcoves or niches into the gallery wall itself, starting at the furthest point and working back towards the area of the open shaft. The cutting of additional alcoves into the gallery system represented the most potentially dangerous part of the working, as excessive flint removal could destroy the structural integrity of the gallery and undermine the whole roof. All chalk rubble dislocated by the removal of the flint seam appears to have been packed back into completed niches, partly to conserve effort and partially perhaps to return a form of stability to finished areas.

Just how many people would be engaged in the cutting of shafts and the extension of galleries is unknown and, probably, unknowable. We do not, for instance, know how long a period each mine was worked or whether more than one shaft was dug simultaneously (though the implication from Grimes Graves, Cissbury, Harrow Hill, and Church Hill is that certain shafts were dug in pairs). The post-medieval mines from Norfolk, for instance, though complex in the nature of subterranean workings, were worked by no more than a single individual, occasionally with an assistant to aid in extraction, all year round. Here mining was a relatively slow business, but perhaps more profitable than having to share the rewards of mining with a larger team of co-workers.

During the British Museum's examination of the Grimes Graves shafts, Gale Sieveking and P.J. Felder calculated that, during the initial digging of the shaft, if one miner required a minimum of one square metre of working space, then at least twenty people could legitimately have been employed in the initial phases of shaft excavation. As the shaft

59 George Holleyman shovelling chalk rubble from the workface of the backfilled gallery in Shaft I at Harrow Hill in 1936. The restricted nature of space available to the miner within the subterranean workplace is abundantly clear, the dimensions of this particular gallery extending to a maximum width and height of no more than 1.3m.

descends, the ratio of 'diggers' to 'spoil shifters' changes dramatically, more people being required to remove large quantities of rubble to the surface. By the time the shaft has attained it desired depth, and the floorstone may be exploited, Sieveking estimated that between six to eight people may still be working in the basal levels, the remaining twelve to fourteen aiding in the extraction of spoil and its dumping out on the surface.

The digging of galleries out from the base of the shaft would require a different strategy concerning the deployment of labour. Sieveking suggested that an average number of galleries extending from any one pit was likely to be four. The dimensions of each gallery, and the way in which each needed to be cut, necessitated that no more than one person could probably be picking the chalk at any one time. Each 'picker' may have had at least one assistant, to remove spoil away from the workface and perhaps to alternate digging duties as required. The average maximum number of people working in the basal levels of each mine, assuming that the galleries were worked together, was in this model unlikely to exceed eight. As galleries extended in length, and the cutting of alcoves and niches increased, then the number of individuals helping to remove flint and chalk would, through necessity, have multiplied. Sieveking and Felder have suggested that the critical distance necessary before an additional helper was required, was around four metres.

60 *Holleyman attempting to remove chalk rubble from the Shaft I gallery at Harrow Hill. © Worthing Museum and Art Gallery*

Longworth and Varndell have further speculated that, in Greenwell's Pit at Grimes Graves, if a single miner was able, with haulage backup, to dig and extract the flint from a 1m area of gallery in a single day, then the time taken to exploit all the floorstone in the basal area of this particular shaft would have been fifteen days. Taking into account the potentially considerable margin for error, especially with regard to number of people employed in the mine and hours worked in a day, then it has been calculated that the minimum time scale necessary to complete all work in Greenwell's shaft would have been around 93 days.

Exactly how much flint was originally extracted from the mines during the Neolithic, is a question that is extremely difficult to answer with any degree of certainty. The major problem with regard to calculating quantity of material removed from a given mine is that the floorstone does not usually form a continuous deposit, but as a discontinuous layer of differentially proportioned nodules. Careful examination of the impressions left in the floor of any shaft may help in calculating how much material has been removed (**63**), though these indications have frequently been erased or otherwise obscured by the

61 Harrow Hill: 'Smithies' removing chalk rubble from the main gallery in Shaft III, at Harrow Hill in 1936.

movements of the original miners and, presumably, by the dragging of baskets laden with rubble. Examination of the hollows left by the prising away of nodules from the walls of the shaft and attendant gallery systems (**64**) may also be used to calculate quantity of flint exploited, though here again problems arise from the obscuring of evidence caused by the movements of the Neolithic mining team.

During the clearance of Greenwell's shaft at Grimes Graves, Felder and the team of Dutch miners calculated that, of a potential 75,735kg of floorstone, at least 63,639kg (or 84%), may originally have been exploited. This suggests that for every square metre worked, around 330kg of flint could have been successfully removed. An estimate for the quantity of floorstone removed from the shaft system of Pit 15D at Grimes Graves suggested that the figure could have been in the region of 312.69 kg per square metre. Longworth and Varndell have calculated that, given a potentially considerable margin of error, if the sample area of the Grimes Graves mining zone had been exploited to the same degree as evidenced in both Pit 15D and Greenwell's shaft, then the total quantity of flint mined could have been in the region of 17,955.63 metric tonnes. Not all floorstone taken

62 Grimes Graves: the 'south-eastern' gallery of Pit 1 as re-examined in 1973. Note the way in which both working areas have been filled with chalk rubble following the initial extraction of floorstone deposits. © The British Museum

63 Grimes Graves: the floor of the 'eastern gallery' in Pit 1, clearly showing the uneven surface produced by the removal of floorstone nodules. Subsequent disturbance, from the movements of the Neolithic miners, has largely obscured much of this information. © The British Museum

1 *The western and north-western slopes of Cissbury as seen from High Salvington in August 1999. The ramparts of the Iron Age enclosure are clearly visible. The area of flint extraction lies behind the central portion of enclosure bank and is partially covered with scrub (author)*

2 *The eastern slopes of Harrow Hill as seen from the north-western slopes of Blackpatch Hill in August 1999. The area of flint extraction covers the upper crest of Harrow Hill to the immediate right of the ploughed field. Just below a single line of trees, in the centre of the photograph, lies the oval earthwork enclosure of Cock Hill, a probable henge monument of the Later Neolithic (author)*

3 *Harrow Hill from the north as seen in August 1999. Notice that the flint mine shafts, visible here as surface indentations against the skyline, cluster along the eastern facing slope of the hill to the left of this photography (author)*

4 *The western slopes of Cissbury from the air in January 1995. Most of the flint mine hollows are now filled with scrub and small trees. Note that some flint mines are visible outside the north-western circuit of the Iron Age rampart at the bottom left of the photograph, whilst the area of mines investigated by John Pull in the 1950s can be seen extending to the south of the ramparts at the top right. English Heritage © Crown Copyright*

5 *Grimes Graves from the air. The custodian's hut and concrete covers marking Pits 1 and 15 are visible in the top right-hand corner next to the car park, whilst Greenwell's Shaft is marked by a concrete cover in the bottom left-hand corner, just before the trees. NMR 15717/27. English Heritage © Crown Copyright*

6 *Harrow Hill from the air in January 1995. The ramparts of the Later Bronze Age enclosure are clearly seen to overlie Shafts approaching the crest of the hill. Rabbit burrowing erosion in those Shafts lying along the eastern slopes of the hill is bringing large quantities of chalk to the surface. NMR 15209/31. English Heritage © Crown Copyright*

7 *Cissbury. Ground level of the western limits of the flint mining area looking south towards the coastal plain of Sussex. Here the spread of backfilled shafts is interrupted by the continuous earthwork circuit of the Iron Age hillfort. This relationship was not understood by the earliest antiquarian investigators at Cissbury who believed that ramparts and shafts were contemporary, the shafts representing the remains of cattle compounds, ponds or sunken feature buildings (author)*

8 *Cissbury. Ground level view of the south-western ramparts of the Iron Age hillfort looking west towards the mining site of Church Hill. Investigation of the ditch circuit here by Lane Fox in the mid-1870s finally revealed that the shafts predated the construction of the enclosure. This shot was taken over the backfilled remains of No.1 Escarp Shaft and should be compared with figure* ***6****, taken in 1875 (author)*

9 Cissbury. Ground level shot of Willet's Shaft No.2 as it appears today, filled with dense vegetation, looking north-east. The pit, excavated in late 1874, was never fully backfilled following the completion of the nineteenth-century fieldwork (author)

10 Cissbury. Ground level shot of the 'Large Pit' partially investigated by Lane Fox in 1875, looking north across the chalk downs. The feature, when originally cleared, measured 20m in diameter and was traced to a depth of 12.8m before the collapse of the standing section renedered all further work too dangerous (author)

11 Ground level view of the backfilled mine shafts of Harrow Hill looking north-east (author)

12 Ground level view of backfilled Shaft 18 at Harrow Hill looking north-east (author)

13 *The surface earthworks comprising Long Down flint mine site looking south-west towards the coastal plain of Sussex (author)*

14 *Ground level view of the conjoined mine shafts of Nore Down, with spoil heap behind, looking south-east (author)*

15 The basal levels of Pit 1 at Grimes Graves as presented today. The floor has been strengthened with concrete to limit visitor wear, whilst much of the lower walls of the shaft have been rebuilt and repointed. Modern iron grilles prevent access into the cleared galleries whilst artificial electric lighting eerily illuminates the subterranean workface beyond. English Heritage © Crown Copyright

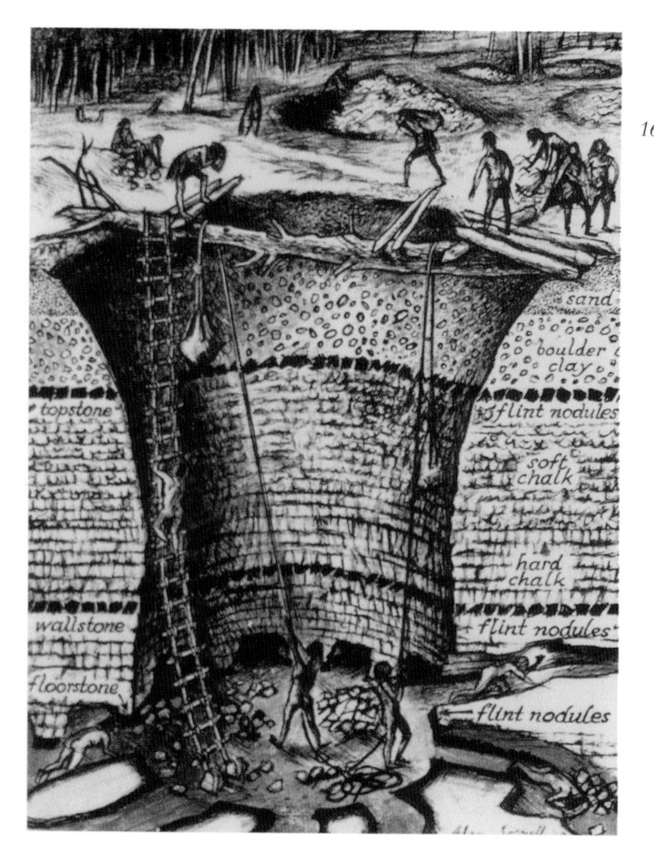

16 Alan Sorrell's reconstruction of Neolithic miners removing flint from the basal levels of a shaft. Both miners are male and are again depicted naked, a solution perhaps to the sometimes hot and cramped working conditions, if not to the cold chalk surfaces and sharp, flesh-piercing flints. The miner to the left lies on his left side in a gallery, removing flint from the chalk wall with an antler hammer or pick. Outside, in the shaft itself, the second miner is engaged in wrapping floorstone nodules in a leather bag, presumably so that they may be removed via ropes hauled by people waiting at the surface. Note the rope and timber ladder held down with flint to the right of the picture, and the antler pick and ox scapula, tied to a wooden handle, in the foreground. English Heritage © Crown Copyright

17 *A drawing by Peter Dunn providing a glimpse directly into the working area of a Grimes Grave shaft. Here three (clothed) males are removing flint from a gallery. One miner is chipping at the workface in a secondary niche with an antler pick, apparently by battering it with a large flint held in his right hand. A second antler pick, a hafted stone axe and an enigmatic chalk cup lie at his feet, while his two assistants drag flint debris by hand and by leather bags pulled by rope, back to the main area of the shaft. English Heritage © Crown Copyright*

Previous page

18 *(above left) This illustration by Alan Sorrell represents one of the earliest attempts to reconstruct a Neolithic flint mine based upon archaeological evidence, in this instance Pit 1 at Grimes Graves. Sorrell's vivid drawing evokes the nature and conditions of prehistoric mining as seen from a 1960s perspective. All the figures in the drawings are apparently male and poorly attired, whilst those working within the galleries are naked. The exact nature of associated ladders and hauling equipment depicted here, leather bags being pulled to the surface with ropes draped over a felled tree and rough planks, must of course remain uncertain. English Heritage © Crown Copyright*

19 *(below left) A reconstructed section through the 1971 Shaft at Grimes Graves drawn by Terry Ball. Here a group of some seventeen males are actively engaged in flint extraction. Ladders are shown providing access to the basal workings, with the miners removing bags of flint rubble on their shoulders via a series of timber platforms built directly into the sides of the shaft, rather than by using ropes as in Sorrell's earlier drawing. English Heritage © Crown Copyright*

20 *Wilmington Hill, East Sussex, as seen from Windover Hill. Here a series of at least 12 irregular hollows and associated spoil heaps, visible at the top right of the picture, on the upper slopes of the chalk escarpment, have traditionally been viewed as representing the remains of Neolithic flint mines. A survey, conducted by the Royal Commission on the Historical Monuments of England in the 1990s, has suggested that these surface hollows represent the remains of medieval or later flint quarries designed to supply stone for buildings in the weald below (author)*

21 Wilmington Hill, East Sussex, looking west towards Windover Hill and the northern scarp slope of the South Downs. The pit visible in the foreground was thought to represent a Neolithic flint mine, but its well-defined nature, together with evidence for vehicular access in the form of cart tracks, may suggest a medieval or later date (author)

22 Wolstonbury Hill, West Sussex. A ground level view of a nineteenth-century flint quarry pit in the course of excavation in 1995. The scale shown is 2m. Flint has been extracted for its building and sparking qualities throughout all periods of human history. Dating of shallow flint quarry features such as this can therefore prove difficult without a thorough archaeological examination (author)

23 Monuments contemporary with the utilization of flint mines 1: the long mound of Bevis' Thumb, near Compton in West Sussex looking north-east. The mound is roughly aligned east to west, surviving to a height of just over 1.6m and a length of around 60m. The overall width of the monument is 8m at the eastern end and 16m at the west, though its southern edge, as seen here, has been denuded by ploughing. The flanking ditches, which originally ran the length of the monument, have been largely obscured by modern agriculture and road building activities (author)

24 Monuments contemporary with the utilization of flint mines 2: the Camel's Humps long mound overlooking Lewes in East Sussex. The mound is orientated north-west/south-east and survives to 34m in length, 18m in width and 3.2m in height. The name 'Camel's Humps' is due to the fact that an irregular pit, cut through the eastern end of the earthwork, has given the surviving ends of single feature the appearance of two partially conjoined round mounds. Traces of flanking ditches survive on either side of mound, though the southern edge of the monument has been disfigured by the construction of a golf fairway (author)

25 *Monuments contemporary with the utilization of flint mines 3: the Belle Tout enclosure on Beachy Head, near Eastbourne in East Sussex. The single circuit of bank and segmented ditch can be seen enclosing the upper slopes of the headland, disappearing over the cliffs just to the left of the lighthouse. Note that this picture was taken shortly after the movement of the lighthouse building in 1999 (author)*

26 *Monuments contemporary with the utilization of flint mines 4: a section excavated across the south-western tangential ditch of Whitehawk causewayed enclosure in 1991. The earthen ramparts of the fourth enclosure circuit, to which the tangential ditch is joined, may be seen behind the wire fence in the background (author)*

27 *Monuments contemporary with the utilization of flint mines 5: detail of the lower ditch cut of the Whitehawk enclosure as revealed in 1991. The distinctive, circular signature of the antler pick, the primary tool used in the construction of both enclosure ditch and mine shaft, may be seen above and to the right of the scale (author)*

28 *Modern depositional practice at Neolithic monuments 1: here the cremated remains of a prestige symbol of social status have been deposited within the uppermost fill of an Early Neolithic enclosure ditch at Whitehawk (author)*

29 *Modern depositional practice at Neolithic monuments 2: here a specific assemblage of artefacts relating to aural entertainment have been deposited close to a long mound at Lavant in West Sussex. Unlike today, there was perhaps no concern in prehistory that discarded material significantly detracted from 'a sense of place'. In fact it might be that human refuse was deliberately allowed to accumulate in shafts and ditches as it was considered to represent a vital component in the reaffirmation of land claims and the subsequent taming of wild or alien places (author)*

30 *Cissbury in 1999, a Scheduled Ancient Monument in the care of the National Trust. The flint mines at Grimes Graves are similarly well looked after by English Heritage, whilst other mine sites, such as Harrow Hill and Long Down are under private ownership. Unfortunately not all mine sites have been so effectively managed, Blackpatch, Church Hill and Stoke Down having been largely obliterated by ploughing in the mid-twentieth century (author)*

64 Grimes Graves: the walls of a gallery in Greenwell's Pit as re-explored in 1974, showing where at least two floorstone nodules have been removed. Note the cutting impressions left by a stone axe (the diagonal striations), between the two main hollows. © The British Museum

from the basal levels of the mines was fully utilised however, large quantities of unused flint apparently being left on the surface, incorporated into flint working floors, redeposited back into abandoned mine shafts or being deliberately reburied, perhaps as a form of offering.

Many of the gallery systems of shafts investigated by Willett, Lane Fox, Harrison and Pull at Cissbury, and Greenwell, Peake, Clarke and Armstrong at Grimes Graves, interlinked, producing a complex plan of short but conjoined shafts and tunnels. This digging regime may reflect a highly organised Neolithic extraction technique whereby the desired seam of flint was systematically removed by the use of multiple interconnected galleries, leaving a network of unexcavated chalk walls to provide structural support. At Blackpatch, in 1932, Pull observed that the extent of subterranean workings meant that in certain areas of the hill 'the neighbourhood rests merely upon thin walls and slender isolated buttresses' (**65**). In this way the repeated digging of vertical shafts down through the bedrock at a series of semi-regular intervals may be interpreted as the deliberate creation of a multiple series of entrance points to aid in the extraction process, exit points in case of sudden roof collapse and a way of bringing additional amounts of air and natural light down into the subterranean work space. It has been further suggested that the system of multiple large shafts in close proximity would originally extract a greater percentage of the floorstone than the cutting of lengthy subterranean systems.

The original Neolithic miners, working at the restricted and dimly lit workface within galleries, may not have experienced too great a problem with regard to the stability of the

65 A view out from Gallery V into the main area of Shaft 1 at Blackpatch, with an oil lamp and hand entrenching tool for scale. The extent of flint extraction at this point supports Pull's comments that the hill of Blackpatch 'rests merely upon thin walls and slender isolated buttresses'. *© The Sussex Archaeological Society*

overhanging rock, given the limited amount of time each gallery may have been left open before abandonment or backfilling, though the skeleton found in Shaft 27 at Cissbury could of course provide a different story. No evidence to suggest the former presence of pit props or other roof supports were located within the radiating basal galleries of the Worthing mine series in Sussex. Indeed at Blackpatch Pull noted that the stability of the chalk bedrock had probably meant that no internal supports had ever been required. Such a view may have been revised when Pull was clearing the galleries of Shafts 24 and 27 at Cissbury between 1953 and 1956, for here the poor nature of the overlying chalk necessitated the use of hefty timber and steel pit props to protect those clearing basal levels of debris. Pull and his team were working within underground voids left empty for over 4,000 years and, in places, it was clear that serious amounts of subsidence and roof collapse had occurred adding to the hazardous nature of gallery re-examination. Where the chalk appeared unstable within the gallery systems explored by Curwen at Harrow Hill, the original miners had apparently shored up areas of the roof with piles of chalk rubble.

Favourable observations regarding the structural integrity of the galleries at Grimes Graves were made by the Dutch mining team during the clearance of subterranean galleries in the 1970s. Here, the careful examination of the structure of basal workings demonstrated that the vertical joints present within the chalk bedrock effectively limited the dimensions of galleries. Galleries needed to be narrow, with good load-bearing walls to support the weight of the overlying bedrock, and, in the absence of pit props, could not extend far out from the area of the shaft wall. Understanding of the properties of the chalk bedrock at the nineteenth-century flint extraction pits at Lingheath in Norfolk, ensured that, though these were dug without recourse to pit-props or other forms of artificial roof support, serious incidents involving the collapse of the overlying chalk, were the exception. The presence of voids within the chalk rubble backfill of some gallery systems at Grimes Graves has, however, prompted the suggestion that rounded timbers may on occasion had been used as roof supports during the initial phases of flint extraction. At least one antler pick at Grimes Graves may have been employed as a type of pit prop, supporting a small area of loose chalk within the roof of a gallery, though it is just as possible that this artefact had been deliberately placed by the original miners as a form of offering.

Windows, or irregular holes linking two, possibly non-contemporary, gallery systems, were first noted by Willett at the base of the shaft opened at Cissbury in 1874. These may, in some cases at least, be viewed as the accidental and partial joining of two non-contemporary working areas. Alternatively the windows could represent an attempt by mining groups to provide more reflected natural light into the galleries from other shafts open at the same time, allow a better circulation of air or even as a more efficient means of exit or escape, via an abandoned or disused mine, should the need arise. Willett noted, in 1874, that a strong draught was observed when a candle was placed at the end of one of the Cissbury galleries, demonstrating that, even after extensive backfill, such windows could well have functioned as a source of additional ventilation for the original miners in the cramped subterranean working space.

Let there be light?

It has at times been suggested that Neolithic miners may originally have encountered problems with regard to lighting and the adequate illumination of the workface. When Greenwell recovered four pieces of cup-shaped chalk from a shaft at Grimes Graves in 1870, he suggested that they were the remains of primitive lamps that had originally brought an artificial source of light to the darkened galleries. Greenwell could not, however, identify any evidence of staining or burning within the cups of a kind that one would expect if the pieces had been used as lamps. Recent tests upon the inner surfaces of some cups have revealed traces of a type of vegetable fat, though whether this gives credence to the suggestion that these artefacts were lamps remains debatable. Willett, when describing a series of miscellaneous objects from the 1874 excavations at Cissbury, noted that a cup-shaped piece of chalk, its edges blackened by fire, had been recovered from Tindall's shaft. Unfortunately this piece could just as easily have been burnt by its

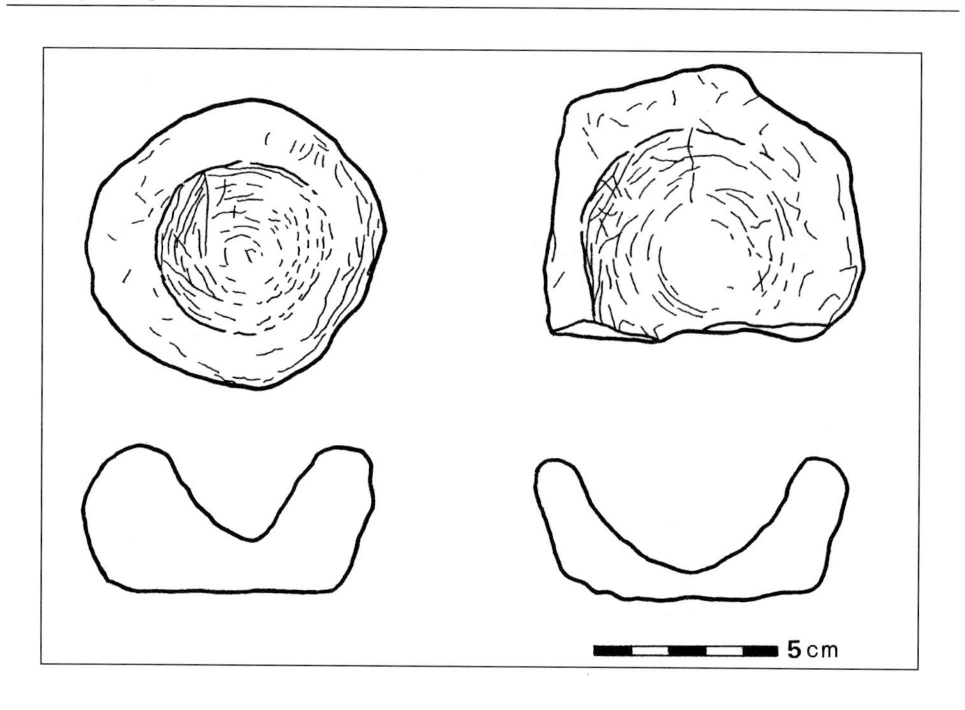

66 Examples of the so-called 'chalk cups' recovered from a number of Early Neolithic contexts in Britain. These two pieces were recorded from Pit 10 at Grimes Graves. Redrawn from Longworth, Herne, Varndell and Needham 1991

incorporation within a fire, rather than as a source of a lamp-like flame.

Quite what the pieces of cup-shaped chalk (**66**) actually meant within the context of the mine remains somewhat of a mystery. Interpretation is not helped either by the extensive range of cup-types that have been recovered or by the fact that a number of such artefacts also occur from non-mine sites such as the Neolithic enclosures of the Trundle and Whitehawk. Given the quantity and basic similarity of these finds across the spectrum of Neolithic type-sites, and the observation that some may have contained vegetable fat, the possibility exists that they may have represented a type of libation cup or small bowl for foodstuffs.

A number of burnt areas or hearths have been noted within the basal levels of mine shafts, sometimes close to gallery entrances. Absence of domestic refuse from these hearths may indicate that food processing did not play a major part in the use of such fires, though they may represent a desire to produce additional warmth or light within subterranean working areas or as a way of aiding the flow of air. Fires may also have been important for the process of hardening antler prior to its use at the workface, or in the process known as 'fire setting' whereby heat is directed onto the rock face to aid in its subsequent removal. Other deposits of charcoal observed within the lower fills of Neolithic mine shafts may relate more to the incorporation of residue from outside of the mine. Charcoal deposits from the floor of Gallery 2 within the 1971 shaft at Grimes Graves have however been interpreted as the possible residue of torch extinguishing activity.

A small amount of charcoal found within the area of the right hand of the human skeleton from Shaft 27 at Cissbury was originally viewed as the possible remains of a taper that the deceased had been carrying at the time of roof collapse. The interpretation of this particular charcoal lens depends upon whether the skeleton it accompanied represented the product of a tragic accident or a formal if unusual burial deposit. If the skeleton does indicate deliberate burial within the mine then the charcoal may represent no more than an extraneous deposit whose location next to the skeleton was purely coincidental.

An area of smoke discoloration, perhaps indicating the use of artificial light in the mines, was noted on the roof of the entrance to Gallery 3 in Blackpatch Shaft 2. Pull suggested that, as the gallery in question was flooded with daylight along its entire length, the soot deposit may have derived from the lamp of someone entering the gallery at night, possibly a Neolithic miner returning to retrieve tools left at the workface. It is just as possible, however, that the soot was of more recent origin, perhaps relating to a lamp or candle belonging to an unauthorised nocturnal visitor to Pull's excavation. A similar deposit of soot, recorded from the roof of gallery IV, Harrow Hill Shaft 21 (**67, 68**) may also be viewed as the result of an illicit night-time visitation to the shaft during the 1924-5 excavations. Not only were no new areas of soot revealed during the re-examination of the gallery in 1982, but the working area would seem to have possessed an ample supply of natural light if originally worked during daylight hours.

Whether those working within the shafts would actually have required a source of lighting to aid in the extraction of flint within all mines is debatable. Pull noted that none of the recorded galleries at Blackpatch were long enough to have required artificial light, though he conceded that lighting may well have been employed within some of the longer galleries recorded from Cissbury. In Shaft 2 at Blackpatch, the walls to every gallery, where they turned a right angle, were pierced with large openings possibly in order to enable daylight from the open shaft to penetrate the workface. All of the subterranean working areas within the galleries of Shaft 2 could, in Pull's view, thus be illuminated to a greater or lesser degree.

At Grimes Graves it has been noted that, once within the basal levels of certain shafts, one's eyes quickly become adjusted to the dark, making a source of artificial light almost unnecessary. In such cases, light reflected in from the area of the shaft was probably sufficient to aid in the removal of flint. Soot marks retrieved from pieces of collapsed roof at the base of the 1971 shaft at Grimes Graves would appear genuine enough, however, and may relate to the use of a form of lamp or fire brand. This in turn could raise questions as to whether shafts and gallery systems were worked solely in the daylight hours, or at night, perhaps through the evenings and early mornings when the need for artificial illumination would have been greatly increased (**69**).

Entrance and exit

Quite how the Neolithic miners extracted both themselves and their flint prize from the basal levels of the deeper mine shafts remains something of a mystery. Evidence relating to the original method of entry and exit to ancient shafts are unlikely to have left a

67 Robert Gurd, site surveyor, making records in gallery IV, Shaft 21 at Harrow Hill in 1925. Note the area of soot discolouration on the ceiling of the gallery, directly above his head. The Curwens interpreted this as evidence of Neolithic artificial illumination within the mines, though it is possible that it may represent evidence of an unauthorised nocturnal visit to the gallery by persons unknown, during the course of the 1924-5 investigations. © The Sussex Archaeological Society

significant trace within the archaeological record, especially if miners originally used ropes or wooden ladders (**colour plate 16, 17**). The modern excavators of Neolithic mines used all manner of ladders, scaffolding and ropes to enter the shafts, whilst buckets attached to rope and pulley systems were often used to great effect to clear the subterranean levels of debris (**70**).

Flint miners working in Norfolk during the nineteenth and early twentieth centuries seemed to have made little use of such rope and pulley techniques, often hoisting out large lumps of floorstone on their heads, making use of footholds cut directly into the wall of the shaft itself. Footholds in the shaft wall do not appear prominently within the Neolithic mines, though examples may have been recorded by Armstrong within Pits III, IV, V, VI and 13 at Grimes Graves (**71**). In Pit II, a 1.2m square ledge, constructed at about 1.4m above the floor of the shaft, seemed to have originally been accessed by a series of chalk-cut stairs within the south-western side of the feature. Unfortunately these do not appear

68 Harrow Hill: further examples of sooting on the ceiling of gallery IV, Shaft 21. © The Sussex Archaeological Society

69 Blackpatch: working in the basal levels of gallery IV, Shaft 1 in 1922. The modern excavation teams often employed oil lamps and candles in their examination and removal of debris from the backfilled gallery systems, especially when working into the evening hours. Whether the Neolithic miners similarly used a source of artificial light is a matter of conjecture. © The Sussex Archaeological Society

70 *An interesting method of soil extraction: two volunteers launch themselves into the void of Harrow Hill Shaft 21, during the course of the 1924-5 excavations. Presumably the landing was considered to be safe, and the chances of meeting the rapidly ascending rubble basket fairly minimal. © The Sussex Archaeological Society*

to have been recorded in significant detail, other than appearing on the published pit section, and in a series of rather blurred site photographs, so their true nature and appearance is difficult to determine. Matters are not helped by the observation that stratigraphy in Pit II is far more complex than Armstrong originally believed, comprising of at least two discrete phases of flint exploitation.

The steps cut into Pit V appear, as with Pit III, to have descended to a short platform or ledge, left in the eastern wall of the cut at a height of 1.2m from the pit floor. Harrison claims to have discovered a rough series of steps or footholds within the Cave Pit at Cissbury, but the strange nature of this particular feature, when combined with the possibility that it may have been modified in the Iron Age, must suggest caution. A ramp of 'boulder clay' found by Armstrong in the northern side of Pit 12 at Grimes Graves was interpreted by the excavator as the original means of exit and entry to the shaft.

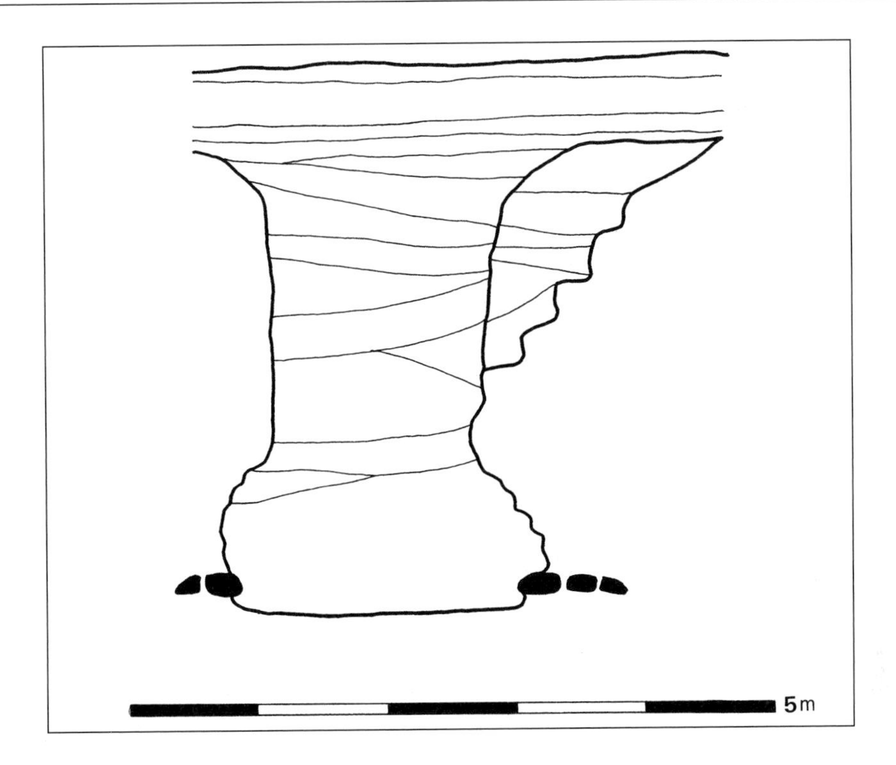

71 *Grimes Graves: section through Pit III. Although the phasing of this particular shaft remains somewhat unclear, Armstrong was adamant that a series of irregular cuts recorded from the south-western edge of the feature (the right hand side of the illustration) represented a series of steps designed to provide access to the lower levels of the mine. Note that the clear undercutting of the basal level of flint in Pit III seems to indicate that the floorstone was originally levered out of position. Redrawn from Longworth and Varndell 1996*

Freshly excavated spoil could have been removed from a shaft by employing a method of shovelling in stages whereby a miner in the deepest part of the shaft heaves rubble up to a platform or step above. At this point a second miner shovels the same spoil to a platform above and so on until all the material has been removed. Longworth and Varndell have suggested that at Grimes Graves such a digging method would, for reasons of safety, have only been practical within the more shallow of extraction pits. In any case, access to the deepest levels of extraction would still, at the point of gallery excavation, have required a more reliable and less time consuming method of flint removal.

Chalk and flint rubble could have been removed by the Neolithic miners from the deeper working areas of shafts by using baskets or bags hauled to the surface with ropes (**colour plate 16**). Whilst investigating Shaft 27 at Cissbury, Pull noted that a projection on the south-western edge of the mine had been rubbed smooth and round, presumably by rope attrition. Similar evidence has also been noted on the walls of Shaft 5 at Blackpatch. More drastic wear patterns in the form of wide grooves, presumably also caused by rope attrition, were observed above the entrance to gallery II, in Pit 1, galleries

IV and VI in Pit 2 and the roof of a gallery connecting the unexcavated Shaft D to Greenwell's Shaft at Grimes Graves. Galleries projecting from the shaft wall of mines at Cissbury and Grimes Graves may have been deliberately so cut as to facilitate the haulage of rubble directly from the workface in bags or baskets via ropes.

Extensive weathering and edge collapse at the mouths of the prehistoric mines may well have destroyed all evidence of potential access platforms or ladder supports, though cuts observed by Peake near the top of Pit 1 at Grimes Graves were interpreted by the excavator as the remains of a wooden cross beam. Some of the best-preserved evidence relating to internal features within Neolithic flint mines has come from three sites at Hov in north-western Denmark. Here, excavations conducted in the late 1950s revealed traces of horizontal posts that had been driven into the sides of the shaft at a height of 2m above the floor. The posts, which measured 8-12cm in diameter, were thought to represent part of a timber platform. A similar group of six horizontal holes, measuring 8-13cm in diameter, were noted from the walls of the 1971 shaft at Grimes Graves. These were set at a distance of 4.6m from the floor of the shaft floor and were also interpreted as the remains of a potential timber platform (**colour plate 17**).

Internal structures such as these could originally have been designed as secure landings for ladders or climbing poles or as places to dump excavated spoil so that the floor of the shaft below would remain relatively clear of debris. Alternatively the timber constructions may originally have represented a form of protection for those working within the basal levels of the mines, from falls of chalk rubble. Little conclusive trace of internal structures relating to extraction was detected within the Sussex mine series, though the narrowing in diameter of certain shaft walls to create narrow ledges, such as at Blackpatch Shaft 2 and Church Hill Shaft 6, may indicate the creation of a step, similar in intent to the timber platforms of Hov and Grimes Graves, to aid in the removal of freshly excavated flint and to provide better access to the subterranean levels. Squared shafts, such as Willett's Shaft No. 2 and the Cave Pit, both reinvestigated by Harrison at Cissbury between 1875 and 1878, may have been so designed to better facilitate the construction of an internal wooden platform. Alternatively it may have been easier to secure the base of a ladder or climbing pole within a shaft possessing distinct corners to it.

It is possible that a form of timber ladder was originally used in the mines, though how substantial such a structure would have been and how definite an impression it would have made upon the archaeology of the site is unclear. At Blackpatch, for example, Pull noted that during the course of emptying Shaft 1, he and his team employed a wooden ladder which, after six months of almost continual use, left no obvious trace either in the floor of the shaft or upon the walls. At Church Hill, two slanting holes measuring between 0.15 and 0.21m in diameter were found 0.4m apart in the chalk at the base of Shaft 7. Pull and Voice suggested that these impressions were probably due to the pressing down of two 'stout wooden poles', possibly a ladder or slide, up which bags of rubble could be pulled. A 1.2m long 0.2m wide vertical break in the fill of Shaft 27 at Cissbury was interpreted by Pull and Salisbury as the remains of a small tree trunk used as a ladder by the original miners (**72**). The hollow has the general appearance of an animal burrow, though its near vertical descent, at the approximate centre-point of the shaft, may, as Pull suggested, indicate an area where a timber was incorporated within shaft backfill. A similar

72 *Cissbury: a linear void, running the vertical length of the middle fill of Shaft 27, was interpreted at the time of its discovery as the decayed remains of a tree trunk or climbing pole, used by the original miners to gain safe access to the subterranean working area. Traces of a similar feature have been found in the fill of a Neolithic mine at Hov in Denmark.* © *Worthing Museum and Art Gallery*

impression, again interpreted as the remains of a tree trunk, with its side branches removed, employed as a climbing pole, was observed for a length of 5m within the fill of Shaft II at Hov in Denmark.

If the evidence from both Cissbury and Hov does relate to ladders or climbing poles, then why had these pieces of equipment been abandoned in shafts and not reused elsewhere on the site? The poles could of course have been broken or compromised by excessive use. They may have been discarded because timber was a resource that could easily be replenished. Alternatively, as with the useable digging tools left by the original miners in abandoned gallery systems, it is possible that the timbers were left as an offering or because they had in some way been spiritually or socially contaminated by their utilisation in the mine, making it impossible for them to be used elsewhere.

Assuming that ladders were used by the original mining team to take the extracted flint to the surface, then we should suppose that, for ease of transportation, the rubble would be carried in baskets or containers which were lashed to some form of back or head frame. Ascending a ladder with only one hand free, the other supporting a basket of mining debris, would not only be extremely difficult, it would, in the context of the mine, be tantamount to suicide. Both hands are required to support oneself whilst climbing in or out of a deep pit, especially if the means of exit is represented by a simple lopped-branch tree trunk. Back frames supported by shoulder and head straps, of the sort known to have been regularly employed by those extracting rubble from later Roman mines, may well have been used here.

Signs and symbols

Attention was first drawn to the existence of a series of distinct markings on the walls of flint mines by Harrison, working at Cissbury in 1875. Harrison was reinvestigating part of Willett's Shaft No.2, when he observed a set of four incisions, two vertical, one horizontal and a diagonal, in the wall immediately opposite the fourth gallery. The ancient appearance of the carving, quite unlike the graffiti that had then recently been added to the entrance to the northern gallery of Shaft No.2, convinced Harrison of the feature's age. A second descent into the pit led to the discovery of another engraving at the entrance to gallery 2. The nature of this second marking, which had the appearance of the number '16', led to some doubt as to its authenticity. A third group of scratch-marks consisting of a series of short straight lines were later noted from Willett's Shaft by Harrison, who interpreted them as 'ancient letters'. Augustus Lane Fox, then president of the Royal Anthropological Institute, noted his worries with regard to the authenticity of these pieces in a discussion that followed the reading of Harrison's paper in 1877.

Two further series of vertical and diagonal incisions were later revealed above an entrance to a basal gallery in Shaft No.2 at Cissbury, whilst a 'rude nondescript figure' was found on the side of the western gallery of No 2 Escarp Shaft by Lane Fox during the excavations of 1875. Of these markings Lane Fox noted that he had no reason to doubt their authenticity. Additional linear incisions were later observed within the Cave Pit at Cissbury by Harrison: vertical and diagonal lines over the entrance to gallery C, two perpendicular lines on the inner western wall of gallery C, and a series of horizontal and parallel lines from over the entrance of gallery B. Harrison suggested that these could be taken as indicating symbols of ownership, religious charms or perhaps an early form of writing. Other possible interpretations, including a form of art, tallies to denote the number of flints obtained from each working area and idle scratchings made 'in some moment of fidgety restfulness'.

The examination of Shaft VI at Cissbury by Harrison in 1876 revealed yet more linear engravings over an unidentified gallery. An unspecified number of 'small cup-shaped marks' were also observed on the walls of the undercuttings for this Shaft, though no illustration of these features appears to have survived. A second series of purposeful marks, consisting of two groups of dots and several straight lines, were observed by Harrison on the northern side of the opening into gallery C in Shaft III. The form of these markings, and their positioning over a gallery entrance, may indicate a point of similarity with the circular marks over the galleries later found in Shaft 4 at Church Hill. The absence of more detailed information at this point is particularly frustrating.

The first group of markings recorded within Pit 2 at Grimes Graves in Norfolk were found over the southern side of the entrance to gallery 6, above the upper level of wallstone and consisted of twelve lightly curving vertical and diagonal strips of varying lengths. Clarke noted that the midday sun shone directly upon the engraving and that the nature and form of the lines could possibly indicate a type of sundial. A second group comprising of horizontal, vertical and diagonal lines was later noted within Pit 2, cut into the buttress dividing galleries 4 and 7. These engravings, later disturbed by an unauthorised visitor to the mines, were interpreted by Clarke as representing tally marks associated with the removal of flint from the galleries.

The scratch marks discovered within Shaft 21 at Harrow Hill consisted of eight roughly parallel lines (**73**) from a block of chalk originally derived from the south jamb of the entrance to the upper western gallery, driven into the second seam of flint encountered within the mine. A group of three incised lines, two parallel with the third crossing at an oblique angle, were noted on the east jamb of gallery 2, while a series of incisions forming an irregular chessboard design was recorded on the shaft wall at the western edge of the entrance to gallery 6 (**74, 75**). Four additional blocks of chalk bearing linear incisions were located within shaft 21 as isolated finds (**76**).

The Curwens wondered whether these pieces of graffiti indicated a primitive type of tally-system, though the chessboard effect of the gallery 6 example could, they postulated, represent no more than a simple doodle such as 'a schoolboy would draw on his blotting paper'. A further series of Neolithic graffiti marks were apparently located at the entrance to gallery 3 in Shaft 13 to the north-west of Shaft 21 at Harrow Hill, which was cleared by Felder in 1982. Unfortunately the precise details of these markings do not appear to have survived. An incised block of chalk with a series of vertical engravings was recorded from the chalk rubble representing the dominant fill of Shaft 1 at Longdown.

Apart from the linear incisions, a number of additional markings have been noted from the Sussex mines. In Shaft 4 at Church Hill, above three of the five gallery entrances, a

73 *Harrow Hill: a series of eight roughly parallel lines incised across a block of chalk 'detached from the south jamb of the upper west gallery' of Shaft 21 which had originally exploited the second seam of flint encountered within the shaft.* © *The Sussex Archaeological Society*

74 *Harrow Hill: a series of linear incisions 'forming an irregular chess-board design' shown in situ on the wall of Shaft 21, to the immediate west of the entrance to gallery VI. On exposure, this area of wall immediately began to fracture, necessitating its hasty removal from the shaft. © The Sussex Archaeological Society*

series of circular impressions were recorded by Pull (**77**). Given the length of time that Shaft 4 was left open during periods of excavation between 1946 and 1948, it is possible that the gallery-head markings are of more modern origin, deriving from the activities of some uninvited visitor. The form and nature of the marks do not automatically trigger alarm however, and certainly Pull seems to have been convinced of their authenticity. Nothing quite like them has been seen from any other flint mine in Britain, though a possible comparison may be made with the groups of dots and small cup-shaped marks observed by Harrison in Shafts III and VI at Cissbury. Unfortunately, as no detailed record of the Cissbury markings would seem to have survived, the comparison may not be taken any further. The apparent uniqueness of the Church Hill examples may be due to their placing over points of entry to subterranean galleries. Similar symbols, if not positioned so obviously or dramatically within a shaft, could always have been overlooked by the

75 Harrow Hill: a close up of the Shaft 21 incised section of wall, following its removal from the shaft in 1925, clearly showing the 'chess-board' and 'ladder-pattern' effect. © The Sussex Archaeological Society

76 Harrow Hill: a detached block of chalk from the lower fill of Shaft 21, bearing a large number of incised lines 'as if made by the serrated edge of a worked flint repeatedly drawn comb-wise across the surface'. This block was found lying across the incised section of shaft wall to the west of gallery VI. © The Sussex Archaeological Society

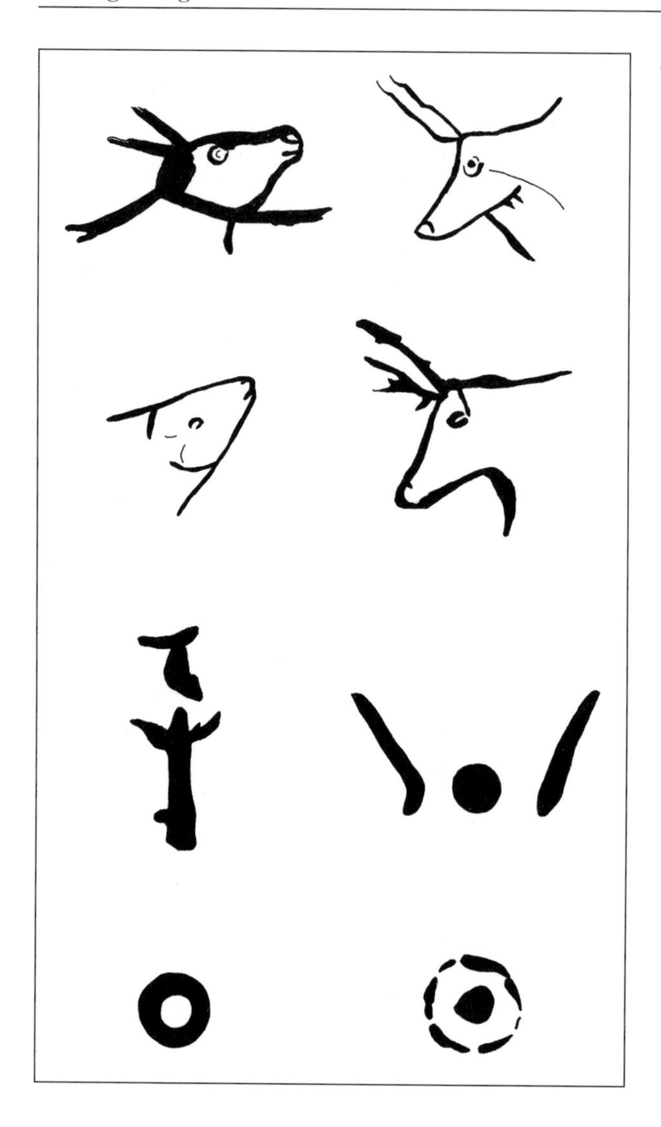

77 *A diverse series of incised marks recorded by Pull from the basal levels of flint mines at Cissbury and Church Hill. The top four, clockwise from top left, comprise the 'short-horned bull', two red deer and the 'fish head' recorded during the examination of Shaft 27 at Cissbury between 1953 and 1954. The bottom four, clockwise from top left, comprise the enigmatic 'miner's symbol' recorded from Shaft 27 at Cissbury and the three circular variations observed between 1946 and 1948 over three of the basal gallery entrances belonging to Church Hill Shaft 4. None of the marks are shown to scale. All redrawn from Russell 2000*

modern excavation team, thinking that they were pick or gouge-marks from the initial phase of shaft exploitation.

There is little chance of misinterpreting the engravings recorded by Pull within gallery 7 at Cissbury (**77**). The first to be discovered here was described as a short-horned bull, whilst the second, facing the first, was interpreted as the head of a red deer. A third engraving, again of a red deer, was later noticed close to the first example to be found. A fourth series of markings, consisting of 'a fish's head and star spread indefinite' were discovered within gallery 8 which was linked to 7. The gallery 7 and 8 markings were sketched and photographed, after they had been highlighted in colour, before rubbings were taken. Copies of the original rubbings exist in the Worthing Museum archive for the short horn bulls head, the second red deer, the fish head and the enigmatic miners symbol. Unfortunately the rubbing of the first red deer to be located within gallery 7 cannot now be traced, although a partially interpretative sketch of the figure, drawn by Pull at the time, does appear in the site archive. It is possible to ascertain the degree of realistic depiction of this first deer by comparing the bull's head that appears in the sketch with its equivalent rubbing.

That these series of markings are both deliberate and contemporary with the prehistoric utilisation of the mine would not appear to be in doubt, though their significance within the mine itself is by no means clear. The naturalistic engravings of red deer noted from the cortex of mined floorstone, retrieved during the examination of Floor 85 at Grimes Graves by Armstrong in 1920, could offer some parallel but, as has already been noted, these flint drawings represent part of a wider modern hoax, intended to promote a secure Palaeolithic date for the Norfolk site.

What then can be made of these diverse groups of subterranean engravings? It may be tempting to view the recorded groups of linear incisions as a tool intended to aid the extraction process. They may have been part of a primitive map of the working areas or, as suggested by Clarke and the Curwens, they may have functioned as tally marks noting the quantity of floorstone removed from a given area. The discovery of similarly incised chalk blocks from the backfill of a number of Neolithic ditched enclosures, including the Trundle and Whitehawk, may contradict such a hypothesis. The discovery of such pieces from non-mine contexts could suggest that the incisions represented a form of common social denominator, possibly a community marker. If this is the case then in Sussex one could potentially draw links between the operation of certain shafts at Harrow Hill, Longdown and Cissbury with phases of activity at the enclosure sites of the Trundle and Whitehawk. Rodney Castleden has speculated that the criss-cross, chessboard-style effect on the chalk may have been intended to represent a ploughed field, which, if correct, could imply agricultural fertility or form of subsistence base.

The combination of circular and linear markings from over three of the galleries within Shaft 4 at Church Hill raise a similar series of problems with regard to interpretation. These unique symbols could have been intended as a way of identifying specific galleries with a specific person or group of people. They may have represented a type of protective symbol intended to placate or appease a specific subterranean deity, fear of the underworld being a common factor within ethnographic studies of mining activity. Alternatively they may have functioned as a form of positioning device or direction finder, the circle in each case representing the position of the central mine shaft, elaboration beyond the area of the circle indicating perhaps the extent, number or direction of particular basal workings.

The diverse series of markings recovered during the examination of galleries connected to Shaft 27 at Cissbury are more difficult to interpret. The deer heads, bull's head, fish head and abstract 'miner's symbol' are unlikely to represent tally-marks, though they could possibly represent the sketching of items familiar to the Neolithic artist that created them. They were possibly a series of tribal deities or spirits associated with the mine. The two left-facing red deer heads, as recorded, appear broadly similar in composition and design. Their portrayal could in part at least be due to the importance of deer within the life of the community or in the production of antler for mining tools. The right-facing short horn bull may also represent a deer, the antlers being removed to indicate loss. Whatever the interpretation of species, its central importance may have lain in the apparent depiction of a harness or rope around the animal's neck. This could indicate a level of domestication and, by implication, of the triumph of human groups over the wild. The markings from the edge of the western recess in gallery 8 are more difficult to quantify, though the star or 'miner's symbol' may have been intended to represent an antler pick or other digging tool. The 'fish head' may indicate a tribal or social signature or an important foodstuff. It might not even represent a fish at all and could, if one is so-minded, be interpreted as a phallus or symbol of fertility.

Backfilling

It would appear that the majority of subterranean prehistoric galleries and working areas had, on completion, been filled with chalk rubble, presumably derived from excavation in other areas of the shaft. This would seem to imply that those engaged in mining deliberately filled recently abandoned working areas with excavated debris from new gallery systems, presumably so as to avoid having to haul the material out of the shaft to the surface. Much of the chalk debris left within surface spoil heaps around the mine sites must therefore relate more to the initial cutting of the shafts than to the subsequent removal of the flint seams. At the termination of mine activity some of the shafts appear to have been backfilled with spoil. Whether this was a economic necessity, designed either to stabilise empty and potentially hazardous mines or to clear the surface of as much unwanted debris as possible before deciding where to sink later shafts, or whether this was an activity of special significance, perhaps intended to heal the wound caused by the sinking of the shaft, is unclear, as is the degree to which shafts were backfilled, as many large heaps of mining debris still remain at ground level to this day.

Much of the discussion concerning the artefacts derived from Neolithic mine shafts, has, as already noted, concentrated either upon the range of digging tools found within basal levels, or upon the unusual finds, such as human remains, recovered from the main body of the fill. This is perhaps understandable, for flint mines are generally interpreted as being purely functional, therefore anything found within the backfill of a shaft, if not related to the original extraction of flint, must be assumed to represent domestic debris or waste products. This sort of argument has unfortunately obscured considerable amounts of useful and interesting data relating to the way that mines were perceived by those who dug, used and backfilled them. Often the nature and quantity of finds within shaft backfill has only been summarised within published reports, when more detailed descriptions would have been more helpful. A direct comparison between the artefacts recovered from shaft backfill and the backfill from other Neolithic monuments, such as enclosures and long mounds, is therefore largely impossible, though a series of broad points may here be outlined.

Mixed in with flint knapping debris in the upper fill of Shaft 1 at Blackpatch were at least 15 sheep mandibles, whilst two thirds of the way down the fill of Shaft 7, a large quantity of animal bones 'principally ribs of oxen' was observed. At Cissbury, in Tindall's shaft, at a depth of around 8.5m, two ox skulls, a human skull, the skull of a wild boar, and a quantity of bones which included otter and roe deer and possibly badger, goat and dog were found. Bones representing pig, ox, goat, roe deer and fox were found with a human skeleton in the Skeleton Shaft at Cissbury. The animal bones referred to by Lane Fox at a depth of 2.4m down in the fill of the Large Pit included goat, pig, roe deer, red deer, horse and ox. In Shaft VI at Cissbury, at a depth of 6.1m into the fill and within the same general context as a human skeleton (**78**), Harrison recovered a larger artefactual assemblage. This comprised of a number of scorched antler picks, large numbers of flints and an ox bone. Pig bones were recovered by Pull at a depth of 2.1m in Cissbury Shaft 24.

At a depth of 2.4m into the fill of Shaft 27 at Cissbury, a large quantity of broken tabular flint was recorded together with bones of 'very small animals', which had presumably fallen into the shaft whilst it remained half backfilled. Below these levels a series of unusual discoveries were made including practically the whole skeleton of an ox, some bones broken for marrow, and some blackened by fire. Some authors have suggested that the ox fell into the shaft whilst it was open, but if so it could hardly have fallen in whilst alive as the splitting and charring of long bones clearly indicates that at least part of the carcass had been cooked and eaten. This must have occurred prior to its inclusion within shaft fill as the immediate area surrounding the bones showed no signs of burning. Whether this partially articulated body, together with the pig bones, represents a high wastage deposit of domestic refuse or the deliberate burial of partly devoured foodstuffs, possibly as an offering, must remain a matter for debate. An extended human skeleton was recorded from the entrance to one of the Shaft 27 basal galleries.

At Grimes Graves, a set of disarticulated human bones comprising the greater part of the lower limbs and parts of the lower jaw, vertebrae and ribs, were recovered from layer 3, Pit 2, to a maximum depth of 5.2m. The bones were thought to represent those of a single individual, a young female aged around 13. Layer 3, referred to by Peake and Clarke as 'the black band', was interpreted as a 'definite occupation layer'. Other finds associated with this layer included a quantity of knapping debris and finished tools, charcoal and faunal remains which included ox, sheep, red deer, roe deer, fox, dog and vole. Some of the ox bones appeared blackened by fire. A piece of human skull, identified as having belonged to a man aged around 30, were recovered from layer 5 in Pit 1 at Grimes Graves, beneath a similar 'black band' as noted in Pit 2. Associated with the skull were 'some fine implements' of flint as well as knapping debris and the bones of roe and red deer, pig and ox.

From these somewhat brief examples it may be possible to suggest a link between human and animal bone within mine shaft backfill, for the faunal remains only ever seem to occur in significant numbers, or in some cases only ever at all, when human remains are also present. Similar observations may also be made with regard to the fill of Neolithic enclosure ditches where human remains are usually attributed with some significance when considering site function of the sites. Enclosures have been considered as necropoli or places where human bodies were disassembled to allow for the selection, removal and formal deposition of certain body parts elsewhere. The discovery of a similar range, if not quantity, of bone material from within the backfill of Neolithic mine shafts may however suggest that such a clear-cut definition is unwarrantable. Human and animal remains, especially upper body parts such as the skull, occur in ditch and mine shaft fills with significant quantities of other Neolithic cultural debris, such as pottery and flintwork. This could suggest the practice of cannibalism, with human body parts being discarded

78 Cissbury: the upper fill of Shaft VI photographed during Harrison's excavation of 1875. The crouched remains of a human skeleton can be seen at the base of the modern ladder. © The Sussex Archaeological Society

with other elements of food residue. Alternatively the mixture of human bone, animal bone, pottery and flint could reflect part of a representative sample of social identifiers which were placed by a specific group into the land via ditches or shafts, so as to indelibly stamp it with their own cultural identity.

If human bone debris was incorporated within ditch and shaft backfill in an attempt to somehow imprint the monument with a specific social label or identity, then discussion concerning 'burial' in the conventional sense becomes invalid. The accumulation of human body parts within subterranean cuts would be seen as representing part of a more general process of structured deposition and not the defining element of that process. The fact that within the disarticulated bone assemblages from enclosure ditch-fill, skulls would appear to predominate, may reflect the desire to incorporate the more identifiable elements of certain individuals into the fill of a construct perceived to lie at the ideological or political centre of one or more territorial zones. Discovery of similar deposits within certain flint mine shafts may also have emphasised their importance within the monument frameworks of the southern English chalk.

A similar claim of imprinting cultural identity in order to claim the land, may be made

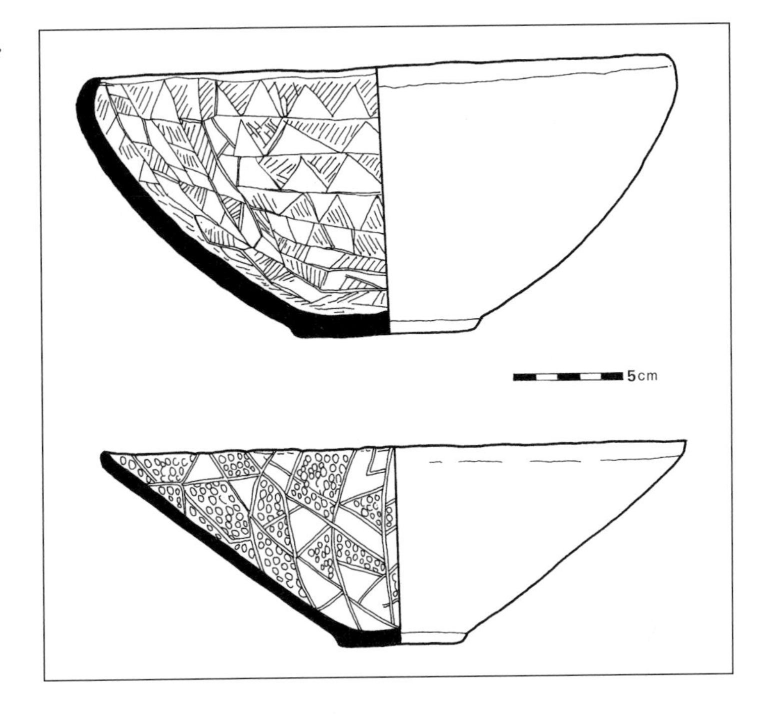

79 Grimes Graves: The reconstructed form of two Grooved Ware bowls recovered, in fragments, from the 1971 Shaft. Redrawn from Mercer 1981

with regards to pottery finds within mine shaft backfill. Nowhere is this perhaps clearer than within Shaft 1 at Church Hill where the pottery assemblage from the upper fill of the shaft included sherds of Beaker, Collared Urn, Grooved Ware and possible Food Vessel and Peterborough Ware. The accumulation of such a varied assemblage could be viewed as an attempt by one or more groups to impress their cultural signature into an abandoned monument or into an area of land. Fragments of Beaker and parts of a possible charred bowl were also noted within the upper fill of Shaft 4 at Church Hill. Three pieces of pottery, the larger fragment representing the rim and shoulder of a carinated bowl, were found 4m into the fill of the Large Pit at Cissbury, whilst a fourth was recovered from a depth of 5m. Seventeen sherds of Grooved Ware were recorded from the upper fill of the 1972 Shaft at Grimes Graves, whilst 72 were derived from the fills of the one examined in 1971 (**79**). Four possible sherds of plain Beaker and pieces of a Neolithic bowl were also noted from the uppermost layers of the 1971 shaft at Grimes Graves.

6 Working on the surface

Flint working floors

The discovery of small but discrete clusters of worked flint within the basal levels of certain Neolithic mine shafts appears to suggest that some form of tool manufacture, modification or sharpening was being conducted at the time of extraction. Much of this flint working was comparatively small scale, and was presumably related to the immediate needs of the miners. The majority of raw material was removed from the basal levels of each shaft, shortly after its removal from the workface, for alteration and modification at the surface.

Surface finds of flint knapping debris from around the mouths of the surviving flint mines indicate that the working and shaping of freshly extracted raw material originally extended over a considerable area. Unfortunately few flint working floors have been scientifically investigated and those that have appear to consist of little more than a solid mass of struck flint, the density of which can obscure whether the material was derived from single or multiple working episodes. In recent years, archaeological attention has recently been drifting away from the prominent mine shafts and towards these surface working areas in an attempt to try and understand the full range of activities that originally took place within the area of extraction.

In the surface workshops around Blackpatch and Church Hill, Pull noted that the flaked axe was the principal implement being manufactured, though other tool types such as drills, scrapers, knives, saws and planes commonly occur. It is of course unclear whether the proportion of finished tools that appear within the make-up of such floors accurately reflect the type or quantity of implements originally being manufactured, or whether the finished material represented offerings or some form of votive deposit. The flake material retrieved from floors 1, 2 and 3 at Cissbury, indicated that blades or knives were the primary product of manufacture here, contrary to the popular modern view that axes were the main concern.

Lane Fox, Armstrong, Pull and others have noted the generally high levels of apparent wastage at the flint manufacturing areas or floors. Similarly large amounts of unutilised though perfectly serviceable flint material sometimes appears to have been incorporated into the backfill of abandoned mine shafts. One explanation for this apparently uneconomical use of both finished artefacts and the hard-won flint is that an excess quantity of tools and raw material could have devalued the price of flint tools at market. To avoid this any potential surplus was deliberately concealed. Quite why any such buried flint was never reclaimed unless there were certain taboos about doing so, remains unclear. At Brandon, in Suffolk, where flint was quarried in the eighteenth and nineteenth centuries for use in flint-lock muskets, excess floorstone was reburied, or otherwise concealed, so as to prevent the extracted stone from drying out prior to use. Such drying and weathering of excavated flint often resulted in a colour change from black to a less distinctive milky-white. It is possible that the Neolithic miners similarly wished to ensure that any potential excess of flint, generated from the cutting of the mines, retained its distinctive colour until such time as it was required.

Alternatively, the deliberate reburial by the Neolithic miners of excess floorstone into a shaft or working floor may be viewed in the same light as the incorporation of large quantities of unused floorstone within the Later Neolithic structured round mounds of Blackpatch. In other words such activity may reflect votive deposition, perhaps to give something of value back to the earth, or as an offering to the spirit of the mining area. Thus the deposits of unutilised flint material may be similar to the deposition of cremated human bone, such as at Blackpatch floor 2 and Church Hill floor 4, and the unused flint axes from surface working floors, such as floor 12 at Church Hill. Whatever the case, the material represents something that does not make obvious economic sense from a modern perspective.

It is not known whether the recorded flint working floors were originally covered or provided with some permanent form of shelter from the natural elements. Evidence for structural features at the surface, such as noted at around Shaft 13 at Harrow Hill, is often vague and inconclusive. It is possible that any form of shelter or covering building may, by reason of being merely a temporary construct, have left little trace in the archaeological record, perhaps failing even to penetrate the chalk bedrock. The absence of reasonable shelters, though easily within the constructional means of those working the mines, may help to explain why some working scatters are concentrated within the hollows of partially backfilled mine shafts as these would certainly have provided some respite from the extreme forces of nature. It is perhaps worth noting that the semi-regular form of at least one surface floor, No. 12 at Church Hill (**80**), could suggest the former presence of a wall or barrier originally limiting the spread of flint debris across the surface of the hill. The presence of hearths and animal bone debris within the make-up of certain surface flint floors may strengthen the suggestion that at least some represent the remains of settlement rather than purely manufacturing activity.

What happened to the finished products?

The first attempts to characterise the trace elements of flint axes from lowland Britain, and thus hopefully determine the provenance of specific artefacts, were conducted by the British Museum in the early 1970s. Initial results seemed to suggest that, of the Neolithic axe forms assessed within East Anglia, Wessex and the south-east of England, the majority, some 67%, probably originated from the South Downs. Such a conclusion would, if taken at face value, underline the early importance of the Sussex mines, implying that the bulk of flint axes in the British Neolithic were derived from seams mined across the south-eastern chalk. A problem with taking the fingerprinting of flint tools too literally was, as those conducting the tests later noted, that the assessment had been conducted on the

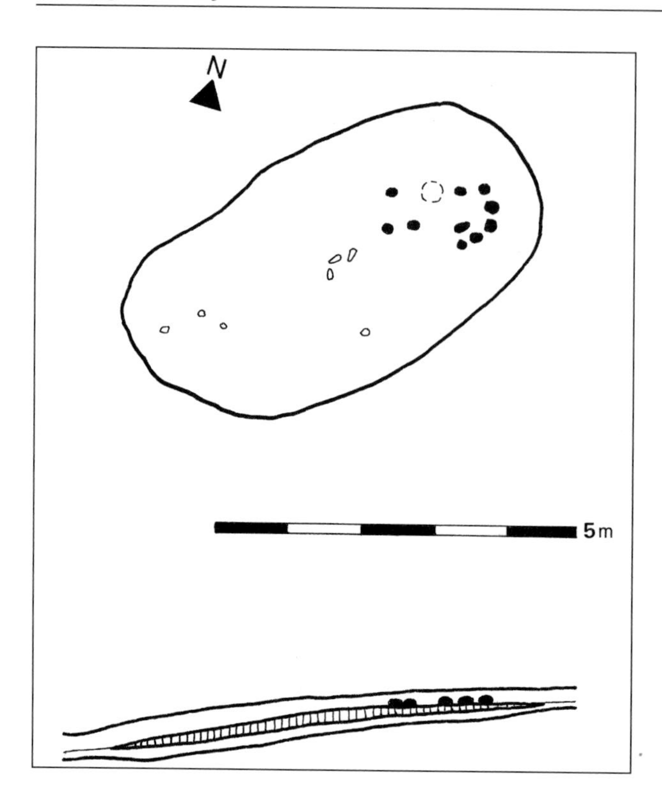

80 Church Hill: plan and section of flint working floor 12. The solid line in the plan represents the limit of flint flakes that define the floor. The hashed circle at the northern end of the floor indicates the position of a burnt area, interpreted by Pull as the remains of a hearth. Surrounding this hearth were ten large nodules of unused mine flint. Within the southern half of the floor, three finished flint axes, and four other unused 'implements' were recorded. Redrawn from Russell 2000

supposition that axes were the major artefact type being manufactured at the mine sites.

Detailed analysis of flintwork derived from the 1971-2 excavations at Grimes Graves has suggested that axes (**81**) represented a relatively unimportant component of the flint assemblage. Alan Saville, when concluding his analysis of the Grimes Graves lithic assemblage, noted that he would prefer to view axe production as representing only one aspect of the Neolithic activities associated with mining, rather than its defining feature. A similar observation has also been made with regard to the Cissbury flint assemblage where Pull's analysis indicated that blades or knives were the primary product of manufacture, with no major indicators of axe making being present. The argument that lowland mine sites represented the major source of flint for axes in Neolithic Britain has also come under close scrutiny, most notably by Julie Gardiner. Her work on flint assemblages has, for example, indicated that surface deposits of clay-with-flint, and not the flint mines, represent the major source for axe manufacture during the Neolithic.

If the output of the mine sites took a variety of forms over time (**82, 83, 84**), including blades, arrowheads, discoidal knives, picks, chisels and sickles, and was not necessarily dominated by distinctive axe-forms, then how can we begin to quantify mine products? Moreover, how can we measure the dispersal rate and ultimate destination of mine products once we move away from the immediate extraction zone? Francis Healy has admitted that, although the quantity of flint extracted from an individual shaft in the Neolithic was likely to have been immense, the 1971 shaft at Grimes Graves being calculated to have produced between 1.12 and 2 tonnes of floorstone, the finished mine product remains 'obstinately close to invisible'. Macroscopic examination of flintwork

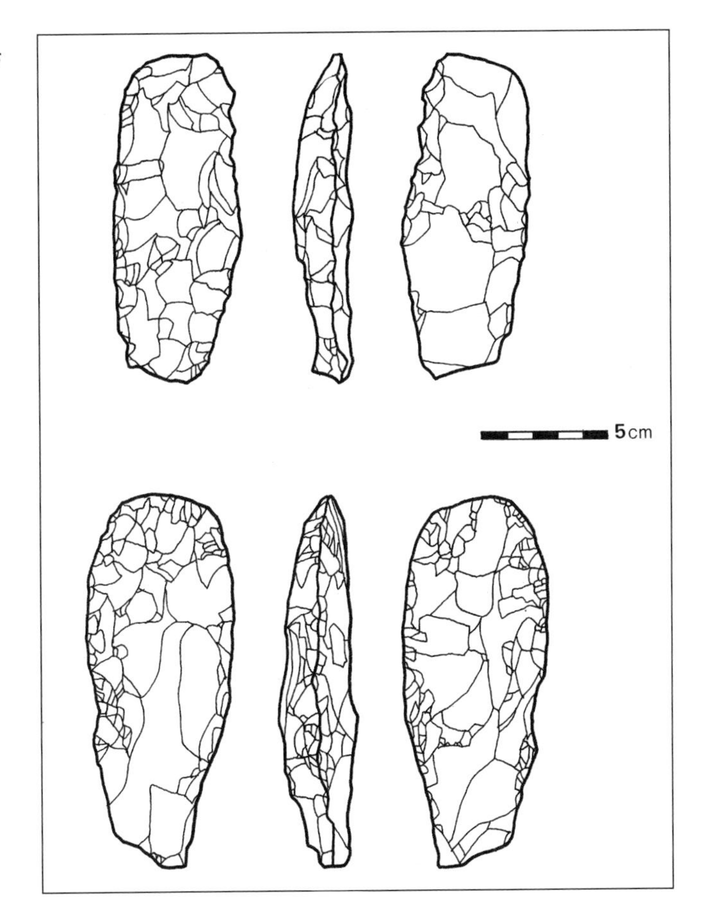

81 Grimes Graves: flaked axes recovered during the excavation of the 1971 Shaft by Mercer. Redrawn from Saville 1981

from the Grimes Graves and Sussex sites has demonstrated not only the distinctive nature of flint derived from the deeper mined seams, but also its marked absence from surrounding Neolithic and Bronze Age settlement assemblages.

Observations such as these, when combined with the fact that finely worked mined flint artefacts would appear most common within formal Neolithic deposits, may be taken to imply that a major element in the desire to mine flint was to generate goods of prestige value. The effort expended in deep seam extraction at sites that may have been dislocated from centres of contemporary settlement would presumably have greatly enhanced the significance of objects made from mined flint. This significance could have considerably added to any perceived tribal, spiritual or magical significance that the objects may otherwise have possessed.

Where did the miners live?

The issue of where those who worked in the mines actually lived is one that, as yet, has not been adequately resolved. Traces of settlement structure in the British Neolithic are notoriously difficult to verify with any certainty, though it is clear that complex settlement

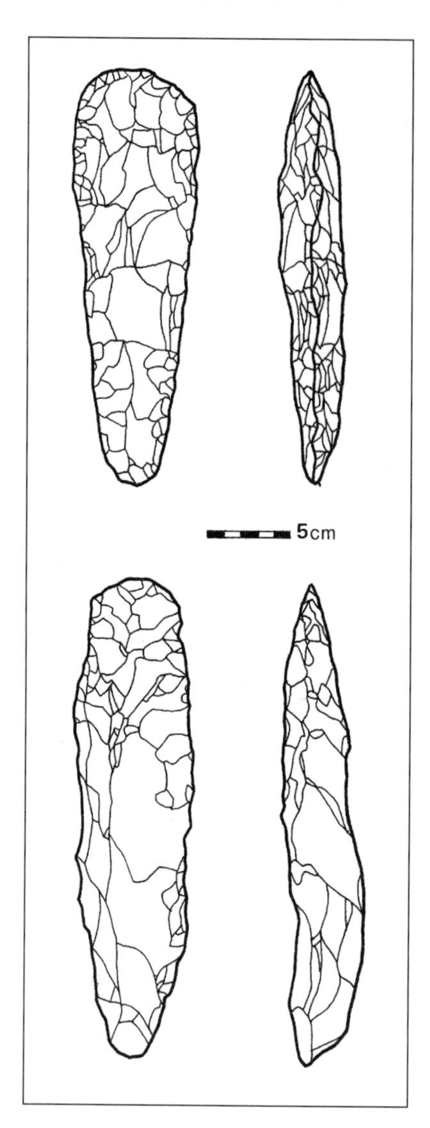

82 (left)
Blackpatch: a flaked axe of 'Cissbury-type' from Shaft 1 (top) and a pick recovered from the surface within the immediate area of Shaft 1 in 1922. Redrawn from Goodman, Frost, Curwen and Curwen 1924

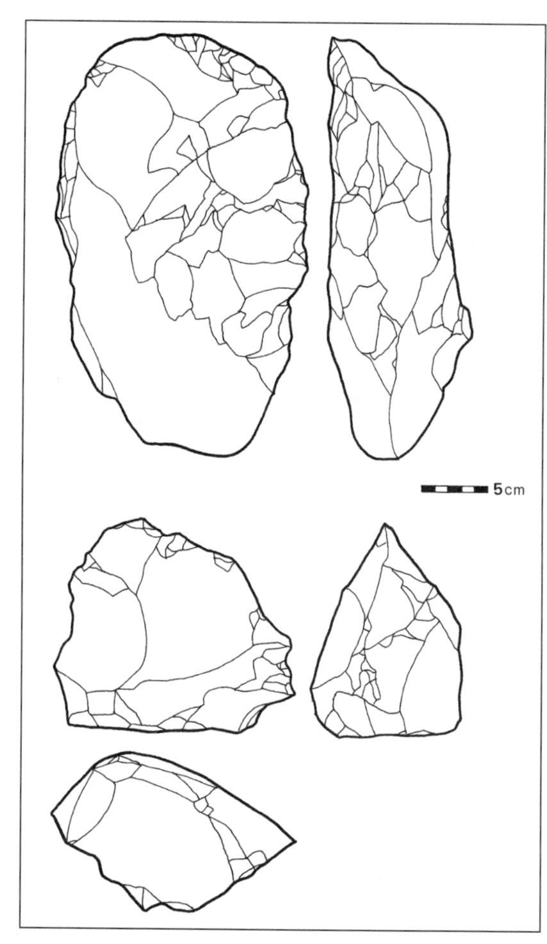

83 (right)
Blackpatch: an axe roughout (top) and a core recovered from the fill of Shaft 1 in 1922. Redrawn from Goodman, Frost, Curwen and Curwen 1924

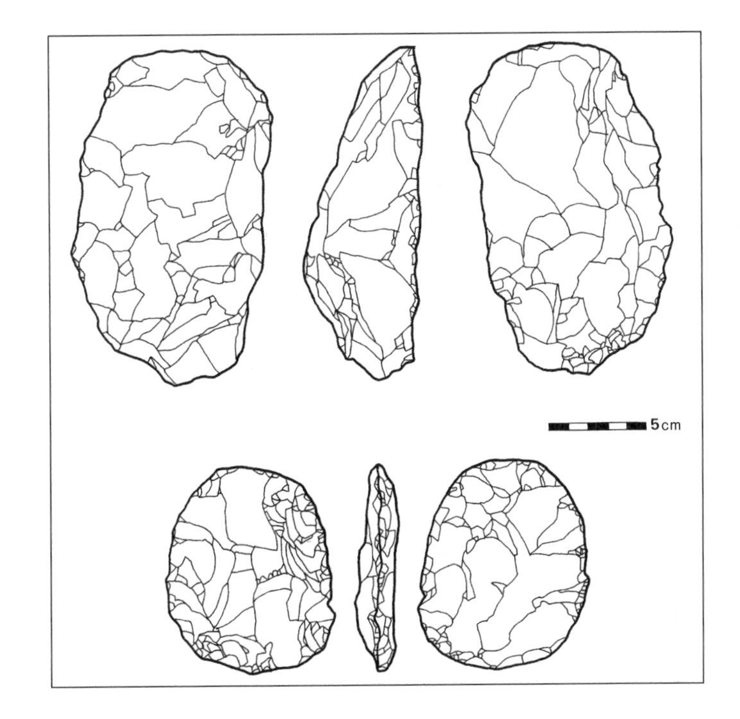

84 Grimes Graves: an axe roughout (top) from the fill of the 1971 Shaft and a discoidal knife found on the surface nearby. Redrawn from Saville 1981

units did exist. In some cases, especially the agriculturally rich southern lowlands of Britain which have been heavily ploughed for millennia, the only certain archaeological trace that Neolithic settlement activity may leave today is surface residue in the form of worked flint and occasionally pottery and bone. Plotting surface concentrations of such artefacts may give us some clue towards the original density and proximity of settlement activity to the areas of mining, though it must be noted that there is no guarantee that any such activity was actually contemporary with a major phase of flint extraction.

What evidence is there with regard to Neolithic settlement within the immediate vicinity of the flint mines themselves? In general terms, absence of clear structural features around the immediate area of the mine shafts may be a result of the continual repositioning of shelters in order to accommodate new extraction pits. Any area of 'settlement' itself could of course be relatively temporary, assuming that people were coming to the areas of extraction sites solely to mine for flint and left once the job was complete. Structures, post-built or otherwise, may not necessarily have even penetrated the chalk subsoil, therefore leaving little in the way of an identifiable footprint. Chemical or plough erosion over the mine sites, however minimal, may have further erased any less substantial features relating to settlement activity.

The major problem with regard to identifying potential areas of contemporary settlement in the immediate vicinity of flint mines is that the surface area exposed around the shafts often represents only a tiny fraction of the original zone of prehistoric activity. Most excavation programmes have, in the past, focused upon the clearly defined shafts or upon certain surface flint working floors. Examination of the apparently 'blank' areas between the archaeologically distinct shafts and working floors has, to date, unfortunately been inadequate. At Harrow Hill, one trench cut to the north of Shaft 13 in 1984 to investigate the nature of possible flint working revealed a number of shallow irregular gullies and at least nineteen small circular and oval hollows. The gullies appeared to relate to a series of natural events, probably water run-off, though the sub-circular hollows at the northern lip of Shaft 13 seemed to be deeper and more regularly defined. The excavators suggested that some of these depressions were structural, possibly post or plank holes representing evidence for a timber building associated with the mine entrance. The possibility that they too may have been formed by natural processes was not, however, entirely ruled out. Indistinct as they are, the irregular features at the lip of Shaft 13 at Harrow Hill represent the best evidence to date of timber structures within the immediate vicinity of the flint mines.

Even if the cutting of each new pit could effectively destroy evidence for the settlement structures at the mine sites, traces of domestic refuse, unless thrown a considerable distance from the living area, should conceivably survive. Evidence for the dumping of settlement waste combined with intensive, possibly in situ, burning, has been recorded from within the upper levels of a number of flint mine shafts, most notably Shaft 5a at Church Hill (**85**) and Shaft 1 at Blackpatch. In relation to such material, Pull commented that this gave 'the appearance of the completely filled shafts having been utilised either for living quarters or at least for domestic purposes'. It has already been noted that the surface depressions of partially filled mine shafts would have provided some basic shelter from the elements, especially for those knapping flint, and it is likely that, in some cases at least, flint working would have been enacted around a central fire or hearth, as seems to be the case with Floor 12 at Church Hill. Whether such activities were conducted within or close to a more permanent type of shelter is at this stage unknown.

Further away from the area of extraction, potential zones of settlement have been detected from at least three sites, namely Easton Down, Church Hill and Blackpatch. At Blackpatch, a series of surface hollows detected in 1929 to the east of the mining area (**86**) were interpreted by Pull and Sainsbury as the remains of dwellings associated with the mines. Unfortunately the excavated evidence is by no means conclusive. Of the two circular features definitely opened, one measured 6.1m in diameter and was 0.2m deep, the other measured 4.6m in diameter and was 0.46m deep. Of the remaining unspecified number investigated, Pull later noted that 'Some proved to be circular . . . with vertical sides and flat bottoms' whilst 'others were saucer-shaped'. Depth varied between 0.23 and 0.46m in depth and between 2.5 and 6m in width. All appear to have naturally silted.

Within the features, Pull claims to have found evidence of habitation in the form of pottery (collared urn), firecracked flint, flint flakes and implements, including 'Cissbury-type' axes, animal bone and sandstone rubbers. In his book *The Flint Miners of Blackpatch*, he argued that these features were huts which 'consisted of a simple scooped hollow surmounted by a series of wooden stakes leaning inwards, and covered or roofed with stretched hides, thatch, or perhaps turves'. Unfortunately, whilst it is true that finds assemblage appears to indicate rubbish related more to settlement than flint extraction, the absence of any clear structural remains, such as post holes, stake holes, pits or hearths, makes a precise interpretation of the hollows somewhat difficult.

A similar series of surface features were noted to the north-west of the Church Hill mines by Pull and Voice in 1946. At least two of these hollows were partially examined by

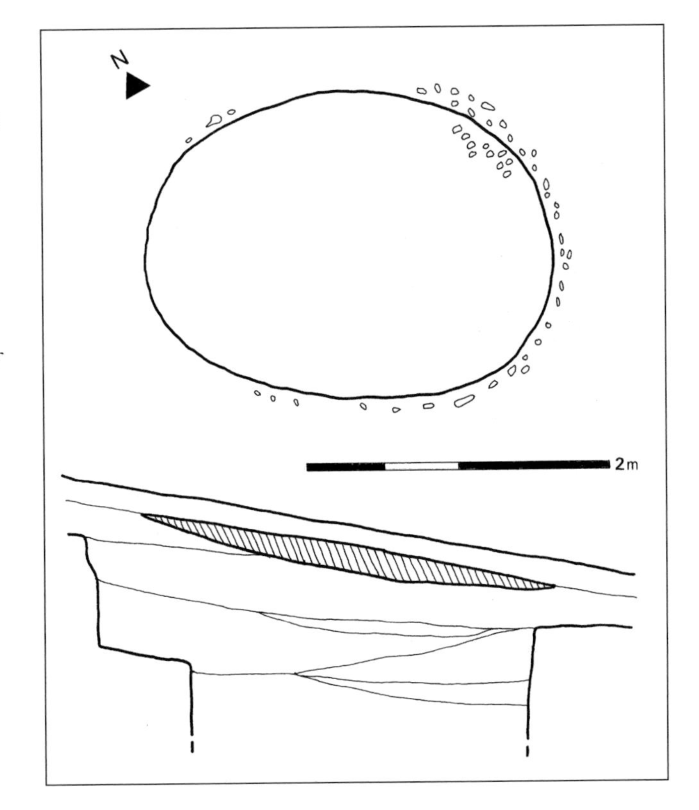

85 Church Hill: plan and section of the hearth site recorded from the uppermost levels of Shaft 5a. Artefacts clustering at the eastern and southern margins of the burnt area included flint flakes, two finished axes, a scraper, a broken flint knife and some bones and teeth of ox. Redrawn from Russell 2000

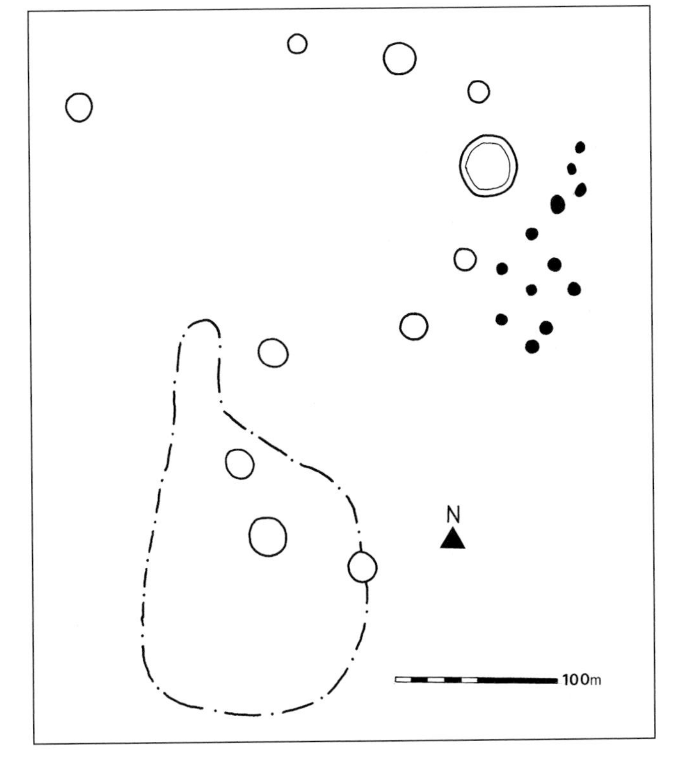

86 Blackpatch: simplified ground plan of the main area of mining (dot-dash line) in relation to the group of round mounds and so-called 'dwelling' pits (shown solid). Redrawn from Russell 2000

Pull, but no indication is given as to their nature or supposed date. A linear spread of surface hollows at Mount Carvey, to the South of Cissbury, High Salvington, to the south of Church Hill, and Myrtlegrove, to the north-west of Blackpatch, were interpreted by Pull as the remains of prehistoric village sites. Judging by the quantity of knapping debris recovered from these three sites, they may, however, actually represent additional areas of Neolithic flint extraction, such as mines or quarries, rather than domestic settlement.

At Easton Down, three 'dwelling pits', identified as Pits A1, A2 and B82, were examined by Stone in 1930. The features lay to the east of the main zone of mining, Pit A1 measuring 3m in length, 1m in width and 0.7m in depth, whilst Pits A2 and B82 both measured 3.3m in width by 0.7m in depth. A series of five irregularly spaced post holes were recorded along the north and north-eastern edge of Pit A1, with Stone suggesting that a further three may have lain at the opposing edge. Finds from this feature included 27 sherds from at least five Beaker vessels, flint tools including an end scraper and a burnt leaf-shaped arrowhead, burnt flint and animal bone comprising mostly jaws and teeth of ox, jaw and a tibia of sheep, and jaws and teeth of pig. Pit A2 contained a similar, if somewhat smaller, artefact assemblage comprising animal bone, burnt flint and Beaker pottery. At least 80 sherds of pottery, derived from two Beakers, a few flint flakes, a hammerstone and a quantity of burnt flint was observed from a 'habitation layer', 0.6m down in Pit B82.

Between 1931 and 1932, Stone began to turn away from the main area of flint extraction at Easton Down in order to concentrate more fully upon the potential settlement zone to the east. A 15.25 square metre area, situated 183m east of Pit 82, was duly opened and a total of ten discrete features, interpreted by Stone as the remains of dwellings, were revealed (**87**). Nine of the features were represented by irregular-shaped hollows, measuring between 3m in width and 1.83m in length, bottoming at a depth of between 0.15 and 0.46m. All of the hollows appeared to have been at least partially surrounded by stake holes measuring around 0.14m in width and 0.15m deep. The tenth 'dwelling' was represented solely by a cluster of six stakeholes, bounding an area of 1.7 by 2.6m. Stone did not provide a detailed description for each feature, but noted that each contained a 'habitation layer' at a depth of around 0.2m. Animal bone, including ox, sheep and pig, pottery, and firecracked and worked flint comprised the major finds recovered from this particular deposit. Much of the pottery seems to have been Beaker, though a few sherds of Early Neolithic 'Windmill Hill Ware' are described. A circular pit filled with ashes, animal bone, Beaker pottery and flint flakes, appeared to have cut through the first dwelling described by Stone.

As with the features described by Pull at Blackpatch and Church Hill, the Easton Hill dwellings are difficult to interpret with any certainty. The hollow features at all three sites were examined at a time when the concept of 'hut-holes', 'ditch-houses', 'pit-dwellings' and other subsurface structures possessed great currency in archaeological circles. Ditches and pits were, in the absence of any more definite structural evidence, seen as houses. The concentration of bone, pottery and flint deposits in these features was seen as evidence that our prehistoric ancestors lived in their accumulated rubbish. This feeling was noted by Curwen, who, when he excavated a Neolithic ditch at Whitehawk in the 1930s, interpreted the artefactual data as evidence for ditch occupation noting that the occupier

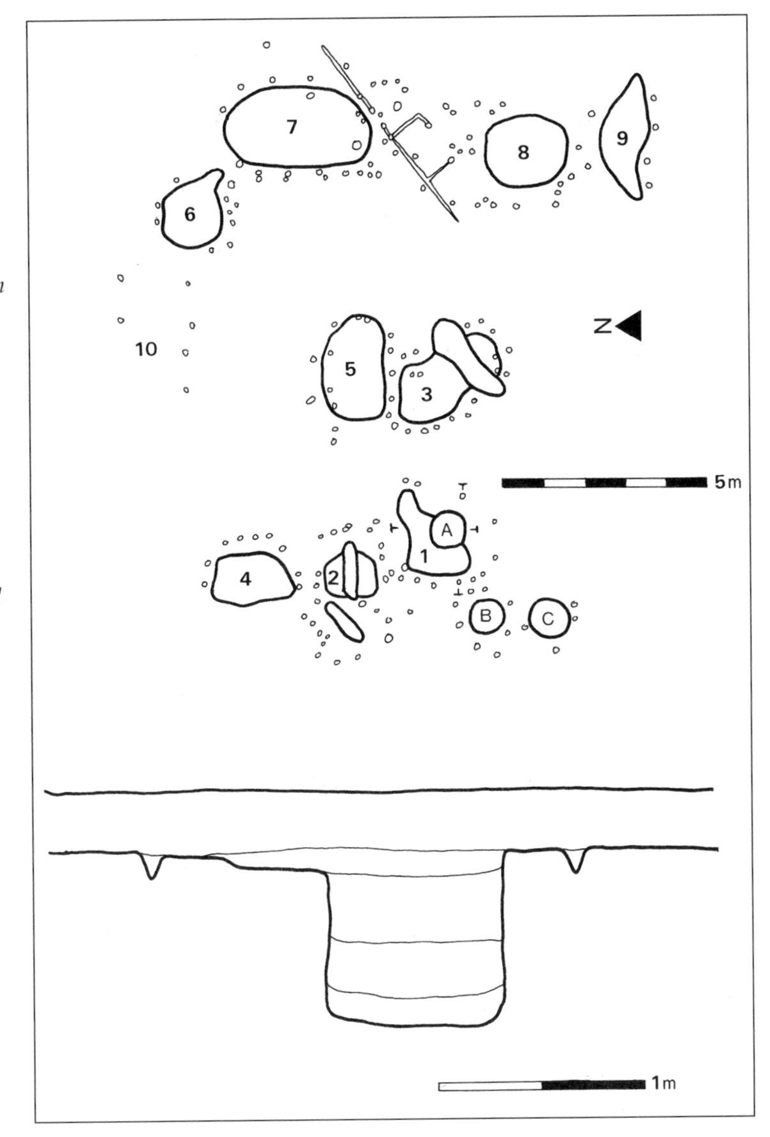

87 Easton Down. Top: ground plan of the 'dwelling pits' and associated postholes recorded by Stone between 1930 and 1932 to the east of the main area of flint extraction. Speculative dwellings are numbered 1-10. The 'ash pits' are lettered A-C. Bottom: a section through dwelling 1 and ash pit A. Redrawn from Stone 1933

in question, 'living amid this filthy litter', was undoubtedly a cannibal. Neolithic man was viewed as primitive and must therefore have lived in primitive, not to say squalid, conditions. The understanding that occupation debris did not automatically equate with in situ occupation effectively destroyed the settlement hypothesis, and, by the mid-1940s, the term pit-dwelling seems to have slipped from the archaeological literature.

The absence of clear structural evidence from the Blackpatch and Church Hill features, as argued above, means that they cannot be viewed as buildings with any certainty. All appear, in their final phases, to have acted as repositories for domestic refuse, though this cannot be ultimately used to define primary function. The features do, however, bear a close resemblance in terms of shape, dimensions, artefact associations, siting and relationship to the mines, to the Easton Down examples which possess a clearer form of structural evidence in the form of an external setting of timber posts. This leaves us with a problem. The shallow features noted at all these sites do not appear to be related to flint extraction (none cut through flint seams), nor would they appear to have functioned well as sunken floor houses, but they do appear to relate to a phase of mining activity, albeit dated to the Later Neolithic. What is needed, at all three sites, is a more scientific and objective analysis of the buried remains in order to ascertain date, form and function. It has to be said, however, that on present evidence, the settlement hypothesis would appear compelling.

Two further pieces of data, sometimes referred to as evidence of settlement contemporary with a phase of mining, should also be noted here. The first site, at Church Hill, consisted of a shallow circular cut set within a larger oval ditch (**88**), both features containing evidence of internal postholes. Pull and Voice interpreted the features as a hut and outer ditched compound, though a ritual interpretation for the outer ditch, which appears to have been sealed in its final phase with large amounts of mined flint, should not perhaps be ruled out. The smaller cut would appear to represent a Later Neolithic feature set within an earlier, and partially backfilled enclosure ditch. Whether this makes the feature a house in the traditional sense is unclear, though the likelihood that it represents a type of domestic structure set at the edge of the mines is more likely than not.

The second site, which has on occasion been referred to as 'a miner's house', is the site at New Barn Down, located upon the lower south-eastern slopes of Harrow Hill. The two features here comprise an oval cut, measuring 1.8m by 2.6m and 0.6m in depth, and a circular cut, measuring 1.2m in diameter and 0.2m in depth. Both were investigated in 1933 and interpreted by Curwen as a Neolithic pit-dwelling. Alternatively, the features could represent the remains of two storage pits backfilled with secondary domestic refuse, itself implying the presence of a nearby settlement, or a series of small scale or abortive flint extraction pits.

Where did the miners bury their dead?

Three categories of human remains have been recorded from the flint mining sites of the central south-eastern chalk: articulated, disarticulated and cremated. As with a similar range of deposits recorded from Neolithic structured mounds and enclosure ditches, such assemblages are often treated as being in some way distinct from other artefact groups. Though the majority of such deposits do not appear to represent primary deposition into the features within which they were found, most would seem to be contemporary with a major phase of Neolithic flint extraction.

Three articulated human skeletons have been recorded from mine fill at Cissbury. In Shaft H (later renamed 'the Skeleton Shaft'), Lane Fox was working in the basal levels, having entered the feature from an adjoining shaft, when a series of animal bones and a human skull appeared at about 0.75m from the floor. Excavation of the shaft demonstrated that the skull was in fact part of a complete skeleton of an adult female lying upside down within the fill. Bones representing pig, ox, goat, roe deer and fox were found associated with the skeleton. Lane Fox and Rolleston suggested that the body represented the

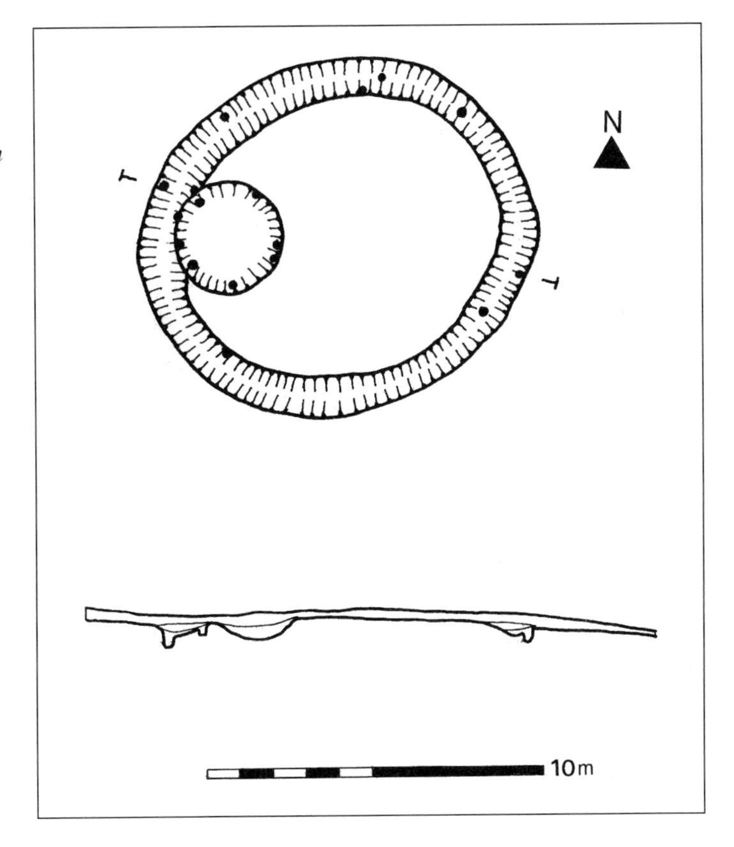

88 Church Hill: surface plan, incorporating subsurface detail revealed from excavation (postholes marked in solid), and section through Hut Site 1 as excavated by Pull and Voice in 1948. It is not known whether the circular 'hut site' and the oval ditch were in any sense contemporary. Redrawn from Russell 2000

remains of a woman who had accidentally fallen into the shaft, whilst Migeod observed that the body must originally have been bound, 'otherwise it would not have kept its upright position'. Pull theorised that the woman had possibly 'been flung head downwards' into the half-backfilled shaft as a sacrifice.

Initial clearance of the western gallery in Shaft 27 by Pull revealed the buried remains of an articulated human skeleton (**89**). At the time of recovery Pull suggested that the skeleton represented the remains of a miner who, whilst entering one of the basal galleries, perhaps to recommence work with tools left at the workface, had been killed by a sudden collapse of the chalk roof. The body was later identified as being that of a female aged around 20, and though Pull dutifully amended his on-site notebook, changing 'he' to 'she' throughout, discussion over the nature and interpretation of the body appears to have progressed no further. A small amount of charcoal within the area of the bones comprising the right hand of the deceased were interpreted as the possible remains of a torch or lit taper that the individual had been carrying when the incident occurred. Some days later, while rubble was being carefully removed, a curious piece of carefully carved bone, in the shape of a fish, was recovered. As noted above, there is now considerable doubt regarding the authenticity of the piece, and it is possible that someone on the excavation team was attempting to play a joke on Pull.

The third articulated skeleton from Cissbury, that of an adult male aged around 25, was recovered by Harrison in a contracted position 4.9m down in the fill of Shaft VI (**90**).

89 Cissbury: the Shaft 27 extended female skeleton, as exposed by Pull in May 1953, lying across the entrance to gallery 1. © Worthing Museum and Art Gallery

The body lay on its right side, the face to the east and had been surrounded by 'a row of chalk blocks and large flints', similar to a feature surrounding a female burial in ditch 3 of the Neolithic enclosure at Whitehawk. Harrison described this construct as a 'quasi-cist'. An unpierced disk of chalk, a burnt pebble and eight shells of land snail were found with the body. Six 'small flint implements' lay outside the quasi-cist and behind the body. In front of the knees and head was found a flaked axe. A large artefactual assemblage, was recovered from beneath the skeleton to a depth of 6.1m, including a number of scorched antler picks, 'a heap of flint flakes between 300 and 400 in number', a single flint implement and the bone of an ox.

Both female burials were retrieved from more primary contexts within their respective shafts than the male, though the question must remain as to whether these represent deliberate depositions or the results of accidental death. Certainly the extended skeleton within Shaft 27 was, when first recovered, thought to represent the body of a miner killed by roof collapse. Alternatively, given its position within the mine, the body may originally have been deliberately placed at the point of entrance to a basal gallery as a symbolic way of sealing off the power or significance of that particular part of the mine. Alternatively the body may have been positioned so as to face into the excavated gallery and towards the subterranean flint source.

A similar interpretational problem, that is to say accidental death versus deliberate deposition, exists for the body recovered head-first from the Skeleton Shaft at Cissbury. If the position of this body relates to a terminal accident then it would imply that the victim

90 Cissbury: the contracted male skeleton recorded by Harrison from the middle fill of Shaft VI in March 1878. Note the 'row of chalk blocks and large flints' which encircle the body. A flaked flint axe lies just in front of the knees. © The Sussex Archaeological Society

originally fell into a half-filled shaft, rather than into a cleared and working mine. As already noted, the body could be viewed either as a sacrifice on behalf of the community, an extreme form of community identifier, or an unusual type of burial, though in this sense the general lack of formality that is recognised from other Neolithic burials would perhaps require some explanation.

Other human body parts recovered from Cissbury during the course of antiquarian exploration there comprise two pieces of human skull. The first, a single piece, was observed above one of the basal galleries in Shaft IV at Cissbury. The second, a more complete example 'wanting only the lower jaw', appears to have been recovered from Tindall's Shaft at Cissbury at some stage in 1874, though the possibility remains that it could have been recovered from elsewhere on the hill. At Grimes Graves, disarticulated human bone comprising the greater part of the lower limbs and parts of the lower jaw, vertebrae and ribs of a young female aged around 13 were recovered to a depth of 5.2m in Pit 2. A piece of human skull, identified as having belonged to a man aged around 30, were recovered from layer 5 in Pit 1. Two articulated skeletons lying in crouched positions were recovered from the upper fill of the 1971 Shaft at Grimes Graves, though artefact and radiocarbon associations suggest that both are no earlier than the Early Iron Age.

At Blackpatch, a series of cremation deposits were noted from the upper fills of Shaft 7, within the flints constituting Floor 2, and within the mounds for Barrows 1 and 3. Cremation deposits were also noted at Church Hill, within Shaft 1 and Floor 4, while a single human fibula came from the fill of Shaft 6. At least seven discrete cremation deposits, most associated with collared urn, were excavated by Stone at Easton Down, to the immediate north-west of the mining area, but it is unclear whether or not they were associated with the main phase of flint extraction.

Human remains have not only been found from the shafts and working floors of Neolithic mine sites, but also, most notably at Blackpatch, from a series of round mounds. Since the mid-1970s it has become clear that the construction of round mounds is something that was not exclusive to the Bronze Age and later periods, and many examples of circular mounds containing complete or disassembled human body parts are now known to have existed in the British Neolithic. The incredible variation in external form and internal structure of such features across Southern Britain, however, makes any comparative statements regarding their morphology difficult. Also, unlike linear mounds, observation of subsurface features cannot be used as a method of recording for Neolithic and some Early Bronze Age round mounds, for the majority do not appear to have originally possessed quarry pits or encircling ditches.

The majority of Neolithic round mounds possess little in the way of a distinctive surface form and the potential for confusion with mounds of later date is considerable. Other problems regarding identification and interpretation of Neolithic round mounds have been outlined by Ian Kinnes as the following: those surrounding the nature of burial rite (disarticulated and articulated skeletal debris are not exclusive to either the Neolithic or Bronze Age); the potential of residual Neolithic flintwork being incorporated into later mounds (a very real problem at Neolithic flint mine sites); and the issues surrounding the erasure of surface form through ploughing. What evidence is available for Neolithic round mounds would suggest the presence of three basic types of form: those composed of soil and rubble derived from the excavation of quarry ditches; those comprising rubble or soil derived from other associated features such as pits, shafts or areas of immediate turf clearance; and cairns, where geological material (usually flint) is selected and piled up to form a discrete surface feature.

At Blackpatch, a series of eleven round mounds and one ring ditch were investigated between 1922 and 1932 by John Pull during the course of the flint mine excavations. All features were designated as 'Barrows' and this form of identification has here been retained to allow for correlation with Pull's data, and not as a form of interpretational inference. Ten of the structures were clearly Neolithic in origin, though one (Barrow 10) may well have been Saxon. None of the round mounds recorded from Blackpatch possessed quarry ditches, material necessary for the construction of Barrows 1, 3, 6, 8 and 12 having been generated from chalk and flint rubble taken from the mines; Barrows 1, 3, 5, 6, 7 and 11 being further capped with a dense layer of floorstone flint, excavated from the basal gallery systems of the surrounding shafts (**91**). A similar deposit of mined floorstone had also apparently sealed the ditch of the only non-mound Barrow feature at Blackpatch, Barrow 9 (**92**). Barrows 4, 5, 7, 10 and 11 were all predominantly composed of chalk, soil and flint 'scraped up' from the immediate surface area. Additional evidence suggested that some of the Barrows had been constructed during a significant phase of flint extraction. Barrows 1, 3 and 12 had, for example, been constructed directly over infilled mine shafts (**93**), the layers comprising Barrow 1 being indistinguishable from the

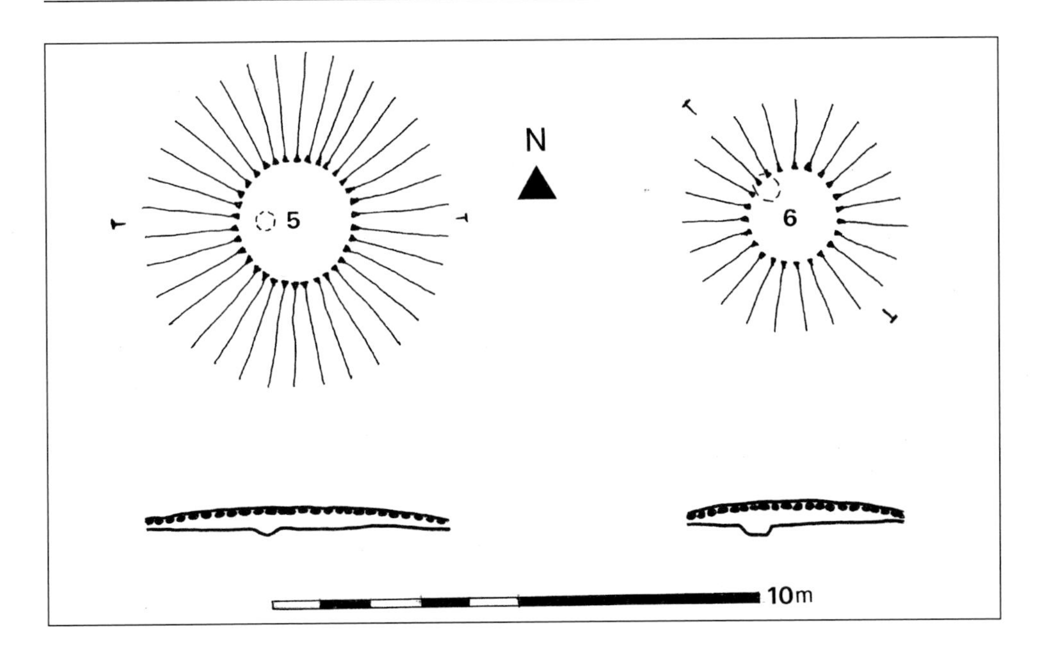

91 Blackpatch: surface plans (showing the positions of subsurface pits) and sections of Barrows 5 and 6. Both mounds were composed of chalk rubble and had been capped with mined flint. Redrawn from Russell 2000

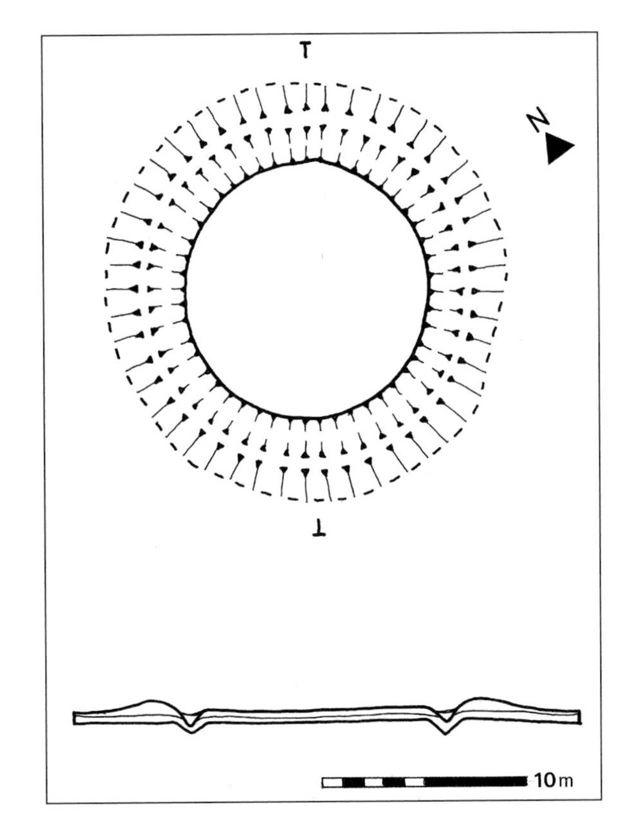

92 Blackpatch: surface plan and section of Barrow 9. This externally banked circular ditch possessed no trace of an internal mound. A deposit of disarticulated human bone associated with Beaker pottery was located in the southern portion of ditch fill. The final phase of ditch fill was composed of mined flint. Redrawn from Russell 2000

fill of the shaft beneath it. The eastern layers constituting Barrow 12 had been further disrupted by the later cutting of a shaft, spoil from this and a shaft somewhere to the north, having been cast out and over the margins of the surface feature.

The constructional form and material composition of the excavated Barrows of Blackpatch has sometimes led to their dismissal as mere spoil heaps which occasionally contained burial elements. This is unfortunately missing the point somewhat, for although the majority of mounds were clearly created from mining debris, the evidence recorded by Pull suggests that such material had been carefully selected and structured, the flint floorstone capping of mounds 1, 3, 5, 6, 7 and 11 being particular relevant in this respect. A second point of interpretational difficulty has been with regard to the diverse nature of human bodies and body parts recorded from within the structured mines, articulated skeletons deriving from Barrows 3 and 12, disarticulated body parts from Barrows 4, 7 and 12, and cremated bone from Barrows 1, 3, 5, 6 and 11.

A partially disarticulated, unsexed skeleton was recorded at the approximate centre of Barrow 12 at Blackpatch. The body appears to have been contracted, lying on its right side with the head to the west. A second skeleton, lying on its right side with the head to the west, was recorded from within the mound of Barrow 12, a flint knife and axe being observed close to the feet. Of the two articulated skeletons from Barrow 3, one, a contracted adult male, was found lying close to the approximate centre of the mound, upon a 4.3m diameter platform of mined flint. The skeleton lay on its left side, with the hands to the face and the head facing east. A leaf-shaped arrowhead from 'behind the shoulders' of the male skeleton, could, if not a residual find, possibly indicate cause of death. Two Cissbury-type axes and a boar's tusk were found near the head of the body, whilst a third axe and 'some teeth of ox and pig' were found to the east. The contracted remains of an adult female, facing east with the hands on the knees, lay off the flint platform to the south-east. A large block of tabular flint 'with an incomplete circle deeply incised through the crust' lay over the lower jaw of the female skeleton, while a 'rough Cissbury type axe' and some pig and cattle teeth lay to the immediate north.

The full nature and extent of the Barrow 3 flint platform is difficult to gauge. It is conceivable that it represents an early attempt at mound roofing or capping to seal off a mine shaft. Alternatively the layer may have been used only at the time of human body deposition, perhaps functioning as a symbolic knapping floor as knapping debris and an unspecified number of hammerstones were recovered from the surface of the layer, together with charcoal and firecracked flint. Alternatively it could be seen as an attempt to deliberately return unutilised floorstone to the soil, together with two representatives of the then contemporary community (a male and a female), at least one of whom may have died violently. A parallel for the flint platform within a round mound may be provided by a structure investigated on Bow Hill, West Sussex, in 1859. Here a chalk mound contained, at its centre 'a remarkable platform of large flints' of 'unusual size and in general nearly flat'. No datable finds were located within the mound, the excavator concluding that the flint pavement was probably 'an altar of sacrifice'.

Disarticulated human body parts comprising the greater part of a single individual, apparently an adult male, were recovered from within the loose flint fill of a 2.4 by 1.5 by 0.7m deep cut at the approximate centre of Barrow 4 at Blackpatch. The 'much decayed'

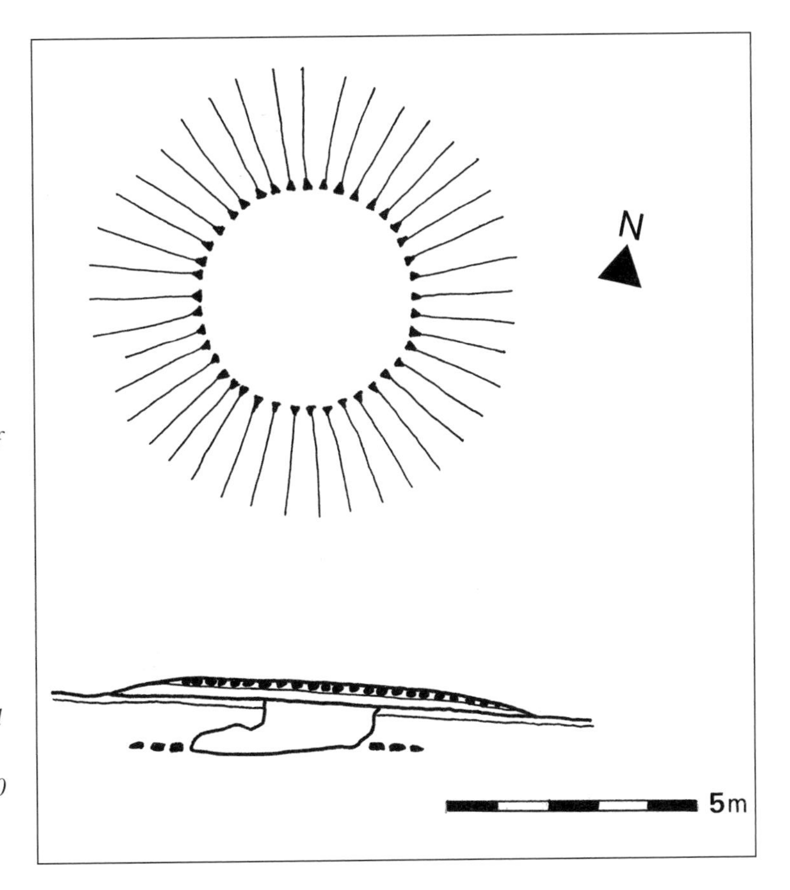

93 Blackpatch: surface plan and section of Barrow 3, which covered, and completely sealed, Shaft 5. Barrow 3, composed predominantly of chalk rubble, contained the skeletal remains of at least two individuals and a cremation overlying a flint platform. The mound itself had been capped with a deposit of mined flint. Redrawn from Russell 2000

skeletal remains of a young adult were found with fragments of collared urn, two leaf-shaped arrowheads, a smoothed piece of chalk, some firecracked flint and fragments of sandstone in a 0.6m diameter, 0.07cm deep cut beneath Barrow 7. Additional disarticulated human bones were found scattered throughout the centre of Barrow 12.

The thoroughly cremated bone deposit from Barrow 1 at Blackpatch was recorded from within the southern make-up of the mound together with charcoal, a small flint axe and an unspecified number of collared urn sherds, apparently constituting the greater part of a single vessel. Cremated bone was also observed 'distributed over a wide area' within the upper levels of Barrow 3, whilst the cremation from Barrow 6 was found together with a bone pin, a sherd of Beaker, some flint flakes and a quantity of firecracked flint within a 1.5ft diameter, 0.25ft deep cut at the base of the mound. The cremation from Barrow 11 was contained within an inverted collared urn, capped with two large blocks of tabular flint. The cremated bone from within Barrow mound 5 was arranged in a crescent. A white quartz pebble and a flint blade lay to the east and a black flint pebble and two arrowheads lay to the south. An upright collared urn was found within a cut close to the centre of the mound. This contained no cremated bone, though a single firecracked flint flake was observed from within.

A series of round mounds on Church Hill, to the north-west of those excavated at Blackpatch, and again described as 'Barrows', were examined by Pull around the neighbouring flint mining zone of Church Hill. Little detailed information exists concerning the majority of investigations here, but the first excavation at least indicates a basic similarity of form to the Blackpatch examples. Barrow 1 measured 4.3m in diameter and was composed of flints representing 'several tons of large waste' and slabs of tabular flint which had 'without doubt been brought from the neighbouring flint mines'. Beneath the flint rubble, a quantity of pottery, some of which could be identified as collared urn, a large amount of flint knapping debris, a small cremation and a flint knife were recorded. A single oval cut, measuring 2.1m by 1.5m and 0.5m and containing a flint blade was located at the base of the mound.

The varied nature of human remains recorded from the Later Neolithic round mounds of the Blackpatch and elsewhere on the southern chalk have at times proved difficult to interpret. It is possible that marked differences between the deposition of human bodies and body parts at Blackpatch may represent the differing belief systems and ideology of varied human groups drawn to the extraction site by the prospect of flint extraction. Alternatively, it may be that, as with the linear mounds of the Earlier Neolithic, problems surrounding the nature and interpretation of perceived 'barrows' may stem from the automatic assumption that such structures were primarily designed for burial, therefore any artefact found within the structure must relate in some way to the deposition of bodies. Human bones therefore represent evidence for primary or secondary burials, animal bones become evidence for feasting, and flint tools and other artefacts become grave goods. This is an interpretation which, although understandable, should not necessarily be adhered to.

The transformation from linear to circular mounds from the Earlier to the Later Neolithic and Early Bronze Age is usually taken as evidence of a developing social system which indicates the rise of the individual. The excavation data from earthen long mounds can, as already noted, demonstrate that the disposal of human remains did not necessarily constitute the primary motive for the building of such earthworks. Sometimes the perceived importance of the mound appears to have lain with its construction, composition and location, rather than with any specific association with the dead. If the linear mounds of the southern Chalk cannot strictly be viewed as burial monuments, then the origins, evolution and development of circular mounds, and also the deposition of single, articulated, and therefore presumably fleshed bodies, may also require more careful reconsideration.

It is possible that the move from linear to circular mounds may represent the abandonment of the community archive or community marker in which the material essence of a particular social group is stored in order to claim an area of land. The fact that circular forms of mound appear at a time when circular domestic structures were more common may alternatively suggest that the concept of mound as symbolic home containing a series of representative community identifiers continued beyond the Early Neolithic. The development of round mounds, with bodies placed at the centre, in the area of a house normally occupied by the hearth, may further add weight to this idea. In this model, the arrival of single articulated bodies may suggest that, by the Later Neolithic, the nature of society had altered to the point that individuals could now, at death, act for the wider community. Individual burials, sometimes with singular dress items, including daggers, hair braids and archery equipment, now appear to have become the main way of imprinting social identity into the land.

The need to establish clear identity and ownership of specific parts of the landscape may have gained in importance throughout the Late Neolithic and Early Bronze Age as social pressures on the land from competing human groups increased. Perhaps communities felt the need to hijack the monuments of earlier periods, such as the enclosures, linear mounds and shafts, in order to strengthen or legitimise their claim. Such capture of sites could have occurred through the addition of Beaker pottery, flintwork or a contemporary and complete member of society, deep into a backfilling ditch, shaft or weathering mound. Such inserted bodies need not be those of the religious leaders, the politically powerful or the financially successful, for these individuals may have been chosen due to the fact that they were perceived as being representative, not unique.

7 The meaning of mines

The shafts from which deeply bedded flint was extracted in the Neolithic have often been categorised as economic structures, associated with the earliest forms of heavy industry detectable within the British Isles. Recent studies into the context of stone tools and the material remains associated with extraction sites, have, however, tended to suggest that although the desire to generate flint suitable for the manufacture of tools provided one of the motivating forces behind the digging of shafts, the quantity and range of non-functional deposits appear to suggest that ritual activities also formed a significant element.

It is important to be aware that we cannot judge the Neolithic mine sites by the standards or mindset of today's modern and highly urbanised society. The mines cannot be treated as simple industrial monuments or functional constructions in the same way that today one may treat a modern coal, tin or gold mine. These sites were operated within a landscape dominated by non-functional, and to the modern mind non-rational, activities. Shafts, though often consigned to the footnotes of prehistoric research, may be viewed as being just as important, from the perspective of monumental architecture, as the long mound or the ditched enclosure. Consideration of the less obvious aspects of Neolithic flint extraction, such as the siting of shafts, the symbolic nature of extraction, the significance of carvings, non-functional artefact deposition and human burial, may provide us with an alternative way of visualising and understanding the prehistoric mining process.

The siting of mines

It has been suggested that the mines of the southern chalk in Sussex and Wessex, though perhaps physically marginal from areas of Neolithic settlement, may have been deliberately false-crested so that the white scars and chalk spoil heaps could be seen over great distances of the landscape. Problems exist with interpreting this observation too literally however, for we can never know with any certainty just how dense the vegetational cover was at the time of mine use, and how seriously this would have impaired the view within particular areas.

The majority of Neolithic monuments on the southern chalk today exist within a treeless environment, devoid of anything but low vegetational cover. Whether this was the case at the time the monuments were constructed is of course debatable. Ken Thomas has argued convincingly, from a series of land snail assemblages, that the South Downs had not been largely cleared of woodland prior to the construction of the first major enclosure sites of Whitehawk and the Trundle in the late fifth millennium BC. What evidence there is would appear to indicate a wide variety of environments at the beginning of the Neolithic, some monuments being constructed within areas of extensive clearance, others within extremely localised zones, and with no certainty as to whether the cleared areas were permanent or temporary. Observations made today with regard to site intervisibility should therefore contain the proviso that they represent a best guess, generated from the perspective of total visibility and that such totality may not have been possible at the time of the monument's construction and use.

Other factors should be noted here. Regardless of the limitations of visibility to or from Neolithic sites, the mines, enclosures and linear mounds would certainly have appeared more dramatic when freshly constructed, with large dumps of white chalk rubble, than they do today after millennia of weathering. The positioning of long mounds, enclosure sites and flint mines at high points along the chalk must indicate a desire to be seen, though how far this desire to see or to be seen may have been taken is unclear. It should also be recognised that any discussion concerning the patterning of Neolithic constructs across the chalk is drawn from an incomplete data set. It is highly likely that additional sites have been erased by later building work or intensive agricultural practices and that other sites remain as yet undetected. Our catalogue of monument types will remain fragmentary, but this should not prevent us from attempting an understanding of their topographic significance.

Despite the obvious limitations, study of geographic setting for Neolithic mines is still considered to be important (**94**). The deeply seated structure of the southern chalk remained largely unchanged from the Neolithic period. As long as one is aware of the constraints upon local environments, changing rivers and coastlines, modern developments, and incomplete data sets, and works safely within them, then valid observations concerning the visualisation and significance of prehistoric structures and the modern landscape may still be made. The siting of extraction pits on specific hills may of course relate to the presence of good flint seams, as well as with conceptual issues such as access and land ownership. Having said this, however, it is interesting to note that though links are often made between the flint mines and the large downland Neolithic enclosures such as the Trundle and Whitehawk, the mine sites appear to be out of sight of these large monuments, which themselves may have been on marginal land. This may have been deliberate.

At Harrow Hill the recorded mine shafts cluster along the eastern slopes of the hill, never once appearing beyond the summit or across the western fringes (**colour plate 2**). This could plausibly result from the nature of the subterranean flint seams and indicate the most economical method of extraction, but assuming that mine shafts had been cut across the western slopes of the hill they would have been clearly visible from the Neolithic enclosure sites of the Trundle, Court Hill, Bury Hill to the west (again assuming an absence of vegetational cover). As it is the mines face out to the north and north-east, across the Downs but not to the Weald beyond, to the east and south-east, across to the Blackpatch mine complex, and to the south, towards a broad stretch of the coastal plain. Similarly the Blackpatch mines face predominantly to the west, towards Harrow Hill, and the south-west and south towards the coastal plain. The positioning of Harrow Hill ensures that this particular group of features upon Blackpatch, cannot be

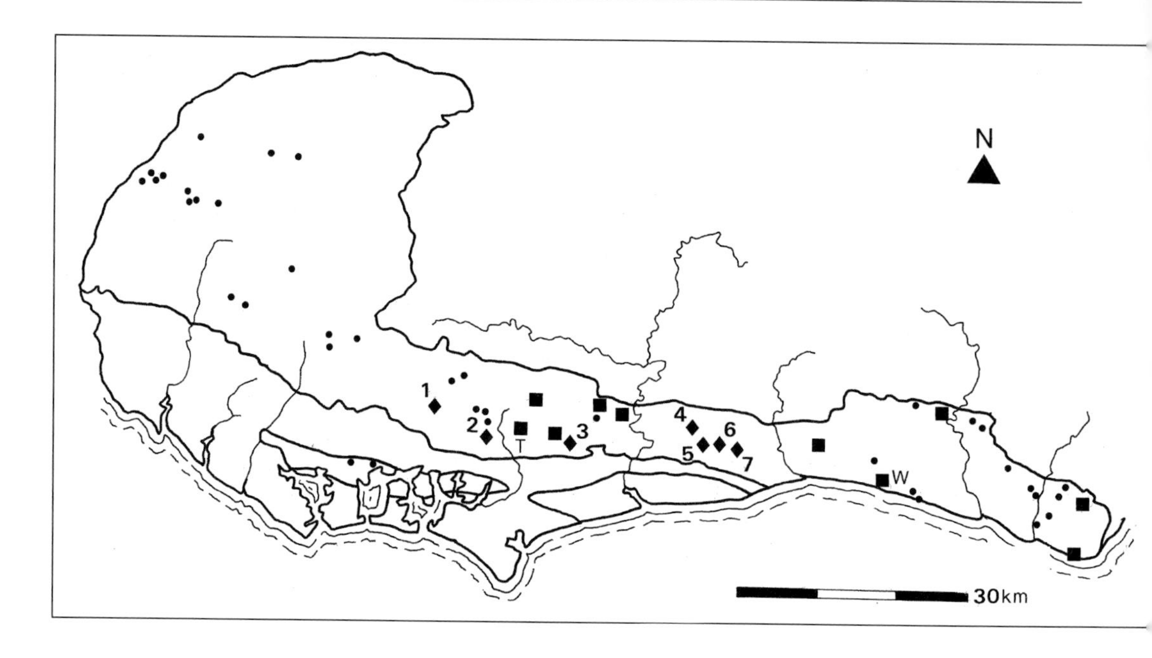

94 The distribution of Early Neolithic monumental architecture upon the chalkland of the South Downs in East Hampshire and Sussex. Long mounds are shown as circles, enclosures as squares and flint mines as diamonds. The two marked enclosures comprise the Trundle and Whitehawk. Numbered flint mines are as follows: 1 Nore Down; 2 Stoke Down; 3 Long Down; 4 Harrow Hill; 5 Blackpatch; 6 Church Hill/Tolmere/High Salvington; 7 Cissbury/Mount Carvey. Redrawn from Russell 2000

seen from the Neolithic enclosure complexes to the west. In effect, with Harrow Hill and Blackpatch we are perhaps seeing two large areas of flint extraction which, though located upon the higher slopes of two of the four most prominent hills within the central block of the Worthing Downs, are facing one another across a wide valley area and are, to a greater extent, invisible from the Weald or from the monument zones to the east and west.

A similar situation may be detectable at Church Hill and Cissbury. The Church Hill mines, which may have started upon the steeper eastern slopes of the hill where flint seams presumably outcrop, face south-east towards Cissbury and the coastal plain, and east and north-east towards a section of the Downs but crucially not the Weald beyond (**colour plate 1**). The larger Cissbury series, where mining may have been instigated upon the north-western slopes, looks north towards the distant northern edge of the chalk Downs, north-west towards the Church Hill mines, west towards High Salvington, and then south west where it commands an impressive view of a broad swath of the now heavily developed coastal plain. Nowhere can the Weald be glimpsed and, though the broad eastern slopes of Blackpatch are visible, both this group of mines and that belonging to Harrow Hill, are obscured. Interestingly, had the mine group extended over and across to the eastern portion of Cissbury, it would have possessed a dominating view out towards the remaining Downs and coastal plain surrounding modern Brighton, the Whitehawk enclosure and out towards Beachy Head and Eastbourne where the chalk hills today reach the sea. As with Harrow Hill and Blackpatch we therefore have two large areas of Neolithic extraction which, though located upon two of the four most prominent hills within the central block of the Sussex Downs, face out towards one another across a wide valley but cannot be seen from the Weald or from the monuments to the east of the river Adur or those to the west around Chichester.

The Long Down mine group is located upon the upper western slopes of a relatively secluded dry valley, overlooking a section of coastal plain to the south. The site directly faces the Neolithic enclosure of Halnaker Hill on the opposing western hill, but visibility to the other main enclosures of this period in the immediate vicinity, namely the Trundle, Court Hill I and II, Bury Hill and Barkhale, is blocked. In a similar, if broader, way the mines of Stoke Down look out across to the Trundle, but visibility to other forms of Early Neolithic monument is blocked. Nore Down possesses no clear view of any other monument, though a number of long mounds exist in the near vicinity. None of the Wessex mines are intervisible, though a single long mound lies less than 150m to the south of Martin's Clump. The mine sites of Grimes Graves and Buckenham Toft in Norfolk possess a different topographic placement to the Sussex and Wessex mines, being set within a more gently undulating landscape (though it must be said that the potential for dramatic location in that part of Britain is somewhat limited).

The apparent wish to partially obscure visibility to and from the southern and south-western mines may have helped enhance their perceived mystery by ensuring that they were hidden from the majority of apparently contemporary enclosures and long mounds. The hills chosen for extraction may have been conceptually important in a spiritual, tribal or ancestral sense to those living in this area, for other hills, which contain just as good a source of accessible seam flint, do not appear to have been in any way worked. The mined hills, and especially those in the Worthing block of the Downs, were specifically chosen. Tools made of the stone extracted from these selected hills may further have been seen to possess significant or magical properties.

Who owned the mines?

Quite who worked the mines and how, if at all, the extractive process was organised and administered remains unclear. Ethnographic studies of mining activity can supply examples as to the nature of prehistoric outcrop working and ownership as well as detailing specific exchange systems, though how applicable these are to the British Neolithic remains to be seen. In New Guinea, work on indigenous stone production systems indicates that in some places quarries were under the careful ownership of one particular tribe, with outside groups being able to directly access newly finished stone tools only by travelling to the source and trading directly with the controlling group, a journey of anything up to four days. Strict codes of access also controlled the native exploitation of stone at the Mt William quarry site in Australia. Here, during the 1830s when the site was first recorded by European settlers, it was noted that although the stone outcrop itself belonged to a particular tribal group, only the members of a specific family within that group were actually allowed to work there. Elsewhere, though tribal control of important outcrops and quarry sites was often carefully maintained, it seems that outside groups were on occasion permitted direct access following the presentation of gifts.

At Lingheath in Norfolk, ownership of the nineteenth- and early twentieth-century flint mines was vested in a group of trustees who extracted groundage rent upon flintknappers for every load of flint removed from the site, the fee being dependent upon the quality of flint taken. Prospective miners would have the edges of their intended pit set out on the ground surface by the trustees, whose job it was to ensure that any new shaft was placed a set distance from the last in the hope that each would exploit a good source of previously untouched subterranean flint. At Lingheath, therefore, we possess evidence of mining activity conducted by people of geographically diverse origins, largely unconnected by family or tribal ties, who came to the same point in the landscape in order to work side by side in the extraction of flint for purely commercial gain.

It is possible that the mines of Neolithic Britain were themselves not owned by any particular social group, and that access to the flint source was conducted on a relatively free and open basis. A number of Native American stone quarry sites, for example, occurred in what appears to have been a type of no-mans land or neutral space within which access may have been fairly open and unrestricted. We have already noted the apparent absence of clear settlement zones around the mine sites, as well as the distant location of other large monument types, notably the large enclosures and linear mounds. If the mines were largely peripheral to the areas of enclosure and were placed in areas away from the main settlements, then the process of extraction would, for those going to the mines, have meant a measure of significant dislocation from their respective communities.

Who worked in the mines?

Such a sense of isolation, not only from the community but also from wider world, would have increased for those working within basal subterranean gallery systems. Anyone who has crawled to the end of one of the Grimes Graves galleries and lain there in the dark will be aware of just how totally divorced one feels from the 'cheerful, sustaining sounds, the songs of birds and human voices' of the world above. It is possible that the act of descending into the dark and cramped working areas of shaft galleries and extracting the flint seam formed part of a rite of passage for the immatures of Neolithic social groups who were about to enter into adulthood. It has after all been already noted that many of the basal galleries of Neolithic pits are extremely constricted making access to some workfaces difficult for all but the slight of build.

Alternatively, working at the mine sites could have been part of a wider social event with people from disparate groups coming together to co-operate in the extraction process and thus affirm their individual community identities and interclan loyalties. Communal activity such as this could be used to explain the visual absence of large enclosures and linear mounds, for in such areas as they were placed, the shafts themselves may have acted as important centres of social activity. This could explain the nature of artefacts recovered from backfilled mine shafts and why such assemblages appear to mirror the range, if not the quantity, of material retrieved from the enclosures and linear mounds. Such deposition of artefacts could represent a type of community or tribal marker with which individual groups hoped to imprint their own identity deep into the earth.

That those who worked the deep flint seams were specialists is clear enough, but only perhaps in the sense that those who farmed the land required specialist knowledge of what crops to grow, and where and how to tender them. We need not automatically view the shafts in the sense of modern mines whereby those who work within them gain their sole livelihood from doing so. In fact the relatively small number of known shafts, when compared with the extensive range of dates provided for the period of extraction, would appear to argue that mining was not the sole activity of a specialist group of mining folk. It has even been suggested that the act of mining in the Neolithic was perhaps conducted on a seasonal basis, at a time when food production was not of paramount importance. It is interesting to note however that the nineteenth- and twentieth-century flint mines of Lingheath in Norfolk were worked by small amounts of people, usually no more than a single individual with perhaps one assistant, all year round. In the summer months the subterranean miners here had protection from summer heat, and in colder months refuge from the extremes of winter, the subterranean levels staying a relatively stable temperature throughout.

Thus far there has perhaps been an unconscious assumption to view those present within Neolithic mines as being male. What was happening to women and children in the Neolithic, is a question that has only recently received serious consideration. This is perhaps due to the male-orientated view of the past as commonly depicted through modern reconstructions. In such recreations there is a marked, perhaps unconscious, tendency to categorize activities for specific members of past communities according to sex. Hence prehistoric males are usually shown returning from a hunt, whilst prehistoric females are grinding foodstuffs or weaving within the main area of settlement. Children are invariably absent from such scenes, something which can be used to query the viability of the community depicted. There is no archaeological evidence from Britain to support these hypothetical divisions of labour within Neolithic society, and there is certainly no material evidence to support the predominance of adult males within the mines and flint extraction areas (**95**).

Whilst it is difficult, if not impossible, to decipher or separate male, female and infant with regard to past activities, some clue to possible differences between the behaviour patterns of such groups in prehistoric society may be gleaned from the differential treatment of the dead. Broad distinctions with regard to spacing, age and gender may be inferred from the differential positioning of later prehistoric adult male, female and immature corpses placed within the major Neolithic monument types of the chalk. Admittedly the sample size is neither large nor securely dated, and is never likely to be complete, but it is interesting to note that, of the articulated burials recovered from Neolithic enclosures and mine sites, adult male and adult female/immature interments have never been recovered from exactly the same context.

At Cissbury, of the three articulated bodies recovered from shaft fill, only that of an adult male appears to have been deposited with any formal solemnity, within the upper fill

95 Speculative recreation of the initial phases of basal flint extraction in Shaft 4 at Church Hill. Mining is being conducted by all ages and sexes. Flint is being extracted in back frames by those ascending a cut tree trunk. Drawn by the author

of Harrison's Shaft VI. The skeleton recovered by Pull from Shaft 27 was first viewed as the 'victim of a mining tragedy', an interpretation which was quietly dropped in later years, perhaps once the body had been identified as that of a young female. This is a somewhat worrying state of affairs, for there is no reason to suggest that prehistoric flint mining was an exclusive preserve of the adult male. Indeed, to extend this argument, it is unlikely that many of the muscle-bound males depicted in certain modern reconstructions of flint mining would ever have been able to fit within small basal galleries and side chambers of excavated shafts. It is certainly clear that many of the modern adult excavators working in the shafts had severe problems negotiating the narrow spaces within cleared galleries (**96**). The possibility that it was individuals of slighter build, perhaps even immatures of either sex, who worked within the basal levels of the mines, is one that should not be overlooked. If only immatures worked within subterranean levels it could further indicate that descent into the mines represented part of a rite of passage towards adulthood (**97**).

The social context of Neolithic mining

As many people are now starting to recognise, the Neolithic is best characterised by a set of new ideas concerning the transformation of the natural world through the building of monumental architecture, rather than by the arrival of agriculture and the subsequent change in social mobility. Monument construction defines the Neolithic, and by at least

96 *Harrow Hill: the entrance to galleries III and IV in Shaft II as exposed in 1936, clearly showing the limited dimensions of the original working space. © Worthing Museum and Art Gallery*

97 *Harrow Hill: view of a young flint mine excavator taken from gallery IIa, Shaft 21 in 1925. © The Sussex Archaeological Society*

4200BC new architectural forms such as the flint mine, the enclosure and the long mound were beginning to impact upon the landscapes of Britain.

It is suggested that throughout the Later Mesolithic, in the sixth and early fifth millennium BC, human social groups were anchoring their mobility to specific points in the landscape. This 'tethering to place' did not involve a radical change towards a sedentary life. The gradual rise in population base across southern Britain, however, appears by the end of the fifth millennium BC to have coincided with the arrival of new ideas concerning the nature and identification of community, new ways of defining and remodelling space, and new ways of ordering the landscape and taming the natural world. These concepts were articulated through the construction of monumental architecture.

The radiocarbon chronology is fragmentary to say the least, but it is suggested that the first monumental forms to impact upon southern Britain were, at around 4200BC, ditched enclosures such as Whitehawk and the Trundle, as well as the first mine shafts such as recorded from Blackpatch and Church Hill and possibly Harrow Hill, Martin's Clump and Long Down. These monuments represent the initial movement of population base away from the more low-lying areas and onto the higher geological ridges. Enclosures represent a form of seasonal or temporary settlement safe zone, imprinted with the identity of the varied social groups involved in its construction, for the dispersed and relatively mobile human population. As such they represented a translation of the strongly defined enclosure circuits identified from earlier periods within central Europe. The cutting of specific vertical shafts into certain high spots in southern Britain occurred at the same time.

Shafts were not primarily intended as an economic necessity, generating material for trade or for everyday use. As with enclosure sites, shafts were probably seasonal anchor points for human groups that remained relatively mobile within their landscape. They were places of initiation and ceremony, places where one could descend into a subterranean world of darkness totally removed from the natural and familiar; places of ancestral significance, where one could claim and tame the land; places from which deeply bedded flint could be won at a cost and prestige items could be manufactured.

Enclosures and shafts were probably built, utilised and maintained by a diverse set of human groups. Both types of site may even have been established at the margins of discrete social boundaries. Selected material derived from settlement waste, and considered to be representative of each varied social group, appears to have been deliberately incorporated within enclosure ditch and mine shaft backfill. All these elements would have helped emergent societies to imprint their own identity into the land and help to establish a control beyond the level of the monument itself.

The white chalk rubble generated from linear ditches and deep shafts would have had a significant impact upon a landscape previously unaffected by deliberate and large-scale human modification. Through the careful topographic placement of shafts and enclosure sites, those involved in their building ensured that the majority were not intervisible. This may reflect the fear of neighbouring communities, or the desire to ensure that the areas visible from monuments did not include the domain of other social groups. Alternatively it may have been part of a deliberate programme of structuring the landscape so that human social units progressing through the land, presumably along seasonal or migrational paths, would increasingly find their movement structured. The landscape was no longer totally wild. Familiar places were being altered and their significance and meaning rewritten in new and more permanent ways. Order was being imposed upon the land.

A third component in the architectural repertoire of Neolithic people was the long barrow or linear mound. As already noted, these structures do not appear to have been designed primarily as burial monuments or tombs, but as visible containers of social identity, designed to imprint new areas of land with the cultural attributes (flint, pottery, animal bone, geological material, occasional human bone) of a particular social group. Their comparative proliferation across Britain in the mid-fourth millennium BC may indicate the increased numbers of people laying claim to specific areas of the land or the desire to increase the fertility of the group and of the land they inhabited. Alternatively they may be interpreted as a form of 'unwelcome' sign such as: 'This territory is ours. Keep away'.

The final period of Neolithic monumental evolution in the later third millennium BC is characterised by the failure to develop enclosure circuits and the proliferation of new small-scale circular architectural forms such as the round barrow and the henge. The development of structured round mounds may reflect the continuation of the concept of mound as a symbolic house containing the cultural attributes of a particular group. Rights of land ownership could have been legitimised by the inclusion of contemporary community members within such forms.

Gradually the nature of individual deposition became more elaborate, but the concept of mound as community archive may have continued, with later generations inserting their dead into the earthworks. Gradually the cutting of vertical shafts comes to an end, the final phases at Blackpatch and possibly Church Hill and Easton Down being marked with an elaborate series of structured round mounds. Symbolically charged flint artefacts were no longer in demand. There were new prestige items of metal in circulation and most flint tools at this time appear to have been generated from surface flint deposits.

The escalation of smaller forms of construct across more varied areas of Britain at the end of the Neolithic presumably reflects the more fragmented nature of society, which was no longer largely composed of mobile groups requiring defined anchor points, but a series of more fixed, if small-scale, social units whose lifestyle was ever more reliant upon agriculture. The more extensively distributed, if smaller-scale monuments that appear across the British landscape in the Early and Middle Bronze Age probably reflect the more evenly spread, sedentary-based social groups that existed at this later time.

Postscript: flint mines and flint mining after the Neolithic

The large scale mining of flint came to an end in Britain in the third millennium BC, at about the same time that new forms of trade and prestige goods, made from copper, tin and gold, were beginning to circulate within society. Flint, though retaining an importance throughout prehistory as a useful, important and readily available source of natural material for the manufacture of tools, does not appear to have been mined again on a large scale until the Roman period. Large amounts of flint were quarried for building projects in southern Britain during the third and fourth centuries AD, most notably for use in town walls, villas and coastal fortifications. Although flint is visible in a wide variety of archaeological contexts from Roman Britain, there is, as yet, no clear understanding of the circumstances under which this material was derived. Presumably there were many well-organised flint quarries in existence, but little detailed work has yet been conducted upon the discovery, identification and recording of such an industry.

Flint remained a very important source of building material for castles, churches, villages and towns in southern and eastern Britain throughout the medieval period, providing a durable, high quality wall surface. From the seventeenth century the material was used in glass making and in the manufacture of china. By the eighteenth century there was a new demand for flint from the military, who were constantly on the lookout for more efficient ways of killing people. Flints formed the vital sparking element of the flintlock musket, and, until the invention of the percussion cap in the early nineteenth century, deep seated flint was extracted from a variety of sources in the British Isles.

One of the most famous mining sites of the gunflint industry was at Lingheath near Brandon in Suffolk. Here miners dug shafts to a depth of 14m in order to extract the required amount of floorstone. Shafts, though of lesser dimensions to their Neolithic predecessors, possessed a similar range of basal galleries and no doubt proved just as laborious, time-consuming and difficult to work. The last of the Brandon miners, one Arthur 'Pony' Ashley, ceased work in April 1934 aged 71. After six thousand years, the history of flint mining in Britain had come to an end.

Visiting the sites today

Grimes Graves and Cissbury represent two of the best preserved and most accessible of mine sites in Britain today, though only at Grimes Graves may one descend into the working space of the Neolithic miners. Many other sites remain visible on the surface, as the recent survey by the Royal Commission on the Historical Monuments of England has shown, but few are either accessible or dramatic, many having been badly hit by plough activity in the latter half of the twentieth century.

Cissbury, West Sussex (NGR TQ 137 078)

Lying 3.2km (2 miles) to the north of Worthing, and around 1.2km (3/4 miles) to the east of Findon, the site at Cissbury is owned by the National Trust. A number of car parks exist close to the site, the closest located at the northern fringes of the Findon Gap, just east of the A24. The site itself is easily accessible by footpath. Artefacts deriving from excavations at Cissbury have been widely dispersed, but the best collections may be found in Worthing Museum and Art Gallery, Museum of Sussex Archaeology, Barbican House in Lewes and the Ashmolean Museum in Oxford.

At 184m above sea level, Cissbury offers extensive views eastwards towards the white cliffs of Beachy Head, northwards across the Downs and Chanctonbury Ring, and westwards to the mining site of Church Hill and across the coastal plain towards Portsmouth and the Isle of Wight. Cissbury Ring itself is an impressive, oval-shaped Iron Age univallate hillfort, enclosing some 24.3 hectares (60 acres). The massive inner rampart, which measures over 9m in width at its base, fronts a flat-bottomed ditch, measuring over 6m in width and surviving to around 2.5m in depth. The flint mines occur mainly within the western part of the hillfort, but also continue under and outside the defences on the southern side of the hill. Over 200 shafts are visible as depressions, some surviving to an impressive 6m in diameter and 3m in depth. Scrub clearance over the hill has in recent years contributed much to the overall visibility of the mines.

Grimes Graves, Norfolk (NGR TL 817 898)

Lying 11km to the north-west of Thetford, Grimes Graves is owned by English Heritage, the site car park being clearly sign posted from the A134. Finds from the excavations may be seen in Norwich Museum and the British Museum. There is also a small exhibition and shop on site. Just over 430 shafts are visible around the covered pit as dramatic surface hollows averaging 5m in diameter and up to 2m deep.

Three of the shafts were not backfilled following modern examination, and are at present sealed beneath concrete covers. Due to safety reasons, however, only one shaft, Pit I, is open to the public. Access to the floor of the shaft is via a fixed ladder. Hard hats are provided. Though substantially modified in order to improve safety, with iron grilles fixed over the gallery entrances to limit access, Pit I is the only place in Britain where the internal nature of a Neolithic flint mine may be experienced at first hand. Opening times for the site and exhibition are usually: 1 April to 31 October, daily 10am to 6pm; 3 November to 30 March, Wednesday to Sunday 10am to 4pm. There is an admission charge.

Harrow Hill, West Sussex (NGR TQ 081 100)

Lying some 4km to the due south of Storrington and 5.8km (3½ miles) to the north-west of Cissbury. A number of car parks exist upon the northern scarp slope of the Downs within a fair walk from the site, the closest being those signposted from just outside of Storrington, on the A283 and B2139. The site itself is accessible from a number of footpaths that traverse the lower slopes of the hill. Artefacts deriving from excavations at Harrow Hill may be found predominantly in Worthing Museum and Art Gallery and the Barbican House Museum of Sussex Archaeology, in Lewes.

Harrow Hill rises to a maximum height of 167m above sea level and possesses commanding views of the immediate Downs to the north and east and coastal plain to the south. A small rectangular, univallate earthwork enclosure, covering an area of 0.3 hectares, overlies the southern edge of the Neolithic mining area. It is presumed to be late Bronze Age in date. Around 160 mines are clearly visible today as a series of impressive oval and circular depressions, measuring between 4 and 6m in diameter and surviving to an average depth of 3m.

Long Down, West Sussex (NGR TQ 933 092)

Lying some 8km to the north-east of Chichester, 3km (2 miles) to the north east of Boxgrove and 0.7km to the west of Eartham. Limited parking is available in Eartham whilst a Forestry Commission car park and a series of unsignposted lay-bys exist to the north and north-east of the site, off the A285. A single footpath traverses the southern edge of the mines. Finds from the site are stored in Chichester and Worthing Museums.

Longdown rises to a maximum height of 95m above sea level, facing across a dry valley towards the Early Neolithic enclosure of Halnaker Hill, 1.1km to the east. At least 38 well-defined mine shafts and their associated spoil heaps are visible today, ploughing having erased the northern and eastern fringes of the site.

Further reading

The list of works that follow is not intended as a complete and authoritative bibliography for all the sites, excavations and topics covered in this book. Instead, the intention has been to produce a list of the more comprehensive summaries and notable excavation reports as well as providing the best 'starting point' to pursue more detailed texts. All works cited here contain the additional references necessary for continued research. The best place to commence a detailed study of flint mines is probably the comprehensive book *The Neolithic Flint Mines of England* by Barber, Field and Topping, which presents the results of survey work conducted by the Royal Commission on the Historical Monuments of England and published by English Heritage in 1999. The journal *The Proceedings of the Prehistoric Society* represents the major outlet for recent academic papers on prehistoric archaeology in Britain and abroad and a number of useful articles may regularly be found here.

General works

Barber, M., Field, D., and Topping P., *The Neolithic Flint Mines of England*. English Heritage and the Royal Commission on the Historical Monuments of England. London. 1999

Becker, C., 'Flint mining in Neolithic Denmark', *Antiquity* 33, 87-92, plate xii. 1959

Clark, G., and Piggott, S., 'The age of the British flint mines', *Antiquity* 7, 166-83. 1933

Clarke, W., 'Are Grime's Graves Neolithic?', *Proceedings of the Prehistoric Society of East Anglia* 2, 339-49. 1917

Curwen, E.C., *The Archaeology of Sussex* (2nd edition). London. Methuen and Co. 1954

Darvill, T., *Prehistoric Britain*. London. Batsford. 1987

Field, D., 'The landscape of extraction: Aspects of the procurement of raw material in the Neolithic' in P.Topping (ed), *Neolithic Landscapes*, Neolithic Studies Group Seminar Papers 2. Oxbow. Oxford, 55-67. 1997a

Forrest, A., *Masters of Flint*. Lavenham Press, Suffolk. 1983

Gardiner, J., 'Flint procurement and Neolithic axe production on the South Downs: A reassessment', *Oxford Journal of Archaeology* 9, 119-40. 1990

Holgate, R., *Prehistoric flint mines*. Shire Publications. Princes Risborough. 1991

Holgate, R., 'Neolithic flint mining in Britain', *Archaeologia Polona* 33, 133-61. 1995a

Piggott, S., *The Neolithic cultures of the British Isles*. Cambridge University Press. 1954

Schild, R., and Sulgostowska, Z. (eds), *Man and Flint. Proccedings of the VIIth international flint Symposium, Warszawa – Ostrowiec Swietokrzyski, September 1995*. Institute of Archaeology and Ethnology Polish Academy of Sciences. 1997

Shepherd, R., *Prehistoric mining and allied industries*. Academic Press. London. 1980

Sieveking, G. de G., and Hart, M. (eds), *The scientific study of flint and chert*. Cambridge University Press. 1986

Sieveking, G. de G., and Newcomer, M. (eds), *The human uses of flint and chert*. Cambridge University Press. 1987

Smith, R., 'On the date of Grime's Graves and Cissbury flint mines', *Archaeologia* 63, 109-58. 1912

Artefacts and their context

Bahn, P., and Vertut, J., *Images of the Ice Age*. Facts on File. Oxford. 1988

Bradley, R., and Edmonds, M., *Interpreting the axe trade* Cambridge University Press. 1993

Craddock, P., Cowell, M., Leese, M., and Huges, M., 'The trace element composition of polished flint axes as an indicator of source', *Archaeometry* 25, 135-63. 1983

Curwen, E.C., 'On the use of Scapulae as shovels', *Sussex Archaeological Collections* 67, 139-45. 1926

Edmonds, M., *Stone tools and society: working stone in Neolithic and Bronze Age Britain* Batsford. London. 1995

Ferguson, J., 'Application of data coding to the differentiation of British flint mine sites', *Journal of Archaeological Science* 7, 277-86. 1980

Mason, H., *Flint: The Versatile Stone* Providence Press, Haddenham. 1978

Pitts, M., 'The stone axe in Neolithic Britain', *Proceedings of the Prehistoric Society* 61, 311-71. 1996

Sieveking, G. de G., Bush, P., Fergusson, J., Craddock, P., Huges, M., and Cowell, M., 'Prehistoric flint mines and their identification as sources of raw material', *Archaeometry* 14, 151-76. 1972

Blackpatch

Goodman, C., Frost, M., Curwen, E., and Curwen, E.C., 'Blackpatch Flint Mine Excavation 1922', *Sussex Archaeological Collections* 65, 69-111. 1924

Pull, J., *The Flint Miners of Blackpatch* Williams and Norgate, London. 1932

Russell, M., *The Neolithic flint mines of Sussex: Excavations by John H Pull at Blackpatch, Church Hill, Tolmere and Cissbury, 1922 – 1956.* Bournemouth University School of Conservation Sciences Occasional Paper 6. Oxbow. Oxford. 2000

Church Hill

Law, H., 'Flint mines on Church Hill, Findon', *Sussex Notes and Queries* 1, 222-4. 1927

Pull, J., 'Some discoveries at Findon 1: The prehistoric antiquities of Church Hill', *Sussex County Magazine* 7, 470-2. 1933a

Pull, J., 'Some discoveries at Findon 2: The fire mound', *Sussex County Magazine* 7, 506-8. 1933b

Pull, J., 'Some discoveries at Findon 3: The burial mounds', *Sussex County Magazine* 7, 597-600. 1933c

Pull, J., 'Some discoveries at Findon 4: The flint industries', *Sussex County Magazine* 7, 653-55. 1933d

Pull, J., 'Some discoveries at Findon 5: The flint implements', *Sussex County Magazine* 7, 727-30. 1933e

Pull, J., 'Some discoveries at Findon 6: The flint mines', *Sussex County Magazine* 7, 810-4. 1933f

Pull, J., 'Further discoveries at Church Hill, Findon', *Sussex County Magazine* 27, 15-21. 1953

Russell, M., *The Neolithic flint mines of Sussex: Excavations by John H Pull at Blackpatch, Church Hill, Tolmere and Cissbury, 1922 – 1956.* Bournemouth University School of Conservation Sciences Occasional Paper 6. Oxbow. Oxford. 2000

Cissbury

Donachie, J., and Field, D., 'Cissbury Ring: A survey by the Royal Commission on the Historical Monuments of England', *Sussex Archaeological Collections* 132, 25-32. 1994

Harrison, J., 'On marks found upon chalk at Cissbury', *Journal of the Royal Anthropological Institute* 6, 263-71. 1877a

Harrison, J., 'Report on some further discoveries at Cissbury', *Journal of the Royal Anthropological Institute* 6, 430-42. 1877b

Harrison, J. 'Additional discoveries at Cissbury', *Journal of the Royal Anthropological Institute* 7, 412-433. 1878

Irving, G., 'On the camps at Cissbury, Sussex', *Journal of the British Archaeological Association* 13, 274-94. 1857

Lane Fox, A., 'An Examination into the Character and Probable Origin of the Hill Forts of Sussex', *Archaeologia* 42, 27-52. 1869a

Lane Fox, A., 'Further remarks on the hillforts of Sussex, being an account of the excavations at Cissbury and Highdown', *Archaeologia* 42, 27-52. 1869b

Lane Fox, A., 'Excavations in Cissbury camp; being a report of the exploration committee of the Anthropological Institute for the year 1875', *Journal of the Anthropological Institute* 5, 357-90. 1875

Rolleston, G., 'Note on the animal remains found at Cissbury', *Journal of the Royal Anthropological Institute* 6, 20-36. 1877

Rolleston, G., 'Notes on skeleton found at Cissbury, April 1878', *Journal of the Royal Anthropological Institute* 8, 377-89. 1879

Russell, M., *The Neolithic flint mines of Sussex: Excavations by John H Pull at Blackpatch, Church Hill, Tolmere and Cissbury, 1922 – 1956.* Bournemouth University School of Conservation Sciences Occasional Paper 6. Oxbow. Oxford. 2000

Stevens, J., 'The Flint-works at Cissbury', *Sussex Archaeological Collections* 24, 145-65. 1872

Toms, H., and Toms, C., 'The Cissbury Earthworks', *Sussex Archaeological Collections* 67, 55-83. 1926

Turner, E., 'On the military earthworks of the South Downs, with a more enlarged account of Cissbury, one of the principal of them', *Sussex Archaeological Collections* 3, 173-84. 1850

Willett, E., 'On flint workings at Cissbury, Sussex', *Archaeologia* 45, 337-48. 1880

Den of Boddam

Saville, A., 'Prehistoric exploitation of flint from the Buchan Ridge Gravels, Grampian Region, north-east Scotland', *Archaeologia Polona* 33, 353-68. 1995

Durrington

Booth, A., and Stone, J., 'A trial flint mine at Durrington, Wilts', *Wiltshire Archaeological and Natural History Magazine* 54, 381-8. 1952

Wainwright, G., and Longworth, I., *Durrington Walls : excavations 1966-1968.* Society of Antiquaries Research Report. London. 1971

Easton Down

Stone, J., 'Easton Down, Winterslow, South Wiltshire, flint mine excavation, 1930', *Wiltshire Archaeological and Natural History Magazine* 45, 350-65. 1932a

Stone, J., 'A settlement site of the Beaker period on Easton Down, Winterslow, South Wiltshire', *Wiltshire Archaeological and Natural History Magazine* 45, 366-72. 1932b

Stone, J., 'A Middle Bronze Age urnfield on Easton Down, Winterslow', *Wiltshire Archaeological and Natural History Magazine* 46, 218-24. 1933a

Stone, J., 'Excavations at Easton Down, Winterslow, 1931-32', *Wiltshire Archaeological and Natural History Magazine* 46, 255-42. 1933b

Stone, J., 'Excavations at Easton Down, Winterslow, 1933-4', *Wiltshire Archaeological and Natural History Magazine* 47, 68-80. 1935

Grimes Graves

Armstrong, A., 'Flint crust engravings and associated implements from Grime's Graves, Norfolk', *Proceedings of the Prehistoric Society of East Anglia* 3, 434-43. 1922a

Armstrong, A., 'Further discoveries of engraved flint-crust and associated implements at Grime's Graves', *Proceedings of the Prehistoric Society of East Anglia* 3, 548-58. 1922b

Armstrong, A., 'Discovery of a new phase of early flint mining at Grime's Graves, Norfolk', *Proceedings of the Prehistoric Society of East Anglia* 4, 113-25. 1923

Armstrong, A., 'The Grime's Graves problem in the light of recent researches', *Proceedings of the Prehistoric Society of East Anglia* 5, 91-136. 1926

Armstrong, A., 'The Percy Sladen Trust excavations, Grimes Graves, Norfolk: interim report 1927-1932', *Proceedings of the Prehistoric Society of East Anglia* 7, 57-61. 1934a

Armstrong, A., 'Grime's Graves, Norfolk. Report on the excavation of Pit 12', *Proceedings of the Prehistoric Society of East Anglia* 7, 382-94. 1934b

Burleigh, R., Clutton-Brock, J., Felder, P., and Sieveking, G., 'A further consideration of Neolithic dogs with special reference to a skeleton from Grimes Graves, Norfolk, England', *Journal of Archaeological Science* 4, 353-66. 1977

Clarke, W. (ed), *Report on the excavations at Grime's Graves, Weeting, Norfolk, March - May 1914* H.K. Lewis. London. 1915

Clutton-Brock, J., *Excavations at Grimes Graves Norfolk 1972-1976: Fasicule 1 - Neolithic antler picks from Grimes Graves, Norfolk and Durrington Walls, Wiltshire; A biometrical analysis* British Museum. 1984

Greenwell, W., 'On the opening of Grime's Graves in Norfolk', *Journal of the Ethnological Society of London* 2, 419-39. 1870

Healy, F., 'The hunting of the Floorstone' in A. Schofield (ed), *Interpreting Artefact Scatters: Contributions to Ploughzone Archaeology*. Oxbow Monograph 4. Oxford, 29-37. 1991

Kendall, H., 'Grime's Graves: Floors 47 to 59', *Proceedings of the Prehistoric Society of East Anglia* 3, 291-305. 1920

Legge, A., *Excavations at Grimes Graves Norfolk 1972-1976. Fasicule 4: Animals, Environment and the Bronze Age Economy*. British Museum Press. 1992

Longworth, I., Ellison, A., and Rigby, V., *Excavations at Grimes Graves Norfolk 1972-1976. Fasicule 2: The Neolithic, Bronze Age and later pottery*. British Museum Press. 1988

Longworth, I., Herne, A., Varndell, G., and Needham, S., *Excavations at Grimes Graves Norfolk 1972-1976. Fasicule 3 - Shaft X: Bronze Age flint, chalk and metalworking*. British Museum Press. 1991

Longworth, I., and Varndell, G., *Excavations at Grimes Graves Norfolk 1972-1976. Fasicule 5: Mining in the deep mines*. British Museum Press. 1996

Manning, C., 'Note on Grimes Graves', *Norfolk Archaeology* 4, 356. 1855

Manning, C., 'Grimes Graves, Weeting', *Norfolk Archaeology* 7, 169-77. 1872

Mercer, R., *Grimes Graves, Norfolk. Excavations 1971-72: Volume 1*. Department of the Environment Archaeological Report 11. 1981

Peake, A., 'Further excavations at Grime's Graves', *Proceedings of the Prehistoric Society of East Anglia* 2, 409-36. 1917

Peake, A., 'Excavations at Grime's Graves during 1917', *Proceedings of the Prehistoric Society of East Anglia* 3, 73-93. 1919

Pettigrew, S., 'Note on Grimes Graves', *Journal of the British Archaeological Association* 8, 77. 1853

Richardson, D., 'A new celt-making floor at Grime's Graves', *Proceedings of the Prehistoric Society of East Anglia* 3, 243-58. 1920

Saville, A., *Grimes Graves, Norfolk, Excavations 1971-72: Volume II the flint assemblage*. Department of the Environment Archaeological report no 11. 1981

Sieveking, G. de G., 'Grime's Graves and Prehistoric European Flint Mining' in Crawford, H. (ed), *Subterranean Britain: Aspects of Underground Archaeology* John Baker, London, 1-43. 1979

Sieveking, G. de G., Longworth, I., Huges, M., and Clark, A., 'A new survey of Grime's Graves', *Proceedings of the Prehistoric Society* 39, 182-218. 1973

Sturge, W., 'The polished axe found by Cannon Greenwell in a flint pit at Grimes Graves' *Man* 8, 166-8. 1908

Harrow Hill

Curwen, E., and Curwen, E. C. 'Harrow Hill Flint Mine Excavation 1924-5', *Sussex Archaeological Collections* 67, 103-38. 1926

Curwen, E.C., 'Flint miner's dwelling and Bronze Age farm in Sussex', *Antiquity* 8, 215. 1934b

Curwen, E.C., 'A Later Bronze Age farm and a Neolithic pit dwelling on New Barn Down, Clapham, near Worthing', *Sussex Archaeological Collections* 75, 137-70. 1934c

Holgate, R., 'Harrow Hill near Findon, West Sussex', *Archaeologia Polona* 33, 347-50. 1995b

Holleyman, G., 'Harrow Hill excavations, 1936', *Sussex Archaeological Collections* 78, 230-51. 1937

McNabb, J., Felder, P., Kinnes, I., and Sieveking, G., 'An archive report on recent excavations at Harrow Hill, Sussex', *Sussex Archaeological Collections* 134, 21-37. 1996

Long Down

Holgate, R., 'Long Down near Chichester, West Sussex', *Archaeologia Polona* 33, 350-2. 1995c

Salisbury, E., 'Prehistoric Flint Mines on Long Down 1955-8', *Sussex Archaeological Collections* 99, 66-73. 1961

Martin's Clump

Stone, J., 'A flint mine at Martin's Clump, Over Wallop', *Proccedings of the Hampshire Field Club and Archaeological Association* 12, 177-80. 1932

Ride, D., 'Excavation of a linear earthwork and flint mines at Martin's Clump, Over Wallop, Hampshire', *Proceedings of the Hampshire Field Club and Archaeological Association* 53, 1-23. 1998

Ride, D., and James, D., 'An account of the prehistoric flint mine at Martin's Clump, Over Wallop, Hampshire, 1954-5' 1989

Nore Down

Aldsworth, F., 'A possible Neolithic oval barrow on Nore Down, West Marden.', *Sussex Archaeological Collections* 117, 251-2. 1979

Aldsworth, F., 'Prehistoric Flint Mines on Nore Down, West Marden', *Sussex Archaeological Collections* 121, 187-90. 1983b

Skelmuir Hill

Saville, A., 'Prehistoric exploitation of flint from the Buchan Ridge Gravels, Grampian Region, north-east Scotland', *Archaeologia Polona* 33, 353-68. 1995

Stoke Down

Wade, A., 'Ancient Flint Mines at Stoke Down, Sussex', *Proceedings of the Prehistoric Society of East Anglia* 4, 82-91. 1922

Tolmere

Curwen, E., and Curwen, E.C., 'Probable flint mines near Tolmere Pond, Findon', *Sussex Notes and Queries* 1, 168-70. 1927

Russell, M., *The Neolithic flint mines of Sussex: Excavations by John H Pull at Blackpatch, Church Hill, Tolmere and Cissbury, 1922 – 1956.* Bournemouth University School of Conservation Sciences Occasional Paper 6. Oxbow. Oxford. 2000

Index